D1528455

# SCOUTING FOR GRANT AND MEADE

# SCOUTING FOR GRANT AND MEADE

The Reminiscences of Judson Knight,
Chief of Scouts, Army of the Potomac

EDITED BY PETER G. TSOURAS
FOREWORD BY WILLIAM B. FEIS

SKYHORSE PUBLISHING

Skyhorse Publishing books may be purchased in bulk at special discounts for sales promotion, corporate gifts, fund-raising, or educational purposes. Special editions can also be created to specifications. For details, contact the Special Sales Department, Skyhorse Publishing, 307 West 36th Street, 11th Floor, New York, NY 10018 or info@skyhorsepublishing.com.

Skyhorse® and Skyhorse Publishing® are registered trademarks of Skyhorse Publishing, Inc.®, a Delaware corporation.

Visit our website at www.skyhorsepublishing.com.

10 9 8 7 6 5 4 3 2 1

Library of Congress Cataloging-in-Publication Data is available on file.

ISBN: 978-1-62873-698-4

Printed in the United States of America

# DEDICATION

This book is dedicated to the memory of Judson Knight
and to the scouts of the United States Army,
Men of Daring, Cunning, and Courage

# CONTENTS

# Foreword:
# "A Knight's Tale"

**WILLIAM B. FEIS**
*Author of Grant's Secret Service: The Intelligence War from Belmont
to Appomattox*

$A$T THE END of the Civil War, Union General Philip H. Sheridan
acknowledged the critical role his scouts played in the final campaigns
when he thanked them for "cheerfully going wherever ordered, to obtain
that great essential of success, information."[1] And his praise was not
misdirected since he and most good commanders knew instinctively
that, as nineteenth-century military theorist Antoine Henri-Jomini
observed, intelligence gathering was an undertaking "unquestionably of
the highest importance." But Jomini also cautioned that procuring good
information on the enemy was also "a thing of the utmost difficulty, not
to say impossibility."[2] Though Sheridan certainly appreciated the con-
tributions of his intelligence operatives and understood the innumerable
difficulties and dangers they encountered trying to keep him informed,
few inside or outside the army knew much at all about the intrepid men
and women who sacrificed in the shadows for the Union cause.

Even today the true nature of Civil War military intelligence
remains overshadowed by the overly romanticized tales spun by

Confederate spies Rose O'Neal Greenhow and Belle Boyd, and their Union counterparts Allan Pinkerton and Lafayette C. Baker. Their truth-challenged and blatantly self-promoting narratives stole the postwar limelight far more effectively than they absconded with enemy secrets. "These tall tales," wrote intelligence historian Edwin C. Fishel, "have been reworked again and again by 'popular' biographers and historians until they have long since hardened into a mythology," or what he called the "magnolia blossom school" of Civil War intelligence.[3]

In addition to the romantic haze enshrouding the literature, Civil War military intelligence operations also remain difficult to decipher because they were predominantly ad hoc affairs conducted with little precise record-keeping. Most commanders instinctively understood the need for information because, as Maj. Gen. Daniel Butterfield so eloquently put it, Union armies could not "go boggling around until we know what we are going after."[4] But no official manual or "do it yourself" guide existed telling how to find information while on campaign or how to use it once you found it. Complicating this inexperience, commanders also had access to a wide array of potential information sources, which could be both good and bad since too much information could be as confounding and bewildering as too little. As a result, most Civil War officers—even those with a West Point pedigree—learned the intelligence "business" on the job and pretty much made it up as they went along. Unfortunately, this also meant officers came to rely heavily upon their equally inexperienced information-gatherers to do their job well.

The most important of these operatives—and the unsung workhorse of military intelligence operations—was the army scout. Usually a civilian or a volunteer from the ranks, these intrepid individuals ventured into no-man's-land seeking information on the enemy, returning (hopefully) to their commander/employer with first-hand observations, local rumors, enemy newspapers, captured mail, and reports on terrain, road networks, railroad traffic, troop deployments, and enemy morale. However, like many soldiers in the ranks, most scouts were military neophytes unschooled in warfare, combat operations, or army organization. This meant the ability to distinguish between a company and a division marching along a road, to effectively sort the signals from the noise, and to escape detection, time and again, would only come (if it did at all) while on the job. The knowledge that a hangman's noose awaited those unlucky enough to be captured, however, made becoming a quick study imperative.

Though most scouts probably served ably and well, employing them could pose unique challenges for information-hungry commanders. For example, the fact that an operative's pay depended upon the perceived value of the information brought in opened the process to abuse by individuals looking to scam the army for financial gain. Tall tales and outright lies, often extremely difficult to corroborate, could bring substantial remuneration if a dishonest scout could convince a commander they were true. Unfortunately, this sort of exploitation by a few miscreants only deepened suspicions of all scouts. "As a general thing," complained one observer, "scouts are perfectly worthless. They are usually plausible fellows who go out [just past] the picket line and *lie* on the ground all night under a tree, and come back to headquarters in the morning and *lie* there, giving wonderful reports about the enemy, fearing no contradiction."[5] [emphasis in original] What a Congressman once said of Lafayette C. Baker, head of the War Department's National Detective Police, probably reflected more general suspicions aimed at anyone involved in secret service. "[I]t is doubtful," he wrote, "whether he has in any one thing told the truth, even by accident."[6] The very nature of Civil War scouting, therefore, could sow far more uncertainty than it dispelled. The antidote was to employ reliable individuals who were familiar with military organizations and operations, willing to risk death if captured, and driven by more pure motives than mere pecuniary gain. Enticed by the chance to escape the drudgery of camp and drill field but otherwise deeply committed to the Union cause, soldiers from the ranks often fit this bill rather well.

One of these recruits was Judson Knight, a New York native who enlisted in the Second New Jersey Volunteer Infantry in May 1861 and became a Union scout for Brig. Gen. Philip Kearny later that summer. A veteran of the Peninsula Campaign, the Seven Days, Second Bull Run, and Antietam, Knight fell ill after the fighting in Maryland and was discharged from the service at year's end. Recovered by fall of 1863, Knight embarked upon what would be an extraordinarily productive career as a civilian scout, rising to the position of "chief of scouts" for the Army of the Potomac's intelligence arm, the Bureau of Military Information (BMI) headed by Col. George H. Sharpe. He participated in the 1864 Overland Campaign and settled in to scout for the Union armies besieging Richmond and Petersburg until Appomattox closed out his career.

When the shooting stopped, Knight picked up a pen and recounted his exploits in a series of articles published in *The National Tribune,* a postwar veterans' periodical and forerunner of the *Stars and Stripes.* For example, his first installment set the tone for the remainder when he dealt with the question: "How did you get inside of the enemy's lines, and travel around there and get information, without being arrested?" His answer provided a rare view into the workings of Sharpe's BMI while on campaign. As with many of these postwar accounts, however, over time Knight's reminiscences slipped from view. Thanks to Peter G. Tsouras, an accomplished historian and well-known author of a series of excellent counterfactual histories, Knight's tale has been given new life. A labor of love, Tsouras collected and edited Knight's *National Tribune* articles and spent years digging deeply into the BMI records at the National Archives in order to document and substantiate—as much as possible—the people, places, and events described by the former scout. This painstaking process entailed poring over hundreds of handwritten letters, reports, telegrams, and pay vouchers as well as mining a multitude of other mundane sources to piece together a puzzle with many missing pieces. Though Knight was undoubtedly a trustworthy fellow (Sharpe certainly thought so), the passage of time, the willful forgetting of unpleasant recollections or embarrassing blunders, and the desire to "puff" oneself for history, a common affliction of many postwar memoirists, could blur and distort memories until they eventually hardened into truth. Postwar memoirs written by secret operatives, moreover, pose even greater challenges since much of their business was done in secret and with minimal paper trails, making reliance on the shifting ground of memory a necessary evil. Believing in the adage "trust but verify," Tsouras's archival labors, judicious editing, and eye for detail uncovers where Knight crossed the line separating fact from fiction. This meticulous detective work gives texture, legitimacy, and greater historical value to the scout's recollections and for that we owe Tsouras a great debt.

Unfortunately, many of the writings of former scouts and spies of the Blue and Gray have not undergone similar treatment, which is why 150 years later the Civil War's intelligence story remains cloaked in mystery and misunderstanding. For various reasons, in the decades after Appomattox the vast majority of those employed in "secret service" maintained the silence and discretion they had so carefully cultivated during the war, even as countless other veterans (and a few marquee spies) put pen to paper to feed the reading public's voracious appetite for war stories. Without their voices, the overly romanticized "cloak and dagger" potboilers written to sell books or to salvage postwar reputations became the benchmark for writings on the intelligence war.

All this is what makes Judson Knight's edited recollections such an important contribution to Civil War intelligence history. Not only was Knight a rarity in that he shared his exploits in public, but he also had much of importance to say, having been a senior scout with the Army of the Potomac during the most critical campaigns of the war.

We owe a great debt to Peter Tsouras for retrieving one of the most important scouts of the war from obscurity and breathing life into his experiences for a modern audience. In the end, Knight's narrative grabs the reader with anecdotes of thrilling exploits and, thanks to Tsouras's editing skill and well-placed commentary, sheds light on the real nature of the intelligence "business" in the Civil War as told by one of its foremost practitioners who "cheerfully" waded into the dark and dangerous shadows "to obtain that great essential of success."[7]

# Introduction

HISTORICAL RESEARCH ALL too often resembles diamond mining. Great effort is needed to sift through vast amounts of material to find a few gems. Happily, the source of this book was a rich vein lying just under the surface in the Library of Congress Newspapers and Periodicals Reading Room among the microfilm rolls of newspapers and records.

The *National Tribune* lay there quietly, not much disturbed by other miners of history, all but forgotten. This weekly publication was the ancestor of the *Stars and Stripes*, the service newspaper of the United States Armed Forces, founded in 1877 "to secure to soldiers and sailors their rights . . ."

> *Later the Tribune became known for its regular feature, "Fighting Them Over: What Our Veterans Have to Say About Their Old Campaigns," which solicited memoirs from veterans of all ranks and backgrounds. This column established the National Tribune as a forum for discussion, debate, and reminiscence for veterans around the country, eventually becoming the official paper of the Grand Army of the Republic.*[8]

This feature is a practically unknown treasure trove of firsthand accounts of America's bloodiest war, the struggle that defined the United States as a nation. Within this trove are the serialized reminiscences of the Chief Scout of the Army of the Potomac, Judson Knight, in the "Fighting Them Over Again" feature, which this book presents for the first time.

*"Fighting Them Over: What Our Veterans Have to Say About Their Old Campaigns,"*
*the regular feature of the* National Tribune *which solicited firsthand accounts from*
*veterans. Cartoon from the* National Tribune.

These reminiscences are unique for a number of reasons. Firsthand accounts by scouts of the North and South are rare, and none are from such a senior member of this select and shadowy fraternity. The closest are the reminiscences of John Landegon, Chief Scout to Sheridan while commanding the Cavalry Corps of the Army of the Potomac, but they are far briefer in length and time covered. Those portions where he served with Knight have been incorporated into this account.[9] Although Knight served as Chief Scout from August 1864 to June 1865, he includes earlier accounts of his adventures and experiences under the redoubtable first Chief Scout, Sgt. Milton Cline (February 1863 to August 1864).

Knight's reminiscences are also noteworthy for how well they were written. The style is personal and almost conversational and still easily accessible to the modern reader. Although on a number of occasions Knight describes his direct contact with Generals Meade and Grant, Assistant Secretary of War Charles Dana, his own chief, Col. George H. Sharpe, and a number of other general officers, his reminiscences are those of the day-to-day life and activities of a scout. What you discover is a continuing narration of scouting trade-craft. Nevertheless, his interactions with general officers often either present new information or confirm other accounts, but from another perspective.

Knight's reminiscences, thirty years after the fact, are remark-ably accurate where accounts, dates, persons, and military units can be verified. It is this editor's experience in studying the scouts of the Civil War and working with their modern counterparts that the best of them have both remarkable powers of observation as well as retention, characteristics Knight clearly shows. Almost every instance where Knight refers to officers and units being at a particular place and at a particular time, the historical record proves him correct. He also had a remarkable range of acquaintances with both fellow enlisted men and units, as well as officers, allowing him to provide personal narratives that are colorful, to say the least.

Knight's accounts of his operations behind Confederate lines are also important for their glimpses into themes not much touched on in most Civil War literature. One of the most interesting themes is his repeated encounters with slaves and white women alone on their farms. Much of the Confederate countryside was empty of adult males of military age. Knight was clearly confident that he could rely on slaves to either overtly help him or at the very least not betray his presence. Both Knight and Col. George H. Sharpe, for whom Knight worked, made clear statements that they never heard an account of a slave betraying a Union soldier behind the lines.

Another element of the white Confederate population with whom he came into contact were Union loyalists, many of whom were prewar immigrants from the North or Great Britain or former non-commissioned officers in the regular army. Not a few loyalists were native-born southerners who would not sever their devotion to the "Old Flag." The most important of these was the ring of Union spies in Richmond headed by Elizabeth Van Lew. One of the most interesting characters of the Civil War, Van Lew was a member of

Richmond society. She was also an ardent Union patriot and abolitionist who was determined to do everything she could to aid the cause of the Union. At first that consisted of providing necessities to Union prisoners in Richmond. That quickly evolved into a system for assisting them in their escape and evasion back to Union lines. At great personal risk she hid many prisoners in her own home. A clever woman, she acquired the perfect cover by giving free room and board to the Provost Marshal of the Confederacy as well as by affecting an eccentric personality. As the Union armies closed on Richmond and Petersburg, she offered her services to provide them with information and succeeded in forwarding an almost constant stream of usually highly accurate information, to the Union armies. Her means were so efficient it was said that along with the information, flowers from her truck farm would arrive for Grant's breakfast table with the dew still on them. When Grant became president he would reward her by making her postmistress of Richmond for eight years. A considerable portion of Knight's reminiscences concern fulfilling orders coming directly from Grant through his chief intelligence officer, Colonel Sharpe, to make contact with Van Lew. Knight's adventures add considerably to the knowledge of Van Lew's operation in Richmond.

## SCOUTS IN THE CIVIL WAR

The study of military intelligence in the Civil War invariably leads to the work of the scouts of the Union and Confederate armies. They were the traditional eyes and ears of an army. Today we would refer to them also as collectors of the information that professional analysts would transform into military intelligence.

Scouts had been with armies since deepest antiquity. Rameses II in his accounts of the battle of Kadesh in 1274 BC recounts the interrogation of captured Hittite scouts. However, the Civil War represented a new stage in the employment of scouts. Luckily for the success of the arms of the Union, Maj. Gen. Joseph Hooker, who had just become commander of the Army of the Potomac in January 1963, had had a taste for the value of military intelligence. Heretofore, generals commanding armies had been their own chief intelligence officers, but by this time Hooker realized that the complexities of modern warfare made it impossible for a general to execute this function by himself in addition to his other duties. Being a transformational man, he hit upon a creative solution.

His innovation was to put military intelligence into the hands of a professional staff to exercise the entire process of military intelligence. That included the collection of information from all available

GENERAL GEORGE H. SHARPE

*The brilliant Col. George H. Sharpe, 120th New York Volunteers, created American all-source military intelligence as Chief of the Bureau of Military Information (BMI) for the Army of the Potomac. He became one of Grant's favored family of generals. Judson Knight always referred to him with respect. Author's collection.*

sources and then subjecting it to a rigorous analytical process which would transform that raw information into what is today called finished intelligence. Surprisingly, this was the first time in military history that this had ever been done. That staff was the Army of the Potomac's Bureau of Military Intelligence (BMI). The man Hooker chose to build and run it was Colonel George H. Sharpe, commander of the 120th New York Infantry. Hooker could not have picked a more perfect man for the job. Sharpe was one of the best educated men in the country, had trained as a lawyer, and had traveled abroad to gain a cosmopolitan polish and depth. His legal training had developed just those analytical tools vital to the conduct of intelligence analysis. He was also a wily and charming man who could extract cooperation from a stone during interrogation. As shown in the photo above, where he is almost hidden in the back row, he left a very light footprint, the ultimate accolade for an intelligence officer. He lived up to

*Maj. Gen. Joseph Hooker, Commander of the Army of the Potomac (front row, seated second from right), founded the first professional military intelligence staff, the Bureau of Military Information, in February 1863 and put it in the hands of Col. George H. Sharpe (last row, standing sixth from left). Timothy O'Sullivan, Library of Congress, LC-DIG-ppmsca-34097.*

the motto of the general staff officer, as stated by the Prussian Field Marshal Helmut von Moltke, to be more than one seems.

In a few months, Sharpe had worked miracles. He had assembled a first-rate team which included a civilian contractor, John C. Babcock, who became the master of the art of order-of-battle. Captain John McEntee, another of Sharpe's deputies, was responsible for running the scouting operations of the BMI. For the first time, all the strands of intelligence were gathered under the direction of one chief and subjected to rigorous analysis. Sharpe was responsible for document exploitation (military correspondence, letters, newspapers, and so on.); prisoner of war interrogation, debriefing of escaped Union prisoners, refugees, and contrabands; spies, agents, and scouts.[10] In addition he closely cooperated with the other collectors of intelligence—the Signal Corps, the Balloon Corps, cavalry, and any other department of the government he deemed fit. Sharpe's organization was a significant combat multiplier for the Army of the Potomac and contributed decisively to the victory at Gettysburg and in the success of its later campaigns. Significantly, throughout the war the BMI employed barely over two hundred men, and its peak strength in May of 1864 was only sixty-seven (see Appendix).

For Sharpe, the band of scouts he recruited was the vital element in the creation of military intelligence. Not only did they directly gather information by personal observation and action, but they also worked closely with Sharpe's network of agents and spies. They were the link by which Sharpe coordinated his agents and spies, and the conduit of their collection of information, and they were highly respected by the senior staffs as well as the rank and file. Col. Horace Porter, one of Grant's personal staff, alluded to that in his memoir by writing that "[Sharpe] rendered invaluable service in obtaining information regarding the enemy by his employment of scouts...."[11] It was a rare kudo, for senior officers were remarkably tight-lipped in discussing the operations of the BMI.

Sharpe's scouts also were not adverse to collecting newspapers and other documents. Newspapers were a rich source of order-of-battle information for they frequently contained casualty figures and other information which allowed Sharpe's small group of analysts to determine with amazing accuracy the organization, strength, and commanders of the Army of Northern Virginia. Sharpe's correspondence is filled with his careful efforts to coordinate, support, and track his scouts. It reveals the degree of independence of action he permitted them as well as the significant amounts of money with which he entrusted them.

The scouts were not nameless sources of information for Sharpe's analytical mill. The commanders of the Army of the Potomac, Joseph Hooker and George G. Meade, as well as Ulysses S. Grant, were personally familiar with many of them. They showed an eager concern in the results of their forays and an anxious interest in their location and return during active operations. Commanders were not above awarding scouts significant cash bonuses for particularly successful missions.

Confederate scouts were every bit as daring and skillful as Sharpe's men, but their reports were not subjected to the same professional and systematic analysis. The Army of Northern Virginia had no organization comparable to the BMI. General Lee was his own chief intelligence officer, following the traditional model, and Jeb Stuart was his chief collector of information. The demands of modern war were to prove that such a model no longer fit the times.

Confederate John Esten Cooke penned a most accurate description of the scouts employed by both the Union and Confederate armies in the Civil War.

> The scout proper is "commanding in the field," with no one near to give him orders. He goes and comes at will, having that about him which all pickets obey. He is "on detached service;" and having procured certain information, reports to the officer who has sent him, without intermediate ceremony. Operating within the enemy's lines at all times, he depends for success and safety on the quickness of his eye and hand – and his reliance on these is great. He is silent in his movements, low-toned in his speech, abstemious in his habits, and as untiring on the track of the enemy as the Cuban blood-hound on the trail of the fugitive. He rarely sleeps in houses, preferring the woods; and always slumbers with "one eye open," on the look out for the enemy.[12]

*A scout of the Army of the Potomac. The scouts of the BMI numbered between thirty and fifty men at any one time. They were paid according to their proven experience and effectiveness. Library of Congress, LC-USZ62-108336.*

To these attributes should be added the skills of an actor and a bold effrontery in the midst of enemy soldiers and civilians that would allow him to brazen his way out of any situation that would compromise a lesser man. No less important were keen powers of observation, an accurate memory, a hardy constitution that could sleep out in all weathers, and the skill to scrounge his own subsistence. The turnover rate among the scouts indicated that not everyone was up to the test and that Sharpe did not hesitate to dismiss them.

Sharpe's scouts included both soldiers and civilians. Most of his scouts though were soldiers, many of whom already had scouting experience in other commands. The 3rd Indiana Cavalry was a particularly effective recruiting source. They had been trained by Lafayette Baker, head of the Secret Service, to support Maj. Gen. Joseph Hooker's operations along the eastern shore of Maryland and Virginia early in the war. After they captured a Confederate sloop, they were given the nickname of Hooker's Horse Marines.

Many of the men hired were civilians who would be considered contractors today. The soldiers among the scouts apparently continued to receive their normal soldier's pay in addition to the special pay. That pay, for soldiers and civilians, ranged from fifty cents to four dollars a day for every day of the month for scouts.

*Governor's Island in New York Harbor with Fort Columbia on the lower part of the island, where Judson Knight served in the garrison during the Mexican War. Library of Congress, LC-USZ62-135430.*

The specific rate for each man depended upon both experience and proven ability. The upper and lower rates worked out to monthly totals of fifteen dollars to $120 a month, a considerable improvement over the private's thirteen dollars a month. The rate of four dollars a day was roughly equivalent to the pay of a first lieutenant ($115.50 a month), and was awarded to very few men. Most of the scouts were paid at two dollars to three dollars a day.

Scouting, as Cooke noted, required men with special abilities that were not easy to find. The risk a Union scout took was extraordinary because he often wore either civilian clothes or Confederate uniforms while on operations. Capture so dressed would earn him a swift hanging by the laws of war. Officers, as gentlemen, did not engage in that sort of thing.

An exception to the top scout rate of four dollars was found with John C. Babcock who was listed among the scouts for pay purposes but did not serve as a scout. He was a civilian who served as the order-of-battle analyst for the BMI and was paid at the rate of $7.50 a day ($225 a month), which was more than the pay of a full colonel ($212 a month), an indication of how valuable he was considered.

In addition to the scouts, the BMI employed guides, local men who had immediate knowledge of a particular area and were employed only on an as-needed basis. Many of these men were loyalist civilians such as the McGees and Skinkers of Northern Virginia or runaway slaves or contrabands. In addition to the scouts and guides, the BMI was allowed a support staff of clerks, teamsters, and cooks. Most of these men were black. However, a few of the men listed as guides were also identified as black.

The BMI scouts were a diverse group by physical type, age, and occupation. Most were very young—in their early twenties; however, the two men who would become chiefs of scouts, Cline and Knight, were in their thirties with more maturity and experience. Their occupations ranged from clerk to boatman to plasterer and to machinist, in Knight's case. What unified them was an independence of character, a cool boldness, a taste for danger, and a good dash of the actor, for they spent much time passing themselves off as Confederates, with remarkable success. Sharpe was to prove a shrewd judge of these qualities, and his careful selection of just the right men would be vital to the success of the BMI.

Constant exposure to the elements in all weather and in all seasons, when most troops were in winter quarters or camp, required the hardiest of men as well. Sharpe mentioned the effect of such exposure in a letter to Maj. Gen. Hancock on May 2, 1864. "We expect to be able to send you two good men as guides. One of them may have to ride in an ambulance having lost part of one of his feet while lying within the enemy's lines during the late snow-storm."[13] Many scouts would suffer its effects decades later in ill-health directly attributed to such exposure, as shown in their applications for pensions.

One of the first scouts Sharpe engaged was the redoubtable fair-haired Sgt. Milton Cline of the 3rd Indiana Cavalry. It was no wonder that Sharpe quickly made him Chief Scout for the Army of the Potomac. He set a high example for the rest of the scouts. Cline was coolness personified as he again and again masqueraded as a Confederate cavalry sergeant. His efforts provided the intelligence that allowed Sharpe to offer Lee's head on a silver platter to Hooker in the plan for the Chancellorsville Campaign. The fact that Hooker failed was not the fault of the intelligence Sharpe provided him. It was Cline's efforts that led to the capture of vital information in the Gettysburg Campaign that contributed to the decision by General Meade to fight it out after the second day of the battle. Cline was mustered out with the rest of his regiment in August 1864 during the Siege of Petersburg. Judson Knight would be a worthy replacement.

### JUDSON KNIGHT

Judson Knight was born in the small town of Boonville, Oneida County, New York, on April 26, 1829. In 1847, as the Mexican War broke out, he wrote, "I was living at Poland, Herkimer County, NY, when I first entered the service—as not working for anyone but had been at school at Little Falls, NY. I boarded myself." He enlisted under the name John King on November 13, 1847 and served on garrison duty at Ft. Columbia on Governor's Island in New York Harbor. The only event of that service was the bout of smallpox that he contracted that winter from which he fully recovered. It was an all-too-common experience in this war and

April 1865 payroll for the Bureau of Military Information in which Lt. Gen. U.S. Grant orders a special service payment to Judson Knight of $2,500. A payment of $6,000 was made in June. Courtesy, National Archives, RG 92, Entry 238, File 0447 (1865), Box 268.

the coming Civil War, in which country boys little exposed to communicable diseases easily came down with them once they joined the army. He was lucky to have survived smallpox. It and other communicable diseases would kill more men in the coming Civil War than died from wounds. His only lasting memento of his service were the smallpox scars on his face. He was discharged on June 30, 1848.[14]

He returned to Poland in New York and took up the trade of machinist. About 1855 he moved to Newark, New Jersey, where he was self-employed in that skill. He married Mabel M. Nicholson in Trenton, New York, on October 16, 1858. When the Civil War broke out, he enlisted on May 26, 1861, in H Co., 2nd New Jersey Infantry. He recalled that he was given no medical examination. It would have been evident he was a prime recruit in the best of health. He was a powerfully-built man at six feet and a quarter inch, sandy-haired, with hazel eyes, and a fair complexion badly marked from smallpox.[15]

The regiment was mustered in at Camp Olden at Trenton where Knight, who apparently had made an impression, was quickly promoted to corporal and then to sergeant on June 3rd. The regiment left for Washington, D.C., on June 28th and was combined with other state regiments into the Jersey Brigade. The regiment was in reserve at the battle of First Bull Run on July 21st. The Jersey Brigade became known as Kearny's Brigade after its new commander, the legendary Indian fighter, Brig. Gen. Phillip Kearny, who trained it into a superb fighting formation. Knight was officially detailed as a scout at Kearny's headquarters on August 20th. He had already been scouting for the regiment, evidently successfully enough to be transferred to work directly for Kearny.[16] He occupied a room in Kearny's headquarters until the winter set in.

With Kearny now its division commander, the brigade moved to the Peninsula and fought in the Seven Days battles before Richmond (June 25th to July 1, 1862), to include the engagements at Gaines Mill, Garnett's Farm, Golding's, Charles City Cross Roads, Glendale, and Malvern Hill. Knight was seeing a great deal of combat under one of the finest commanders in the Union Army.

He served as a scout during the battle of Second Bull Run on August 30th. The next day at the battle of Chantilly, Brig. Gen. Kearny was killed. Knight then took part in the Antietam Campaign where his

Division saw action at the battles of Crampton's Gap, South Mountain, and Antietam itself. He remained at Sharpsburg, Maryland, with his division after the battle, where he learned that his wife had died on September 26th. Shortly thereafter he entered the military hospital in Hampton, Virginia, for a serious illness.[17]

He remained there for two months suffering from scorfulosis (swelling of the lymph gland of the neck) and ulceration of the glands of the neck. On December 1st for some unknown reason his company muster roll notes that he was "reduced to [the] ranks from Sergeant." His illness proved serious enough to earn him a discharge from the army on the last day of 1862.[18]

In the spring he was working for Baker's Secret Service (known officially as the War Department's National Detective Police) in Fairfax County, Virginia. Scouting apparently had been an exciting experience for Knight. Scouts were men apart from the rest of the army, and they wanted it that way. If it were commonly known a man was a scout, it would be all too easy to compromise him. The small scouting community was then a very much closed group whose members were known to each other. Perhaps from that group Knight heard of the new Bureau of Military Information that had been just established in the Army of the Potomac in February 1863. As the organization began to grow, Sharpe was sifting the army for good scouts and began assembling an excellent team.

Knight related that he came to army headquarters in April and presented testimonials of his service with the late General Kearny that were evidently impressive enough for Sharpe to later write, "He was immediately engaged by me to serve with us." His name first appeared on the BMI's October 1864 payroll; however, just as he said, he started working for Sharpe in early April of 1863, despite the evidence of the payroll. On April 13, 1863, the assistant adjutant of a cavalry division requested the officer commanding the pickets to "pass within your lines two scouts viz: William Blake and Judson Knight; they both are furnished with passes from Headquarters . . ."[19] Also, Maj. Gen. Daniel Butterfield, who served as Hooker's chief of staff, wrote a testimonial for Sharpe more than twenty-five years later in support of his request for a pension. Maj. Gen. George G. Meade, who replaced Hooker as commander of the army, replaced Butterfield with Brig. Gen. A. A. Humphreys shortly after the battle of Gettysburg in July 1863. Knight would come to enjoy, according to Sharpe, an "enviable reputation as a man to whom a bold enterprise could be entrusted without endangering the confidence of his superior officers."[20]

Unlike most of the rest of the scouts, Knight was a civilian employee or, as could be said today, a contractor. Despite that civilian status, he would be referred to as Sergeant Knight both during and after the war. He first shows up on the payroll of the BMI in October 1863 where he is immediately shown as being paid the near top rate of three dollars a day.[21] The men he spoke highly of were Dan Plew, Dan Cole, Martin Hogan, Pat McEneany, and the Carneys—Anson, Edward, and Philip, almost all veterans of the 1st and 3rd Indiana and 5th U.S. Cavalry Regiments.[22] Their shadowy exploits appear here and there in the massive compilation of the *War of the Rebellion: The Official Records of the Union and Confederate Armies*, often referred to as the *Official Records* or the *OR*.

Apparently Knight was held in high regard by other scouts. Maj. Gen. Philip Sheridan's chief scout, William Landegon, remarked that Knight was a cool and accomplished liar in the performance of his duties in dealing with southern civilians and possessed the other higher qualities of the scout as well.[23]

Knight's descriptions of Colonel Sharpe are unfailingly positive. Sharpe had a lot invested in Knight, and the man delivered, but Knight's comments on the chief of the BMI reflect a solid personal as well as professional relationship. The one man of whom Knight held a negative opinion was Brig. Gen. Marsena R. Patrick (1811–1888), Provost Marshal General of the Army of the Potomac. The BMI fell under Patrick's Provost Marshal General's department, and Sharpe served as his deputy. No more unconventional group than the scouts could be found in the army and were frequently under Patrick's demanding eye. A devout man, Patrick did everything in his power to shield civilians from the depredations of war. However, he was an unbending and strict disciplinarian whose harsh manner engendered no affection from the troops, of which Knight's recollections are an accurate reflection.[24]

Knight's narrative begins in the winter of 1863–1864 with cold and miserable duty in the "Debatable Land" bordering the Rappahannock and Rapidan Rivers. There he worked with Sharpe's Unionist agents in the vicinity, such as Isaac Silver, referred to at army headquarters as "the old man."[25] Silver was one of Sharpe's most valuable agents, able to travel easily to nearby Confederate camps and railroad stations and obtain highly accurate information from a number of his own contacts. Scouts regularly visited his home to bring back that information. His home also became the safe house from which scouts set out on their missions or rested on their return.

The cold waters of these two rivers had to be crossed again and again which would lead to the rheumatism that would torment Knight's last years. Yet as unglamorous and rigorous as it was, it was a vital element in Sharpe's constant effort to collect intelligence on the Army of Northern Virginia in the season when the weather shut down campaigning and confined most of both armies to their camps.

Knight then relates the adventures of his two comrades, Wood Dodd and Frank McCord, in their encounters with and escape from the South's two most notorious partisan commanders in Northern Virginia, Col. John Singleton Mosby and Maj. Harry Gilmor, just before the Overland Campaign of 1864. With this account are other near-death experiences of scouts John Landegon and Anson Carney. That campaign would see Knight roaming the jagged edges of the endless battlefields between Wilderness and the crossing of the Chickahominy River on the army's way to Petersburg. He would recall how he and a few other scouts arrived at the defenses of that city to find them practically empty and ready to fall at the push of only a hundred aggressive men. Yet, the commanders that Grant had expected to do just that were still haunted by the Cold Harbor assault and hesitated just long enough for Lee's hard-breathing veterans to fill the trenches.

The next month Knight was given the mission that would lead to his most important contribution in the war: to connect Sharpe with Elizabeth Van Lew, the Union patriot who had held the loyal population of Richmond together. By coincidence, Knight had already met John Van Lew, her brother, who had escaped through the lines to avoid Confederate conscription and had been questioned by the BMI which is where Knight encountered him. Despite his best efforts, neither patriotism nor money would induce John Van Lew to join the Union Army. He did offer some valuable parting advice to Knight. "I will tell you something that may be of value to you. If you can ever get into communication with my mother or sister, they are in a position where they might furnish you with valuable information. Their names are both Elizabeth N. Van Lew." For Knight it would be something of a prophecy.[26]

Elizabeth Van Lew was eager to do more and had communicated this to Maj. Gen. Butler, commanding the nearby Army of the James in early 1864. This information was passed on to Sharpe. At the same time, the failure to track Confederate Lt. Gen. Jubal Early's drive on Washington convinced Grant that he needed a major source of intelligence from within Richmond itself. He directed Sharpe to find it. Sharpe then moved his operation and a picked group of scouts to Grant's headquarters at City Point. It was mid-July.

Sharpe could have given the mission to Sergeant Cline, but he knew that the chief scout was due to be mustered out the following month. Sharpe already had his eye on Knight as Cline's replacement. In August 1864, Sergeant Cline was duly mustered out of the service with his regiment. Sharpe immediately chose Knight to replace him, and by the end of September he was the only scout receiving four dollars a day.[27] It was a transitional time for the scouts of the BMI; most of the experienced soldier scouts were mustered out of the army at this time with their regiments because their three-year terms of enlistment had expired.

Even before Cline left, Sharpe turned to Knight and gave him the mission as soon as he and his scouts had moved into a building at City Point. Knight took advantage of the Union Navy's control of the James River to ferry him across to Confederate controlled territory around Richmond. Yet once across the river, time and time again Knight was unable to penetrate the Confederate lines and was turned back. Though, like a dog worrying a bone, he persevered and finally succeeded in making contact with Van Lew, establishing a regular courier system for the transmission of intelligence collection priorities from Sharpe and Van Lew's responses. It was after this that Sharpe's intelligence reports began making numerous cryptic references to Union agents in Richmond. No agent was ever mentioned by name, though her name became known to a select few in the BMI and to Meade, Grant, and a few of their senior staff. Knight was a frequent visitor to Van Lew and must have developed a good relationship for he made a point of calling on her twenty years after the war when visiting Richmond.

They made a good team that provided a steady flow of largely accurate and especially timely information to Sharpe, which was the pivot upon which Grant was able to hold Lee in check and gradually strangle the Confederate capital. It has been reported that the channels of information were so quick that flowers cut in the morning on Van Lew's truck farm would be on Grant's breakfast table. Yet, this smoothly running espionage system would come close to ruin due to a double-agent.

In February Knight visited Van Lew and explained, "I'm directed to tell you that there will be an Englishman sent through the lines, whose duty it will be to oblige and bring you information to send through." The agent was an Englishman named Pole, a mechanic who would find employment as a skilled machinist and engineer by posing as a southern sympathizer. Van Lew was instantly suspicious and rightly so. The day after Pole arrived in the city he betrayed a number of Union agents within the city. Pole later explained that he had been the "chosen emissary" of Mason and Slidell, the Confederate emissaries to Britain and France. He had come to the United States and joined the Army hoping to get close enough to desert. When that proved impossible, he apparently sold himself to Sharpe at the BMI as a useful agent. If so, it was one of Sharpe's few blunders.[28] Nevertheless, despite the arrest of a number of Van Lew's ring, her operation was not fundamentally compromised and continued with Knight's participation to ably support Sharpe and Grant.

Knight's successes were well-enough thought of that he was awarded for special services with cash grants of $300 in December 1864, $520 in January 1965, and $393.58 in February, a total of $1,213 or a little less than the yearly pay of a first lieutenant ($1,386). His monthly pay was already equivalent to a first lieutenant ($1,480). This would all be small change. The April 1865 payroll shows him receiving an astounding $6,000! That was more than the pay of a major general ($5,489). Only Grant, as the Army's only lieutenant general, made more ($9,776). The BMI payrolls identify only two other men to receive cash grants. They were Ebenezer Halleck and Alexander Myers (one of Van Lew's Richmond couriers), both of whom were awarded $500.[29]

*Members of the Ku Klux Klan captured by Treasury agents in 1871, just the sort of work Judson Knight was doing after the Civil War.* Harper's Weekly, *January 1872. Author's Collection.*

After his discharge in April of 1865 following Lee's surrender at Appomattox and the disbanding of the BMI, Knight went to Richmond with the remnants of the staff where he was paid off in June. At the direction of Grant himself, he was awarded another $2,500 for special services. That was a year's pay for a full colonel ($2,544), exactly what Sharpe was making. Given that Grant awarded at the same time $2,000 for Elizabeth Van Lew, the incomparable spy mistress of Richmond, it was an extraordinary recognition of his achievements. The awards were well-paired, for Grant was making it clear that without Knight's efforts to establish and maintain contact with Van Lew, her irreplaceable contributions would have never happened.[30]

Apparently, Knight lingered in the South to continue to work for the government in a clandestine police role. He stated in an 1899 deposition that he then went back to Poland, New York, for a year or so, and returned to Newark for a short time. He then wrote that after leaving Newark, "I was in the Secret Service—looking after Ku Klux in Georgia." Interestingly, President Grant's attorney general ordered the new head of the Secret Service, Hiram Whitley, in 1871 to dispatch eight operatives to six former Confederate states, to include Georgia, to investigate the activities of the Ku Klux Klan. After this Knight then moved to New York City for a number of years. By then he had given up on "the iron business" and made plaster-of-paris models for bonnets for ladies and little girls, a strange line of work for a man who had engaged in such adventures during the war. Like so many men who have come back to the quiet of civilian life from the adrenaline rush of war, he may have found the tranquil days of peace something of a letdown.[31]

Apparently, he was not one to keep his family in touch. In early 1867, his worried brother wrote Major General Meade asking about his whereabouts. He wrote that the family had had no communication from him since 1862. Meade forwarded the request through channels to Sharpe, who had kept track of most of the men in the BMI. In his reply he was able to state that Knight was paid off in the spring of 1865 at the end of the war and that he had "received some appointment under a treasury agency in Virginia. I heard of him somewhere in southwestern Virginia during the last year, and I think he is there yet, tho' I am unable to recall the name of the place." He then suggested a number of distinguished men in Richmond who would have knowledge of him as would "any prominent authorities in Richmond to all of whom he is well known." Sharpe may have been toning down Knight's activities for public consumption; the "treasury agency" surely was the new incarnation of the Secret Service with which he had worked after his initial discharge at the end of 1862 and before he joined Sharpe and the BMI.[32]

From New York City he moved to Washington in 1885 for about five years and then moved to Le Roy, Bradford County, Pennsylvania, for a year before moving back to Washington for good, where from 1890 to 1894 he wrote his reminiscences for *The National Tribune*. Ironically, these articles of his personal experiences as a scout in the BMI, which form the substance of this book, are the only extensive account by any surviving member of that organization. Sharpe's son had encouraged his father to come stay with him in Washington while he wrote his memoirs of the war. Unfortunately, Sharpe died shortly thereafter in January 1900.

Within twenty years of the end of the war, Knight's health began to fail due to injuries and ailments incurred during the war, especially during the cold and wet times in the field in the spring of 1864. In Washington he was cared for in his illness by his sister, Mrs. Julia Neary. In 1887 he was awarded a pension of eight dollars a month for his service in the Mexican War. His appeals for a pension for his Civil War service about that time led to the support of a number of the senior men he had served in the war. They included Major Generals Sharpe, Daniel Butterfield, Winfield Scott Hancock, and William S. Rosecrans. Their support was necessary to get Congress to pass a special piece of legislation on his behalf to provide a pension because as a civilian contractor he did not fall under the existing Civil War pension law.

Sharpe's hearty testimonial added the weight that pushed the bill through and was printed by both pension committees reporting the bill.

> *During a considerable part of the time that I served on the general staff of the Army of the Potomac, and afterwards on the general staff of the armies operating against Richmond,*

*in Virginia, Judson Knight was employed at these headquarters as a scout. He enjoyed an enviable reputation as a man to whom a bold enterprise could be intrusted without endangering the confidence of his superior officers. At times he rendered services that received signal praise of the major-general [Meade] commanding the Army of the Potomac and the lieutenant-general [Grant] commanding the armies operating against Richmond.*

*When he came to the headquarters he brought high testimonials of his service with the late General Phil. Kearny. He was immediately engaged by me to serve with us. In 1864 he was made chief of scouts of the Army of the Potomac, and in that capacity, and until the close of the war, rendered the most efficient service. Throughout his service his reports were always relied on, and I take pleasure in saying he is a man who deserves well of his country. He is now crippled from the effects of these services, and it affords me pleasure to make this testimonial in behalf of one who was always faithful and gallant in the performance of his duty.[33]*

Maj. Gen. Rosecran's letter to the Secretary of War in support of Knight's claim was equally fulsome.

*Captain Judson Knight's services in the late war laid the foundation of his present grave disability; but he has hitherto forborne to ask a pension. After reading the high testimonials he has of service as scout and chief of scouts, and knowing the rare combination of courage, intelligence, and fidelity demanded in that service, I feel a warm interest in his case, and shall introduce a bill for pensioning him. I unite with Senator Sewall in asking you to interest yourself in securing him some suitable employment by which he can support himself until he gets legal relief.[34]*

Also included was a letter to Knight from Hancock which stated, "I can state with pleasure that I knew you in the Army as one of the chiefs of scouts, and recall on one occasion when you came to me on duty. My remembrance of you is that you were a meritorious person and performed good service."[35]

The bill was so heavily endorsed that it sailed right through the Senate on March 31 and the House on April 3, 1888, even though as the committee reports stated, "The pension laws do not cover this case, but it is evident that he had earned a pension and needs it." The bill was passed on July 9 and read:

> *Be it enacted by the Senate and House of Representatives of the United States in Congress assembled, That the Secretary of the Interior be, and he is hereby authorized and direct-ed to place on the pension-roll the name of Judson Knight, late chief of scouts at headquarters of the armies operating against Richmond, subject to the provisions and limitations of the pension laws, as though he had been regularly mus-tered into the United States Army, with the rank of captain of volunteers.[36]*

Knight's health continued to worsen, and in 1899 he petitioned for an increase in his pension, only to be overwhelmed by the bureau-cracy in a story that many of the wounded from the Iraq and Afghan wars today can appreciate. His attorney wrote in an appeal in 1902:

> *It should not be lost sight of that the reports of the several boards of examining surgeons are in as much uncertainty and confusion, and even the same report contains contradic-tions of what is stated before; surely there is as wide a differ-ence as in the medical certificates of the physicians who have testified in the claimants behalf. When the doctors disagree who then is to say? This poor claimant has been examined until the doctors are all at sea, and we are no nearer the right of the matter. There must be a way out.[37]*

For Knight there was no way out. The Bureau of Pensions simply waited him out. His last appeal was overcome by his death (1902) and simply stamped "dead."[38]

# Editor's Notes

ALTHOUGH THE ARTICLES of Judson Knight, William Landegon, and Anson B. Carney that make up this work were well written, the passage of almost thirty years from the end of the Civil War blurred a few details. A few names were misremembered or garbled, such as when Knight wrote of Isaac Silver, one of Sharpe's most valuable southern agents, as a Mr. Sylvia. A few place names were misspelled, such as Spottsylvania for Spotsylvania, a mistake made by almost every northern writer during and after the Civil War. Culpeper, Virginia, was also universally misspelled as Culpepper by Union men. I have corrected these minor errors. We can afford to be charitable; after all, they did not have spell-check or the Internet to verify spellings and facts. As it was, their memory for details was extraordinary. A few other spelling oddities that were acceptable at the time, I have retained for the historical flavor.

Because these men were writing for an audience of veterans, they assumed that their readers would understand the context of military life and events of the war which the modern reader cannot always do. For that reason, I have heavily endnoted their articles and, where it was necessary for the flow of the narratives, included that context as either editor's notes or explanatory documents in text boxes. At the same time, these efforts serve to support the authors' facts to a remarkable extent.

# Acknowledgments

T HIS BOOK OWES an immense debt to the support, advice, and insightful review of my friend, William B. Feis, professor of history at Buena Vista University in Storm Lake, Iowa, the acknowledged expert on Civil War military intelligence. Bill was a protégé of Edwin Fishel, author of the magisterial and groundbreaking *The Secret War for the Union: The Untold Story of Military Intelligence in the Civil War* (1996), and his own book, *Grant's Secret Service: The Intelligence War from Belmont to Appomattox* (2002), was a worthy continuation of his mentor's work. In the finest tradition of scholarship, Professor Feis has been as generous with me as Fishel was with him. I cannot thank him too much.

To the dedicated researchers at the National Archive, I can only offer my deepest appreciation for their positive assistance in searching the military service records, pension files, payrolls, and other resources without which the history of Judson Knight and so much of the context of this book could not have been written. I particularly want to thank Achivist DeAnne Blanton; Archives Specialists Jill D'Andra and Rebecca Crawford; and Archives Technicians Dorothy Simmons, Andrew Brethauer, Ray Bottorff, and Alison Gavin. At the Library of Congress, the help of American History Specialist and Curator of Rare Americana Rosemary Plakas and Reference Librarian Meagan Halsband was of inestimable value in completing this book. The Prints and Photographs Division was a treasure house of Civil War art and photographs that grace this book and breathe a little life back into a bygone era. The Library's collection of the drawings of Edwin

Forbes are especially evocative and a favorite of mine. I wish also to thank for all their assistance Alisa M. Monheim and Jaeda Snow at the Huntington Library in Pasadena. These researchers, archivists, and librarians at these great institutions are the quiet guardians and stewards of our civilization, and the vital allies of the historian.

My thanks also goes to James A. Goecker who generously provided vital details from his own extensive research on the BMI scouts from Indiana regiments. Last but not least, I wish to thank my old high school friend and eminent botanist, Stephen K. Langer, for his assistance in identifying the specific chestnut trees referred to by Knight.

As always it has been my wife, Patty, who has been a font of loving support and encouragement without which I could never have stepped out onto the writer's path.

# I
# Major General Philip Kearny

REMINISCENCES OF THE ONE-ARMED HERO OF TWO WARS

*EDITOR'S NOTE: Judson Knight served as a scout for Maj. Gen. Philip Kearny in 1861 and until his death at the battle of Chantilly on September 1, 1862. That service with Kearny left an indelible impression on Knight.*

*For anyone who has served under a truly charismatic and exceptional leader in the military, Knight's account of Kearny will not be difficult to understand. Such a leader exerts so powerful an attraction that the beholder is almost high in his presence. In a case where that leader is a moral example, it is easy to develop a case of hero worship that would last him all of a lifetime. Knight's following account is a reflection of that feeling. In this case, it seeks to commemorate that overwhelming experience with a memoir twenty-nine years after his hero's death in battle.*

*Knight's account also provides fresh historical information, particularly the origin of the unit patch, the award of a*

*Maj. Gen. Philip Kearny, as commander of the Jersey Brigade, gave Judson Knight his start as a scout. It was the testimonials from this service that convinced Col. Sharpe to hire Knight as a scout on the spot. Author's collection.*

precursor to the Purple Heart, and Stonewall Jackson's reaction to seeing Kearny's body on the battlefield of Chantilly.

Knight's conduct as a scout for Kearny provided him with ample testimonials to his ability such that he quickly earned himself a place in the Army of the Potomac's new *military intelligence organization, the Bureau of Military Information. Those abilities eventually earned him a promotion to become the chief of scouts to succeed the remarkable Milton Cline.*

*The following summary of Kearny's life will put much of Knight's account in context.*

*Maj. Gen. Philip Kearny (pronounced Kárni) 1815–1862, was one of the finest leaders in American military history and a man of even greater but unfulfilled promise. Although he inherited great wealth, Kearny's ambition was to be a soldier. In 1837 he obtained a commission in the 1ˢᵗ Dragoons and served in the West for three years until he was sent to France to study cavalry tactics at the famous cavalry school at Samar. He accompanied the Chasseurs d'Afrique on campaign in Algeria where he rode into battle chasseur-style, with a pistol in one hand, a saber in another, and the reins in his teeth, earning the title Kearny le Magnifique.*

*Upon his return he served as aide-de-camp to Maj. Gen. Winfield Scott and then served again in the West. In the Mexican War, the dragoon troop he raised was the personal bodyguard of General Scott. He fought at the battles of Contreras and Churubusco, and in the latter led a daring charge in which his arm was mangled by grapeshot and had to be amputated. Scott called him "a perfect soldier" and the "bravest man I ever knew." Scott honored him by allowing him to be the first American soldier to enter the main gate of Mexico City after its surrender.[39]*

*He resigned his commission in 1851, and in 1859 he returned to France to rejoin the Chasseurs d'Afrique in the war against Austria. He was with Napoleon III's Imperial Guard at the battle of Solferino and charged with the cavalry that broke the Austrian center. For his dash and heroism on the field, he was the first American to be awarded the Legion d'honneur.*

*When the Civil War broke out, he returned to the United States and was appointed brigadier general of volunteers in command of the newly formed Jersey Brigade, which he trained to a high level of efficiency such that it would later achieve a great military reputation in combat. He was noted not only for his superb leadership and tactical skills but also for the great attention he took in the care of his men.*

*It was Kearny who first devised the system of unit patches that survives to this day and has been adopted worldwide. He ordered his officers to wear a red piece of cloth on their caps, and the men followed suit on their own. He said to them then, "You are marked men, you must ever be in the front." The patch was later systematized by Maj. Gen. Butterfield in 1863 to give each corps its own symbol and each subordinate division that symbol in a different color.[40]*

*Kearny was promoted to major general on July 4, 1862 and given command of the 3rd Division of III Corps. Kearny would go on to prove repeatedly that he was utterly fearless in battle and that he had that coolness and clarity of mind in the midst of deadly chaos that distinguishes the very best combat leaders. He led in the battles of Williamsburg and Fair Oaks in the Peninsular Campaign. His corps commander was unsure of his ability to command a division, to which Kearny retorted, "General, I can make men follow me to hell." At Williamsburg, he was summoned to take pressure off another sorely pressed division, and he drove his division forward through mud and rain in an act of sheer will. Blocked by wagons on the road, he roared, "I've been ordered up to fight! I'll permit no wagons to hamper me!" and had the wagons tipped over and burned to make a way for his division. He personally scouted ahead to find the front line in the chaos and rode so far out in front that the Confederates in the woods started shooting at him, calling out to target "that one-armed devil." Yet he escaped. He led his men into battle shouting, "I'm a one-armed Jersey son-of-a-gun, Follow me!" Knowing he was leading unbloodied troops into their first fight, he led consistently from the front; his courage was infectious, and the men surged forward. Kearny light-heartedly encouraged his men by saying, "Don't worry, men, they'll all be shooting at me!" as he charged with his saber in his one hand and his reins in his teeth, chasseur-style, as the Confederates were swept from the field. It was a demonstration of leadership well worthy of the epithet the French had given him. His efforts saved the Army of the Potomac from an embarrassing defeat. His only comment was, "It was incumbent upon me to inspire those men."[41]*

*Rather than take advantage of Kearny's achievement, Gen. McClellan did nothing to follow it up, earning Kearny's growing contempt. Kearny detested him for his constant retreating, writing that it could only be explained by "cowardice or treason."*

*Kearny led his division in the battle of Second Bull Run in late August 1862, and on September 1st held off the pursuing Confederates at the battle of Chantilly. In a driving rainstorm he rode to investigate a gap in the lines. Cautioned by an aide, he said, "The Rebel bullet that can kill me has not yet been molded." He stumbled upon the enemy and defied their demand to surrender. He slipped onto the side of his horse Comanche-style to shield himself from their fire, but a bullet fired by Sgt. John McCrimmon of Jacksonville, Georgia, hit him at the base of the spine, killing him instantly. Confederate Maj. Gen. A.P. Hill exclaimed when he saw the body, "You've killed Phil Kearny, he deserved a better fate than to die in the mud." Gen. Robert E. Lee, commanding the Army of Northern Virginia, returned the body to the Union side with his condolences. At the time of his death, there were rumors in Washington that Lincoln planned to replace McClellan with Kearny the Magnificent.*

*A Union soldier wearing a 6ᵗʰ Corps badge. Kearny originated the idea of unit badges which Maj. Gen. Daniel Butterfield later formalized for the Army of the Potomac under the command of Maj. Gen. Joseph Hooker. Library of Congress, LC-DIG-ppmsca-36890.*

*The National Tribune*
October 8, 1891
Judson Knight, Washington, D.C.

KNIGHT. WHILE IT is true that the idea of badges in the Army of the Potomac was originated by Gen. Kearny, it is not equally true that the red diamond or, as it has been frequently called, the "Kearny Patch," was the first badge ever worn by members of that army. Early in the Fall of 1861 Kearny had a badge made of fine yellow cloth in the form of a Maltese cross trimmed around the edge with gold cord. These he gave to men of his brigade who were wounded. His first command consisted of the 1st, 2nd, and 3rd N.J., and later on the 4th. A German soldier of Co. I, 2nd N.J. made them, and the writer of this saw Kearny present one of them to a soldier who had lost an eye by gunshot received while on a scouting expedition, and with it either $50 or $100 in gold, for the purpose of procuring an artificial eye.

The writer was detached from his regiment [2d New Jersey] for special duty about the 17th of August, 1861 at Kearny's head-quarters, and from that time until winter occupied a room in the house used by Kearny as headquarters.[42] Before such detail he had

*Kearny was killed at the Second Battle of Bull Run on September 1, 1862.*
*Author's collection.*

been serving as a scout for the General, and upon one occasion the General said: "Lieut. Custer tells me that he had heard from citizens that the secesh had a masked battery between us and the village of Annandale.[43] I don't believe it. How long will it take you to find out the truth of the matter?" Lieut. Custer afterward Gen. Custer was Acting Assistant Adjutant General for Kearny at this

time and commanding a troop of the 2d U.S. Cavalry.[44] At this time
the rebels had an outpost a short distance beyond what was known
as Padgets's wagon-stand. On the opposite side of the road, which
was the Little River pike, was a place marked Daingerfield, where
one of the Lees (W.H.F.) lives now. From Padget's a road ran north
until it led into the Columbia pike, which led into the Little River
pike at Annandale.

In answer to the general's query, I told him that by the next morning I could let him know. About 3 p.m. I crossed the road running
between the Little River and Columbia pike, and cautiously made
my way through the woods until the village of Annandale was in
plain sight. A convenient pine thicket near by afforded a safe retreat.
Ensconsing myself therein, with paper and pencil I soon had a map
of the village as it appeared from my retreat.

On the Columbia pike, near a church, within 50 yards of my
position, sat two videts [also vedette-mounted sentinel stationed in
advance of pickets]. One of them had his hat brim hanging over his
eyes on account of a break, and both wore ostrich plumes. They
were probably not as villainous as they looked. On my left, a little farther away, was Little River pike. A steam saw-mill with its
smoke stack perforated with bullet holes stood on the near side,
while on the other side, was another videt on a gray horse which he
presently dismounted from, as a heavy rain storm commenced. He
crawled into a bush hut which was probably no more of a protection
during the storm which lasted for hours, than was my pine thicket.
Soon after dark I made a thorough examination of both sides of
the road from Annandale down toward our lines as far as Padget's
wagon-stand.

On coming to our lines about midnight a Lieutenant of Co. F.,
2nd N.J., and I met in the road. His name is forgotten, but the way his
sword leaped from its scabbard is not. The next morning on showing
Kearny the map I made, and telling him of the color of the horses the
videts were mounted on, and showing one house that was octagon in
shape, he asked "How were you armed?" Upon being shown a pen-
knife, and told that I had carried nothing but that he turned to a field
desk and took up a silver-mounted Colt's revolver, and presenting it to

me, said: "Keep this and practice with it until you find how it shoots." Afterward, in company with Joe E. [C.] Jackson, a Lieutenant on Kearny's staff, who became a Brigadier-General before the close of the war, I practiced in an apple orchard in rear of Kearny's headquarters until I became quite proficient.[45]

At one time during that Fall we had a reserve picket post at a house we called the Territt Mansion. In passing by this post one day, one of the soldiers invited me to dismount and have some corn, of which they had a quantity already cooked. Accepting the invitation, I joined them. After eating as much as I cared for, I began looking over a lot of papers, with which the yard was strewn, and discovered a document reading like this as near as I remembered:

FORT LEAVENWORTH, July -, 1841
Received of Lieut. -----------------Territt, A. Q. M., 64 horses
PHIL. KEARNY
First Lieutenant, Com'd'g – Co., 1st Dragoons

When I returned to Headquarters I laid it upon his desk. After reading it he said to me, "Where on earth did you get this?" After hearing my account he asked if knew any of the family, and said he had danced at the house years before and wanted to know if I knew if any of the family were in the neighborhood. I mentioned a Mrs. Gardner, who lived near Cloud's Mills, and also a man by the name of Territt, who lived inside our lines, on Holmes Run below Barcroft Mill and he renewed his acquaintances.

Early in the fall of 1861, for a short time, it was a part of my duty to visit our pickets, who went out by entire companies and staid a week at a time, to inquire of the men if they had on that day received everything in the shape of rations they were entitled to. "Don't ask the officers but see the men privately and find out," were Kearny's orders. At first there were numerous complaints, which speedily became fewer and fewer until one day two of the regiments, the men said, they had everything; in the other the man I asked said, they had everything but their molasses, and that was not worth mentioning, and if I were you I should say nothing to the General about it.

I reported exactly what the man said. "Humph! Not worth reporting, is it. You ride over to Lieut. --------------- with my compliments and say I want to see him." Corp'l [Madison M.] Cannon, afterward colonel of the 40th N.Y., who was a clerk in Kearny's office, afterward said he never heard a man get such a scoring.[46] "How is this, Lieutenant, with good roads, and plenty of transportation, with not over six miles hauling, my men can't get what they're entitled to? This must not happen again."

When Kearny first came to us the three regiments were not camped near each other: the 3rd (Col. Taylor) was near Cloud's Mills; the 2d (Col. McLean) at Roach's Mill, and the 1st (Col. Morrison) somewhere else. He issued an order that the 1st and 2nd should proceed to the place where the 3rd was. After we had our tents pitched a number of us strolled over to where Kearny's headquarters tents were pitched hoping to get a sight of him. He was not visible and after waiting quite a time, we had started to go back, when we heard the music of a brass band down the Little River pike toward Alexandria. Knowing that the 1st regiment was to come from that way, we waited. Soon they turned into a farm road leading up toward the General's headquarters, and he came out of his tent and stood at a bend in the road. When about 30 feet from Kearny three men straggled from the ranks, and with clubbed muskets approached a peach tree that stood within a few feet of him and began knocking some hard, not fully grown peaches off. It was a study to watch him, and see the different expressions that swept over his face; at first incredulity, as though he could not believe what he saw, then that was succeeded by indignation, and at last by rage. He commenced using scriptural language in a vigorous manner, so much so that it was fully as interesting to see the play of the features of the men he was addressing as his own had been. When they finally realized that he was talking to them, and calling them pet names, they stood in surprise as if it could not be possible he meant them; when at last they became convinced he was really talking to them, they hastened to merge their individuality with that of their comrades and slunk back into the ranks with a grieved expression on their faces that plainly expressed the fact that they considered themselves very much aggrieved and Kearny a very unreasonable man.

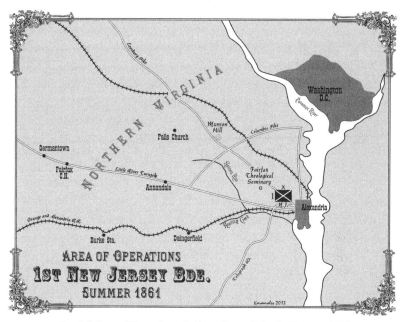

*Map 1-1 Area of Operations, 1st New Jersey Brigade, Summer 1861*

After getting out of his sight as individuals, he turned his attention to the regiment collectively, from colonel to private, and called them moles instead of soldiers. And yet, within two months of that time, I heard him take Capt. Wilson to task for the same thing. He said to him, "Wilson, these men are not soldiers to make a living. They have gone into the army from patriotism, and plenty of them have held positions better than you ever did. You must not talk to them as you do. That night probably found no better hated man in the army than Phil. Kearny, but it did not last long. The enlisted men found Kearny was their friend; their rations improved, their duties became pleasanter under a regular system, and when he issued his last order as their commander at Ship Point, whence he took command of Hamilton's Division, there were but few dry eyes in the brigade. All knew he had been offered more important commands, but would not take them because he could not take his brigade with him. He was sincerely mourned, while all felt proud of the reason he gave for leaving them. He was offered the command of troops under fire. That expressed all. He established a brigade bakery and slaughter-house during the

Fall of '61, and when the army left their camps in the spring of '62 each company in the brigade had $100 in cash in the company fund. I doubt if its parallel could be found in the Army of the Potomac.

Soon after the trip to Annandale, he showed me the only map extent in our army of the country to our front. It was one that had been made for Gen. [Irvin] McDowell by a man named Warrenton Gillingham, then as now, a resident on the old Mount Vernon estate. Mr. Gillingham is and was a "Friend." His map had the main roads, but was in no sense a military map, and the General asked me if I thought I could make it one, after explaining that all houses, small roads, streams, the position of forests, and the names of the inhabitants would have to appear. He had a Co. I man named Peter Goeitchus detailed to fill up and make a military map from data mostly obtained by me. I got Jonathan Roberts to fill in a portion east of the Accotink pike and west of the Potomac river. A man named Stiles filled in a section on the Occoquan and near where the Widow Violet lived, but a large part of what is known as Duane's Map of Northern Virginia would not be in existence today had it not been for Phil Kearny; and the first map furnished from the War Department in 1862 said on the margin that the information from which that map was compiled, of that section of the country, from Alexandria to Fairfax Courthouse, south of the Little River Turnpike to the Occoquan, was furnished by Gen. Kearny.[47]

At first I tried to fill in the map on the north side of the turnpike as well as on the south, but after being arrested and handcuffed by drunken officers, I quit trying to go out of our lines anywhere except in our brigade front. McClellan issued an order forbidding anything of the kind, but in my own case no attention was paid to it in our brigade.[48]

Kearny was indefatigable in his efforts to procure information and know how things were going along our lines. On my telling him one day that there was a place in front and to the left of our brigade picket where there was no post for over half a mile, he expressed an interest to see the spot. Ordering two horses from his own stable, he went with me and was shown the place. Proceeding across the flat just where Holme's Run empties into Hunting Creek, we went through the woods south until we came to Gen. O. O. Howard's headquarters. The conversation between Howard and Kearny was soon over, and he asked how far we could go out on the road; we were then in front of Gen. Howard's line. I told him that unless we met a patrol from the Confederate side we could go six or eight miles, but that the day before a party of 60 had come down to within a mile of where we were then. "Well, come on; let's go out, any way."

After going a mile and a half or more, he told me to call a man who was plowing some distance from the road. I called, and he did not appear to care to leave his work, and I had to call him two or three times before he started to come to the road, and when he did he came very slowly. "Tell him to come a ----------sight faster." I repeated the order verbatim upon which he quickened his steps somewhat. He had a very sullen look on his face as he came to a halt at the fence; and scarcely answered Kearny's first question; but there was very little hesitation after the second one, put in Kearny's quick, incisive manner. After talking with him a short time, as it was nearly night and we several miles to go, we turned and went back.

One day a box came for the colonel not long after we had taken possession of the Fairfax Theological Seminary for quarters. The General said to the boys in the office, "Would you like to see a French officer?" Of course, all said yes. "Well, bring that box to my room." In a short time he came out in the uniform of a French staff officer of the rank of major, as he explained. It was a magnificent uniform, and when he had it on I could think of nothing he looked more like than a game cock, a fighter every inch.

The morning that the Confederates took possession of Munson's Hill, Va., I rode with Kearny to the foot of the hill in the road. There were probably a 100 men in sight on top of the hill who all quit work. They were throwing up breastworks. An officer rode down into the road, and they sat and looked at each other for some time, not over 150 yards apart. Not a move was made while we staid there. Kearny finally said, "It would not take five minutes to brush them away." We rode away without being fired at. Kearny would have made a splendid mark, for he was wearing a white rubber coat and was riding a white or gray horse.

*After the battle of Second Bull Run a serious illness put an end to Judson's Knight scouting career while on active duty. He spent the rest of the year sick in the hospital and was discharged at the end of December. Library of Congress, LC-DIG-ppmsca-33755.*

During the Fall and Summer of '61, I became acquainted with a boy who was a clerk in Milburn's drug store in Alexandria, Va., and have seen him often since the war, so that he has not forgotten me. Some two years ago he said to me, "Sergeant, you used to be with Kearny, did you not, when he had his headquarters out at the Seminary and Bishop John's house?"

"Yes, I said."

"Well, I heard something a few days ago from Major Barrett, of Leesburg. He was on Stonewall Jackson's staff. He told me that Jackson had come along a few minutes after Kearny had been killed, and seeing a crowd inquired the meaning of it. On being told they had the body of a federal general who had just been killed, Jackson dismounted, went to where the body lay, and soon as he saw him said, 'My God, men, you have killed the bravest man in the Union Army,' and then put his hands together and offered up a silent prayer. What a picture that would make."

So spoke Samuel J. Lunt. A few weeks ago I went to Alexandria again to see if I could verify the story. Lunt told me that Maj. Barrett had died since he told me that story, but his brother C. Boyd Barrett, from South Dakota, was in Washington, and probably had heard his brother speak of it. I saw him the next day, and was told that his brother, the Major, had repeatedly told the story, and his brother was the officer who brought Kearny's body into our lines. I said to Mr. Barrett, "You have no doubt of the truth of this story?"

"None at all," he answered. "My name is C. Boyd Barrett, and I live in Aberdeen, S.D. When I first went there I was the only Confederate soldier in the district. Your boys," alluding to the G.A.R. [Grand Army of the Republic] "always invite me to their meetings. Sometimes I make a speech, and we get along first-rate. I bought the Aberdeen *Republican*, and while I did not change the name of the paper, I did change its politics. There are quite a number of ex-Confederate soldiers there now, and we all live in harmony."

Two years ago I wanted to get the address of a relative of Gen. Joe E. Johnston and called at his office to get it. He very cheerfully gave it, and seeing the G.A.R. button on my coat, said, "I see you have been a soldier," and asked what service I had seen. On telling him I was with Phil Kearny in the earlier days of the war, he became much interested, and asked me to sit down. He told me that many years ago he had known Kearny intimately. After quite a long conversation, I said:

"General, I heard Kearny make a remark about two men in the Fall of 1861 which I never forgot. You were one of the men he mentioned and the other was on our side. I watched his career and yours as far as I could, from the newspaper accounts, and have made up my mind that Kearny knew what he was talking about."

"Ah, what was that?"

"I laid a new army register before him in 1861, and as he looked down the list of Brigadiers, he came to one and said: 'Humph. Put me under him. He will not fight unless obliged to.' He was saying that more to himself than to me. I don't believe he thought I heard him. On another occasion I heard him say that, "Joe Johnston is the best military man in America."

*Former Confederate Gen. Joseph Johnston as he looked when Judson Knight met him after the Civil War. Author's collection.*

I could see Gen. Johnston felt gratified, as he turned with a smile, saying as he did so:

"I am glad you received your impressions of me as a military man from so friendly a critic as Gen. Kearny."

Gen. Johnston appeared to be in a reminiscent mood and related several anecdotes of "Phil," only one of which I remember with sufficient distinctness to relate.

"At one time," he said, "When Phil and I were both staff lieutenants on duty here in Washington, he said to me one day, 'Joe, I want you to carry a challenge for me to Col. Harney.'[49]

'What for, Phil?'

'I am told he never speaks of the 1st Dragoons, except as the lying 1st, and as I am the only officer of the 1st in Washington, it is my duty to call him out.'

'Phil, where did you get your information?'

'From Lieut. _____.'

'Did he put it in writing?'

'No.'

'Well, you get it in writing and I'll carry your challenge.'

The General's eyes fairly twinkled as he said, "Do you know that was the end of it?"

# II

# Adventures in the Debatable Land

*EDITOR'S NOTE: The following account is the best existing description of the comings and goings of scouts across what was called the "Debatable Land," between the Army of the Potomac and the Army of Northern Virginia, in that area of Virginia bisected by the Rappahannock and Rapidan Rivers. The term "Debatable Land" was borrowed from that region of the English-Scottish border that was never fully controlled by either side and through which spies and raiding parties penetrated with ease. This American Debatable Land was an equally porous region open to the penetration of scouts for both sides, and in fact, Knight gives an account of passing a Confederate agent at night going in the opposite direction. He also rightly describes how a network of Union agents, all Virginia residents, immensely aided the ability of the scouts to exploit this area by providing shelter and information. It would be in the cold and wet of the winters of 1863 and 1864 that Knight would suffer debilitating injuries that would haunt him to his last days.*

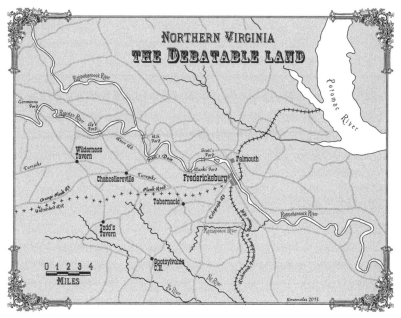

*The Debatable Land*

*The National Tribune*
March 2, 1893
Judson Knight, Washington, D.C.

KNIGHT. THE QUESTION: "How did you get inside of the enemy's lines, and travel around there and get information, without being arrested?" has been asked of me so often, that I have concluded to explain how the Army Headquarters scouts operated generally.

First, it will be understood that in no part of Virginia where the scouts of the Army of the Potomac principally were employed could you travel many miles without finding Union men and women. Sometimes they were natives of the state; not infrequently they were born in some of the Northern States, while quite a number of foreign birth, principally Englishmen, were found who rendered faithful and efficient service. Where we found one of these Union People, if there was another within 30 miles, he or she, as the case might be, were sure to know them; and it made no difference as regarded their social positions, they fully trusted each other. Such being the case, it will readily be seen that if the scouts could reach a Union family living within the enemy's lines, their danger of captivity or death was reduced to a minimum.

### UNION LOYALISTS BEHIND CONFEDERATE LINES

EDITOR'S NOTE: Col. Sharpe identified another group of loyal Union men that his scouts dealt with.

*Many of them had been non-commissioned officers of the Army be-fore the war, and it was curious that while hundreds of Army officers had turned traitors, not a single non-commissioned officer or private could be found who would desert the old flag.*

Col. George H. Sharpe, Chief, Bureau of Military Information, "Last Hours of the Confederacy," *The New York Times*, January 21, 1876.

Living on the south side of the Rapidan River were two of these Union families. As it is well known to everyone of their neighbors during the war that they were in sympathy with the Government, and did all they could to help it, I shall not hesitate to mention their names. One was McGee and the other Silver.[50]

The first that was known of them at Army Headquarters came about in this way: Ebenezer McGee did not want to go into the rebel army, so that about the beginning of the year 1863 he crossed the river and came down upon the north side of the Rappahannock, and was forwarded to Headquarters by the soldiers who first received him. His story was believed, and when he offered to go back and take some of the Headquarters scouts with him and teach them the route, and introduce them to his own and to Mr. Silver, it is needless to say his offer was joyfully accepted, and a party was sent out with him.

The place where he had crossed the river was below the United States Dam and Ford. The two families lived about four or five miles south of the Rapidan [EDITOR'S NOTE: Rappahannock River], in that portion of the State known as the Wilderness.[51] Coming down to the edge of the river from the south was a ravine, which commenced about half a mile from the river, and gradually grew steeper and narrower as it approached the river, until at the river's edge the sides of the ravine were very precipitous and at least 100 feet high. At some time in the past, and not many years previous to the war, a wind-storm had thrown nearly all the trees down, and they now lay across the ravine, some broken in two, so that one had to crawl under them; in a few places you could stand upright. The place was considered utterly impassable, and no attempt was made to have any pickets in the ravine, they always being stationed on the top on each side. The boys went through and came out a half mile inside enemy lines.

A small run emptying into the river on the north side through a thick fringe of bushes made a capital hiding-place for a boat, which was filled with stones and then sunk until again wanted. A small party of scouts were always left hid in the woods to take care of the horses and bring the men back across the river when they returned. The crossing was used for two years. Sometimes we had to go 15 miles to get there. Later we had rubber floats which could be taken apart and carried on our horses, so that we could go to any point we chose to make a crossing.

Long before the Army of the Potomac left Brandy Station, on the Wilderness campaign, we had a wall tent pitched in an almost inaccessible swamp near Silver's. On one occasion during the early part of the Winter of 1864 a party of scouts arrived at the tent before daylight and found it occupied by three men, who were entire strangers to all of our party. Upon being questioned they were very reticent as to who they were, where they came from, or where they were going. One of the strangers had a bad cough, and was constantly barking loud enough to be heard at a considerable distance, and while the bulk of the rebel army were several miles west of us, around and near Orange Courthouse, there were numerous detachments of rebel cavalry all around the neighborhood. Our boys did not want their rendezvous to be betrayed, and the result was a quarrel and nearly a fight. It eventually came out that the strangers were a man giving the name of Maj. Howard, a red-headed Irishman named Plunkett, and the third a boyish-looking fellow, a rebel deserter, name forgotten. Howard and Plunkett had gone into Richmond by way of the Peninsula, and after getting in either could not return or were afraid to [go] the same way they went. They had found someone who knew of Silver, who had sent them on to get out of rebeldom by the way of the Army of the Potomac, and rejoin Gen. Butler at Fortress Monroe by way of Washington. They had picked up the rebel deserter somewhere, and had brought him along.

Both parties remained in the tent all day, which was so crowded as to be very uncomfortable, and the strangers made themselves as disagreeable as they could by refusing to give us any news at all, even if they had learned any, which I have always doubted. When night came all hands were glad to leave the tent and start for the river, which was reached without mishap. Upon giving the proper signal the boat was brought to the south side of the river, and the first men to enter it as soon as it touched the shore were Howard, Plunkett and the deserter. When told to get out and wait, that the boat would be sent back for them, a more abject exhibition of cowardice and selfishness was never shown. They clung to the sides of the boat and would not leave. At last two of our men got out, S. [Sanford] McGee, brother of Ebenezer, and James Doughty.

The boat had been kept so constantly under water for nearly two years that it had become so soaked that the gunwales were not over an inch out of water. Every one was cautioned to sit still. When about three-fourths of the way across one of the jonahs made a lurch and the boat immediately filled and sank, leaving the party in the water. Our own crowd had sense enough to make as little noise as possible, and all hands made for the shore. Upon mustering, the rebel deserter was missing, and the boat was gone. McGee and Doughty had heard the noise and were prepared to stay. They were informed very quietly to go back and come to-morrow night. Howard and Plunkett refused to give Col. George H. Sharpe, Assistant Provost Marshal-General, any information, and found themselves in the "bull-pen," where they stayed until Gen. Butler was communicated with, after which they were released.[52]

> *12:30 pm, March 4, 1864, sent in cipher*
>
> *[Major General BENJAMIN BUTLER]*
>
> *A large man, fair complexion, fat full and smooth, calling himself H.S. Howard of Iowa has come into our lines with our scouts. He represents himself as being in your employ and as having just come from Richmond. Is he all right and what shall be done with him.*
>
> *SHARPE*
>
> *Colonel, Provost Marshal*
>
> Source: National Archives and Records Administration (NARA), Microcopy 504, Roll 303

Carpenters were detailed from a regiment at Headquarters and set to work making a boat, so that Mac and Doughty could be brought out of rebeldom that night. The boat was finished in time and loaded into an army wagon, and with about a dozen men, consisting of scouts and cavalrymen, started to relieve the boys. At this time we did not occupy the entire peninsula formed by the junction of the Rapidan and Rappahannock Rivers; on the contrary, our picket-line ran across from one river to the other, leaving about 10 miles of country below our lines open to the scouts of both armies, and the rebels availed themselves of the opportunity, and Serg't Shadbourne, who was chief scout for Wade Hampton, was continually prowling through that country at night.[53]

## SERGEANT GEORGE D. SHADBURNE

### Chief of Scouts (The Iron Scouts), Cavalry Corps,

### Army of Northern Virginia

*Shadburne was detailed as a scout by Gen. Hampton and he was constantly engaged on this duty until the end of the war. He was a young man of very prepossessing appearance, tall, active and resolute. Ordinarily, he appeared to be only a handsome young fellow,*

*with large, soft, mild eyes, but as soon as a fight began, became trans-*
*formed instantly into the dashing cavalryman; his whole soul seemed*
*to be in the battle, and his black eye blazed like fire—armed with at*
*least two pistols, and often three, he would dash against the enemy,*
*firing with a rapidity and precision not surpassed by even Mosby,*
*who was "very handy with a pistol." But in the excitement of battle,*
*Shadburne was perfectly cool, ready for any emergency or to avail*
*himself of any advantage.*

*The Land We Love*, Vol. III, May–Oct 1867, p. 349. An anonymous
article, possibly by Gen. Wade Hampton himself.

*The Confederate scout. Sergeant George D. Shadburne, Chief of Scouts (The Iron*
*Scouts), Cavalry Corps, Army of Northern Virginia, was too fond of bushwhacking,*
*according to Judson Knight, who thought that violated the understanding that scouts*
*did not seek to kill each other. Author's collection.*

Shadburne was the man who laid the plans and really captured the
beeves near City Point the next year. He was not known to the country
at large, and I take pleasure in giving him his just dues. He was a good
scout and had but one fault, he was too fond of bushwhacking.[54]

We did not leave our picket-line until dark, because we did not want citizens to see the boat so that they would recognize what it was. One man did come out to the road and got a glimpse of it and was told it was a case for a coffin; that we were going to exhume the body of an officer who had been killed at Mine Run a month or two previous, and that we had buried him on the north side of the river, and had not had an opportunity to go after his body until now. He sympathized with us in our loss, of course, and I don't suppose had any doubt of the story being correct. It was about five miles outside the lines where we had to go. We stopped at some distance from the road in an open field and all hands passed a very uncomfortable night, as we dared not build a fire and the weather was cold; it was some time in January 1864.

The scouts went down to the riverside and waited on the shore anxiously watching for the signal, hoping against hope as the small hours wore away. About half past four we left, so as to pass the citizens' houses before it would be light enough for them to see what was in the wagon. We staid all day with the picket reserves, and went back the next night and lay in the cold again. Just as we were approaching the picket-line in the morning a cavalryman shouted: "Your boys are in." The gratitude and relief felt by all hands was intense, and when the boys were met and their hands shaken, the beaming eyes and halting voices must have convinced them they were beloved by their comrades. They had tried to come down to the river the next night after the loss of the boat, but were prevented by a detachment of cavalry who had encamped almost across the southern end of the ravine. They had then gone down the river hunting for a boat. They did not find one that night, but on the following had better luck, and found one chained and padlocked, which took them a long time to get loose, as they had nothing but stones to break the chain or lock with, and it took a long while to accomplish it.

Everyone at Headquarters was glad when the boys got back. I can't remember that the crossing was used again until a few days before the opening of the Wilderness campaign under Grant, when three of us went over, Cline, Forrestall, and myself. As usual, our friends were on the *qui vive,* and on the second day we were there Silver came to us in the swamp. He had just got back from Orange Courthouse, which was Gen. Lee's headquarters at that time. He told us the number of rations that were being issued at Headquarters, Army of Northern Virginia. The exact number has escaped my memory, but I know it was not far from 90,000. He assured us that it was authentic. We considered this of importance enough so that one of us must go back to Brandy Station with the news.

The lot fell to me, and Cline and [Charles] Forrestall volunteered to accompany me to the river. After going about half way I urged them to go back, which they did, and I kept on going.

When about half way through the ravine, in a place where one could stand upright, I suddenly ran against a man who was coming up from the river. It was very dark, and I had not been taking any heed or keeping still, and I judged the one I met was in the same fix as myself— neither of us knew that anyone was near until we came breast to breast. To say I was not frightened would be untrue. I actually felt my hair rise, and thought of the "quills upon the fretful porcupine." I have always thought he recovered from the shock sooner than I did, for I heard him almost instantly trying to scramble up the side of the ravine. As soon as I heard that I thought to myself, "You are as much frightened as I am; let me alone and I will you," and immediately went on my way. Neither of us spoke. When I had gotten on the north side of the river and told the boys of my adventure they said they had heard from a citizen that day that a mail was going to cross the river that night for Richmond. I made my report at Headquarters and staid in camp until the 4th of May on which day we left Headquarters on the Wilderness campaign. Cline and Forrestall staid until our cavalry came across, when they joined them, and, if my memory serves, they had two or three prisoners.

*EDITOR'S NOTE: The Rappahannock and Rapidan Rivers ran through that part of northern Virginia known as the Debatable Land because it was for so long fought over. The name was borrowed from the Scottish-English border over which raids were conducted for centuries. Passage through this area and across these rivers was vital for scouts. Both sides heavily picketed the rivers. The following photograph and drawing show how open the terrain was then, unlike its present heavily wooded condition, making the work of the scout much more difficult.*

*Germanna Ford on the Rapidan River. Author's collection.*

*Kelly's Ford on the Rappahannock River. Edwin Forbes, Library of Congress,
LC-DIG-ppmsca-20625.*

*Our Boys in Blue: Heroic Deeds, Sketches and Reminiscences of Bradford County Soldiers in the Civil War, Vol. 1, 1899, by C. F. Heverely*
   Anson B. Carney

* * *

*EDITOR'S NOTE: Scout Carney provides another account of the operations in the passage of the Rapidan River in this local county history.*

CARNEY. IN THE fall of 1863 we were kept quite busy. Two or three scouts were regularly sent out once or twice a week, especially on dark nights, to obtain information. We would start early in the afternoon with a mule team, and would conceal our outfit and provisions in the thick woods, which skirted the Rapidan river. While one would cook supper, the other two would carefully examine the opposite bank of the river, to discover and locate the rebel pickets and select a suitable crossing place at night. We were provided with two rubber tubes shaped like a cigar. These we would inflate with a hand bellow and place slats crosswise; it would float two of us. We would take off our shoes and roll up our pants and get on, letting our feet hang in the water and paddle with our hands. From 9 to 12 o'clock, when we deemed it best, we would paddle cautiously out upon the dark water of the river; we would direct our course by some overhanging tree or dark ravine which had been selected. The little craft would be paddled as rapidly as the requisite silence would permit. After landing, the craft would be hauled out and concealed; then we would endeavor to gain the rear of the rebel lines, avoiding the enemy, whose whereabouts would be plainly indicated by the camp-fires.

A few miles back in the country there lived a Union man, who would go in the daytime with an old go-cart to the grist mill and stroll leisurely through the rebel camps, obtaining a good deal of information and this would be communicated to us scouts; then we would return to our rubber boat and recross the river. On these trips the scouts would often carry the old man sugar and coffee as well as money, coffee being highly prized on account of its scarcity in rebel territory.

Sometimes on dark nights some of us scouts would mount our horses and dash across a ford of the river, risking the bullets of the rebel pickets who, however, would not aim accurately at night. That ford would be lined with rebels a few hours later to await the return of the scouts. But Union scouts were too wary to be caught in such a trap. On our return we would re-cross at another ford. Scouting required courage, but our men rarely got hurt on these occasions; it would be done so quickly the surprised Johnnies would not collect themselves before we would be out of danger. A slight flesh wound would often be the extent of the casualties.

Another method of keeping posted was by questioning rebel deserters and prisoners at army headquarters. Prisoners frequently sought to conceal what information they possessed, but by skillful questioning the truth was generally wrested from them. A few weeks before the battle of the Wilderness while still in camp I was directed to copy for General [Winfield Scott] Hancock [commanding II Corps, Army of the Potomac] complete rosters of General Lee's infantry, cavalry and artillery. This had been compiled from the testimony of rebel deserters and prisoners. By ascertaining what regiment a rebel belonged to one could from this roster find out what particular force had been fighting us or where it was stationed. Military men will appreciate the value of such information.

*Confederate prisoners from Johnson's Division, taken at Spotsylvania on May 12, 1864. Army of the Potomac SOP quickly forwarded prisoners to the BMI for interrogation, a work in which Judson Knight sometimes took part. Library of Congress, LC-DIG-ppmsca-33763.*

# III

# Brushes with Death: Escaping Gilmor and Mosby

*EDITOR'S NOTE: Death at the hands of the enemy, if captured behind the lines, was an all too real fate for Union scouts as illustrated not only by Knight's record of the encounters with the deadly Confederate partisan commanders, Col. John Singleton Mosby and Maj. Harry Gilmor, but by the personal experiences of John W. Landegon and Anson B. Carney as well.*

The National Tribune,
July 21, 1892
Judson Knight, Washington, D.C.

## ESCAPING GILMOR & MOSBY

KNIGHT. THE SKETCH accompanying this is designed by the writer to illustrate an incident that happened soon after the return of the Army of the Potomac from the Mine Run campaign [early December 1863]. During that campaign a party of scouts from Army Headquarters found themselves in the vicinity of "Old Vidersville,"

*Sneaking across the Rapidan.*

[Verdiersville], about 12 miles south of Culpeper, Va, in the neighbor-hood of the farmhouse that looked as though food for man and beast might be procured. Upon the party riding up to the house they were met by an old Virginia farmer who anxiously asked if they were "Yan-kees." He was told that they were, to which he replied: "I am mighty glad to see you-all."

"Oh! Give us a rest; we have heard that kind of talk before," was the reply from some of the scouts. The old farmer looked anxiously and rapidly from one to another, and a shade of fear swept over his face as he observed the motley dress of several of the party, until his eyes rested upon one who wore a full Federal uniform. He scrutinized him carefully, while the boys were still chaffing him, and addressing him personally, said: "Are you Yankees?"

"Yes, we are!" And the reply was so emphatic and made in such a tone as though the speaker was proud of the fact and of the chance of telling one whom he supposed to be an enemy of the government, that his face instantly cleared and all could see that his assertion of "I am mighty glad to see you all," was a fact.

"Come, gentlemen, light," was his next salutation; and they "lit."

"Can you furnish us a dinner and a feed for our horses?"

"Yes, and glad to do it, too."

While discussing the news the old farmer said: "I am glad you-all came out here today, for I have a son that I want you-all to take with you when you leave here."

He was told that it would not be done, as there was no spare horse for his son to ride.

"Never mind about the horse. I have got as good a horse as any of you-all, and he can have him, if you will only take him along with you."

All hands saw by this time the old man was a Unionist, and in dead earnest. He told the party his son had been in a neighboring State, and had been able to keep out of the army until the previous June, when he was conscripted and allowed to go home to join a Virginia regiment. He had been home about six months, hid in one of the chambers, and had not been out of doors in daylight in all that time. Stepping to the stairway he called him down. His son was about

"ARE YOU YANKS."

*"Are You Yankees?" Cartoon from the* National Tribune.

32 years of age, and about five feet 10 inches in hight, and as white as ghosts are supposed to be, from his enforced seclusion during all those weeks. He was taken along, and when Gen. Meade fell back across the Rapidan he went with us.

Some time during the month of December, 1863, it was concluded at Headquarters that if we could find a good crossing just above Jacob's or Germanna Fords, we would start a line between Headquarters of our army and Headquarters of the Army of Northern Virginia by sending relays of men to the house of the old Unionist, whose name I am not going to divulge; neither shall I tell the name of his son, but in future will refer to him as "Bob."

One morning in the month of December, 1863 a party of about ten of us started for the Rapidan, in the vicinity of the fords mentioned above and after diligent search selected the spot shown in the sketch as the easiest to cross the river without being seen by the enemy, and as the one most desirable by Bob; for he told us he had, as a boy, hunted all through the woods between there and his father's.

By waiting until night we found that the Johnnies after dark put two pickets at the riverside to watch the ford, which, in the vernacular of Virginia, was a "blind ford," called blind because people other than those living in the neighborhood never saw it, as no public road led to it. It was about one hundred and fifty yards across the bottom-land to where the land began to rise, and terminated in a bluff, on which were three pickets. From the bluff to the river ran a fence made of pine poles, with one end on the ground and the other end supported by a pair of stakes, making the fence straight. This fence was above the blind ford, which was called Willis's. For about one hundred yards the bank of the river was about two feet high, with a few trees and bushes near the fence, and at this point was a still pool of water from one side of the river to the opposite one. It was fully decided that the attempt to establish a line of communications with Lee's Headquarters should be made from this point. We made up our minds that it was the most favorable spot for crossing and getting through the videts without detection of any in the vicinity, as after landing, by keeping close to the pole fence, and crouching down so that one's head should not show above the fence, they would escape notice by the pickets down by the ford, while the fence would at the same time so blend forms of men in dark clothes that they would not be seen by the three men on the bluff. As soon as the bluff was reached by walking close to it they would be out of view from the pickets, who stood at some distance back from the edge of the bluff, until they came near the pine thicket, shown at the left. There was the critical point, but the distance was short, and a flock of sheep in the field suggested going on hands and knees until the cover of the pines was reached. It turned out afterward that one had to keep on his hands and knees until the pine thicket was passed; for the branches came up so near the ground there was no other means of locomotion through them.

After the selection of the crossing-place, and stopping long enough after dark to see them make the change for their night-watch which was easily done by keeping watch of them through a field-glass from before until after dark, (by keeping one's eyes constantly to the glass, one could see them when it became so dark that it is doubtful if they could have been found by a casual observer); we then went back 14 miles to Headquarters, starting the next day in time to reach the crossing before dark, so as to give the ones who were to cross a chance to see the arrangements for the night.

Two young fellows from Battery B, 1st Ohio L.A. [Light Artillery] named Wood [Henry W.] Dodd and [Benjamin] Frank McCord[55], had been detailed from their battery by order of Edwin M. Stanton, then Secretary of War. McCord and Dodd had written to the Secretary asking for the detail, as they thought they could render their country better service in that capacity than they could simply as members of Battery B. They had been selected as the first ones to accompany "Bob" to his father's. I think it was the 5th Michigan Cavalry who were on picket on our side of the river that night. When we told them that three of the party were going over to Lee's Headquarters they were incredulous, and it did look to be an impossible thing to do, as the moon was shining brightly and the ground was white with snow. A few of them accompanied us down to the river bank, carrying their carbines along to protect the men if they should be discovered and have to fall back to the rubber float shaped like the mattress of a bed and filled with air. This rubber float would carry six people, and the three of us who were not going on the trip to Lee's Headquarters, paddled them over and stayed by the bank to bring them back if they should be discovered. They landed, and Bob took the lead, with McCord and Dodd following in the order named, stepping in each other's tracks, so as not to make too broad a trail that might attract notice next morning.

We anxiously watched them until they disappeared in the pines, and no alarm had been raised.

It was as cool an exhibition of courage as I ever saw. What other dangers they might meet in their tramp of nearly 20 miles of course no one could tell anything about; but the first stage had been successfully accomplished, and we retired to our side of the river, very much relieved of the tension on our minds to which we had been subjected. The arrangements were for us to stay until the following night, taking care of our own and the absent scouts' horses, and to go after them upon their showing three lights. Sometimes the three lights were omitted, and three stones would be thrown into the water near the shore on which the watchers were, for the signal.

Of course it was not possible to predict with certainty at what hour on the following night they would return, and we went as early as they could possibly be expected, and had a long and cold time waiting. At last the gleam of a burning match rewarded us. We did not wait a moment after the third light was shown before we had our rubber float in the water, and soon had them safely on it. The squeeze their hands received as we met them must have satisfied them of our delight in seeing them safe in our lines again.

Of course there have been many exhibitions of bravery among the soldiers who served during the war of the rebellion on both sides. I knew of instances of Confederate scouts who came into our lines and did some daring deeds, and have known some of our own scouts who did things that would seem to the uninitiated, as very bold and daring. For instance, Martin E. Hogan, with a few of the Headquarters scouts, three months later, lower down the same stream, with some volunteers from the cavalry comprising the raiding party of Kilpatrick and Dahlgren, volunteered to wade the river at Ely's Ford, carrying their arms over their heads to keep them dry. Hogan was in the advance, and he crept up to the first rebel picket, surprised, disarmed, and made him show the way to the next post, telling him to answer properly when challenged, or he was a dead man; and from him to the third and last post, whom he also captured without firing a shot; after which exploit the house where the reserve picket was quartered was surrounded, and Hogan told the boys when they heard a shot inside the house to smash the windows and cover the party inside with their carbines. Then boldly marching to the door he threw it wide open and sprang inside shouting, "SURRENDER, YOU REBEL SONS OF GUNS!" firing his pistol into the floor as he said it. Instantly several carbines were thrust through the glass, and over 20 men, including a Captain and Lieutenant of a South Carolina cavalry regiment surrendered. Taking his prisoners to the river Hogan told them that as he and his men had waded the river to pay their respects to them, they might wade it back, while he and his men would ride their horses across, which they did, and the Confederate Captain complained bitterly to Gen. Kilpatrick of the indignity of his treatment.

But in the case of Dodd and McCord, there was not excitement to sustain them. It was nearly as light as day, and the whole things [*sic*] hinged on their successfully sneaking through. They did not know where the reserves were posted, and how quickly they could be drawn on and they overwhelmed [*sic*]. It has always seemed to me that it was a very cold-blooded act of bravery performed in the interest of their duty, with an eye to the benefit of their country solely. Both of the boys are now dead, and it affords me much satisfaction to make this slight testimonial to them, who were always gallant and discreet in the performance of what they were ordered to do. They were once sent into the Valley on foot. After performing what they were sent to do, they were to rejoin the army the best way they could, whatever it might be. This was in the spring of 1864.

About the 1st of April they started off, well dressed in suits of light-colored corduroy, with light calfskin boots reaching above the knees. One day while sitting on a fence they had just climbed after crossing a field Harry Gilmor suddenly came round a turn in the road close by them. Of course they sat perfectly still until Gilmor came up. Before he reached them Dodd said to McCord, "Let me do the talking."[56]

*Meeting Harry Gilmor, the Guerrilla Chieftain. Cartoon from the* National Tribune.

## Colonel Harry Gilmor

Harry Gilmor (1838–1883) was, after the famed Colonel Mosby, the most famous of the southern partisan leaders. The Marylander Gilmor scouted for Stonewall Jackson in the Valley Campaign and then fought with Jeb Stuart, and when the Confederate congress authorized the creation of partisan groups, Gilmor organized several companies of Marylanders who called themselves "The Band" and were a "rough and ready lot of freebooters who often operated behind enemy lines." After Gettysburg, he established himself in the Shenandoah Valley and was raiding Union convoys, railroads, telegraph lines, depots, bridges, and encampments. In July 1864 he made one of the most daring raids of the Civil War reaching near Baltimore. He was finally captured in West Virginia in February 1865.

*Maj. Harry Gilmor commanded a particularly daring band of Confederate raiders though two Union scouts were able to deceive him of their identity. LC-DIG-cwpb-05420.*

Upon Gilmor asking who they were and where they were going, Dodd told this story: They were both deserters from the Union army, and had deserted because they did not enlist to fight for the nigger, and that was what it had come to. They were tired of the whole thing and had come to the conclusion to go home, and were on their way there at present. As they were sitting on top of the fence he could not of course tell which way they were going. He was so much pleased with their apparent candor and appearance, that he was completely deceived, and instead of treating them as prisoners, he invited them to share his apple brandy and supper, to which they were nothing loth [modern spelling: loath]. He also did the best for them he could in the way of sleeping accommodations, and furnished them as good a breakfast as he had himself.

Before starting off in the morning he regretted very much his inability to furnish them with horses, as he had no spare ones, but told them to be of good cheer as the Provost Marshal at Staunton was a friend of his, and he would speak to him in their behalf; and concluded by telling them that when they reached Staunton they would find themselves among friends. He and his command then rode off. As Staunton was not their goal, they proceeded toward it very reluctantly and slowly, for fear that Gilmor might become suspicious and send some of his command back to see if they were all right. After they had gone toward Staunton a few miles they concluded to take another course, which they did, exhibiting much more speed on the new course than on the previous one. They made good time all that day, and just before sundown sat down to rest, and, while resting, were surprised in the same manner they had the day before by Mosby.

They pursued the same tactics with him that had worked so successfully with Gilmor. Mosby listened to Dodd's romance, and when they had finished, politely said: "You are a _____ damned liar! Such men as you don't desert. I can tell you what you are. You are two Yankee spies, and if I could prove it I would string you up to the limbs of some of these trees."

He told them he should send them off in the morning to Gordonsville with other prisoners he had. They found themselves turned over to the tender mercies of his men, who immediately commenced "going through" them. They first took what money they found, and then "went for" their clothing. McCord's corduroy suit, hat and boots soon found new owners. "Little Dodd's" size saved him; not one of the crowd could wear a single article he wore. All hands were very anxious for his boots, but not one of them could anywhere near get them on.

---

### Colonel John Singleton Mosby

John S. Mosby (1833–1916), nicknamed the "Gray Ghost," was the most famous Confederate partisan leader in the Civil War. His command, the 43rd Battalion, 1st Virginia Cavalry, was known as Mosby's Rangers or Mosby's Raiders, known for its lightning raids that inflicted losses on Union communications and logistics which were all out of proportion to the size of the unit. His command was equally famous for its ability to elude Union Army pursuers and disappear, blending in with local population. The area of northern central Virginia in which Mosby operated with impunity was known during the war and ever since as Mosby's Confederacy. No single Confederate more enraged the Union than did Mosby as he explained,

*"My purpose was to weaken the armies invading Virginia, by harassing their rear . . . To destroy supply trains, to break up the means of conveying intelligence, and thus isolating an army from its base, as well as its different corps from each other, to confuse their plans by capturing their dispatches, are the objects of partisan war. It is just as legitimate to fight an enemy in the rear as in the front. The only difference is in the danger. . . ."*

*Col. John Singleton Mosby, "The Grey Ghost" commanding the 43rd Virginia Battalion, tormented the Union forces with his guerilla attacks. He would have hanged two Union scouts had they not outwitted their guards. LC-B813- 6786 A.*

The next day they were started under guard for Gordonsville, and as the route for the first day, and I am not now sure but the second as well, led in the direction they wanted to go, they went along apparently contented and got the good will of the men guarding them. At night when they went into camp Dodd took one of the guards to one side, where their conversation could not be overheard, and asked him if he could get some apple brandy in the neighborhood. "No trouble at all to get all you want if you only have the money to get it with. I have none, and the other men with me have none either," said the guard.

Dodd then told him that he had money, at which the Johnny expressed surprise. "I thought our fellows got all you had."

"Not by a long shot," said Dodd, and after swearing him to secrecy he untied a rag he had wound around one of his fingers and produced greenbacks enough to purchase six canteens full. The friendly guard went away, after telling his fellows how cute the "little Yank" had been; at which they were all delighted, and he soon returned with the six canteens full of very fair applejack. None of the other prisoners were allowed to have any. The four guards, Dodd, and McCord all began drinking, passing the canteen around. It was understood by our two boys that while they pretended to "take their licker fair," in reality but little was swallowed. It did not take long for all hands to become garrulous, and as the potations became deeper McCord began to show signs of drunkenness, which at the end of about the fourth canteen completely overpowered him and he stretched himself out on the ground in a drunken stupor, at which sight the guards who were getting pretty hilarious, loudly laughed and complimented the "little Yank" on his capacity and being able to "lay out" his companion. With drunken gravity he declared he could "lay out" the whole crowd if the liquor was commissary whiskey, such as he had been used to. At every drink he became more asser-tive in his convictions that he could get the best of them, individually and collectively, if they would "drink fair" every time he did. All this time he was in such an inebriated condition he could with great dif-ficulty maintain an upright position as he sat on the ground.

At last, after an unusually long drink, he succumbed and fell over backward, and lay like a log, and upon a chorus of snores showed the guards that the Yanks were in a condition where they would not have to be watched very closely. They all admitted the "little Yank" a prowess in drinking as long as he did, and wondered why Mosby had pronounced them spies.

"That be _____," said the Sergeant in charge; "anyone can see they tell the truth. They are tired of fighting for the nigger, and for my part I believe what they say, that most of the Yanks are tired of it."

GETTING THE GUARDS DRUNK.

*Getting the Guards Drunk. Cartoon from the* National Tribune.

It was late—at least 10 o'clock before Dodd succumbed, and there were nearly two canteens full when he fell. The guards continued their carouse until after midnight, when the last one succumbed to the influence of apple brandy, and all slept. Then a transformation scene not down on the Confederate program took place. The two drunken Yanks arose and were remarkably steady on their pins, and, like the Arab, they "silently stole away."

I cannot now recall the point where they joined the army, but will never forget how Frank McCord looked in a very dilapidated old hat, a very disreputable gray uniform, and an old pair of shoes run over at the heel, so that he walked partly on the uppers. Dodd, thanks to his size, made a much better appearance; but both were infested with graybacks [lice]. Peace to their ashes! Good boys and true in the verdict of their old comrades, and especially of the writer.

### "HE DIED RIGHT THERE."[57]

He [John W. Landegon] smoked for a time in silence, and I sought to set him talking again. "You said you were nearly hanged once?" He shook his head and frowned slightly, but said nothing.

"When was it?" I persisted.

"May 12, '62," he answered, dryly. He lay back in his big chair, with his eyes closed as though to shut out something he did not care to see. For a long time neither of us spoke; suddenly he opened his eyes and sat sharply forward in the chair.

"Do you know that there are nights even yet when I dream of that day? Do you know but of course you don't! Well, you've got me to thinking of it again, and I might as well tell you, even of that, too.

"There was a cavalry skirmish a couple of miles from Massaponax Church about twelve or fifteen miles south of Fredericksburg; it was going hard against us, and I was sent back to bring up help. I was about half-way to the church when I saw a lot of dust, and I rode harder thinking, you understand, it was the advance of some of our troops; there was so much dust that I rode right into them before I found that they were Confederates that had got round our flank and were coming up behind our men. It was just a scouting party...more coming, I learned. There wasn't a chance to get away, or even to fight; they had never made any mistake about me...grabbed me the minute I got in reach. I was in my gray uniform, mind! They were in a hurry, but they said they had time to hang me. They just hauled off to the roadside and said they would have a trial, anyway that they always tried the men they hanged. So they got up a drumhead court that wasn't any more a court than is our talking here. There was a lot of laughing and joking, the rest of the men all sitting around on the grass at the side of the road, holding their horses by the bridles to let them graze; some of the men smoked their pipes. It was all good fun for them.

"Back around the hills I could hear the popping of the carbines of the men of my regiment that I'd left not half an hour before.

"I didn't get five minutes of trial; they asked me again where I'd been going, and I told them again lying the best I knew that I was only a camp servant...it had got too hot for me up there at the front, and I was scared, and getting back to the camp where I belonged.

"Some one yelled, 'He's a spy; look at his clothes.'"

"And I turned on him and says: 'I'm no spy. I'm just a servant, an' these 's all the clothes I have; I don't get a uniform; I got to wear just what I can find'—all that sort of thing. Anyway, if I wasn't a spy, one of 'em said: I was a 'damned Yankee, that had stole the clothes off some pore dead Confederate soldier.' And they all said: 'That's so, all right! Stole 'em off some pore dead soldier. He had ought to be hung!'

"The president of the court got up and said, 'You're guilty, Yank, and it is the sentence o' this court that we hang you by the neck until you're dead.'

"They all laughed at that, and got up and stood around to see me get hung. We all moved over a hundred yards or so to a tree, and some one started to climb up with a rope—they had a rope, all right—and then some one said 'they'd ought to have some grease, for the rope noose wouldn't slip good without the rope was greased,' and one of the men was sent riding hard across the fields to a farm-house to get some. They got the rope tied to a limb, then they kept showing me the noose...telling me how I'd dance on air. They weren't going to tie my hands and feet, they said; and they danced and waved their hands to show me how I'd do.

"These weren't guerrillas; they were regularly enlisted men. But it was '62, mind, and they were a lot more bitter in those days than they were later in the war; but I never did see, before or after, such ones as these.

"I had been scared nearly to death up till then, but when they got to talking like that I got mad they might hang me, all right, but they weren't going to torture me that way before I died. I tried to pull away from the fellows holding me, and I cursed them all, and called them murderers and cowards, and I told them I'd fight any three of them, any five, any number at once, if they would give me my saber and pistol, but that I wouldn't be hung.

"Just then the man with the grease got back; he'd only been able to get some butter! 'Don't waste good butter hanging a damn Yankee; string him up without greasing the rope, and be quick about it,' some one said.

"So they dragged and lifted me onto a horse, and led it under the limb, and they put the noose around my neck. I didn't see anything or think anything from the time I got put on the horse, and I didn't see that some of them were standing in a little party off to one side. Just then one stepped out and said that I was not to be hung; that I was a brave man; and it wasn't so much that they didn't want me to be hanged, but the other fellows weren't going to do it; I was as much their prisoner as I was theirs that they hadn't any of them been selected for the court...more of that sort of thing (they were from two regiments do you understand?); and that they had decided to send me back to the main column and have me tried right! Some of the fellows drew their revolvers, and some got on their horses, and it looked as if there was going to be a fight right there. But they talked it over with me sitting on the horse, and the rope around my neck all the time, and finally decided that they would send me on.

"They took the rope off, and I began to get some of my senses back, and I saw that the man who was to take me forward was a great, surly-looking devil, one of them that had been so anxious to hang me; he was standing talking to his officer, and they looked over at me, and he kind of smiled and nodded his head; I knew right there that he meant to kill me on the way.

"The whole business hadn't taken more than twenty minutes, but it was a month to me. They wouldn't give me a horse; the fellow rode, but I had to run along at the horse's head. The horse he rode was one of the biggest I ever saw; when it walked I had to trot, and when he rode at a trot I had to run. I had lost my hat, and the sun hurt my head, and the dust choked and blinded me; I was so sick and weak, mind you, the reaction from such fear is a sickening thing that I staggered as I ran, and the fellow kept leanin' over and prodding me with his saber to make me go faster; that began to make me mad, then I got conscious of it, and I felt my strength coming back again.

"I kept on the off side of the horse, so that he would have to cut across with his saber instead of down, when the time came for me to try to run. I can see that road now long and straight, with the unfenced fields sloping down to the road on either side, and sumac bushes along where the fences had been before the war; ahead, the road ran like a tunnel into a big woods that looked all hazy and blue. Beyond the woods a little way was Massaponax Church; I made up my mind that what was to be would take place in that woods, and I sort of felt that the Confederate had made up his mind to end it in the woods, too.

"Just then he called to me: 'Halt, Yank! Till I tighten the girth; saddle's slippin'!'"

"He was dismounting; you know, of course, how a man gets off a horse? his left foot in the stirrup, and swings his right leg back over the horse for just a second his back was toward me, and at that moment he dropped his drawn saber to the ground. . . . He died right there!"

\* \* \*

*EDITOR'S NOTE: This next account by Anson Carney of his brush with death while scouting behind Confederate lines is preceded by a long opening statement by another veteran of the Bureau of Military Information, H.M. Coburn. setting the stage for Carney's story.*

*The National Tribune*
January 4, 1894
Anson B. Carney

## The Close Call of a Scout Experienced in the Hands of Bloodless Secessionists

*EDITOR'S NOTE:* This is the story of Anson B. Carney, given without any attempt at embellishment, and many other hazardous adventures of Knight, Edward A. Carney, and of McEneany, Myers, Hatch, Dodd and Phelps might be related.

H. M. COBURN. Several narratives of scouting adventures have already been printed in the *National Tribune*, but, so far as I know, the following has not heretofore appeared.

During a portion of the last years of the war it was my lot to be detailed among a company of scouts, and at that time the duties devolving upon us all required a great secrecy, care, and attention to business. A good General will always endeavor to obtain as far as possible definite information in regard to the movements of the enemy, and for this purpose scouts constitute a very important part of an active army in the field. Though few in number, they have unusually hazardous duties to perform; and skill, energy, watchfulness and promptness of action are required.

The scouts of whom I desire to speak were attached to the Bureau of Information of the Army of the Potomac, and had to go wherever they were sent, if it was at all possible for them to get there. They frequently made trips for miles inside of the lines of the enemy, and if their adventures were written and gathered into book-form, it would take a very large volume to hold them all.

While the Army of the Potomac was encamped near Brandy Station, Va., and in the vicinity of Culpeper Court-house, the scouts made frequent excursions across the Rapidan River once or twice a week. The objective was if the rebels were doing anything to find it out; and if they were doing nothing, it was important to ascertain that also. Our men used to go many miles back into the country, and visit a Union man, who secured such information as he could from time to time, and when our boys visited him he told them all he had been able to learn about the movements of the Army of Northern Virginia.

Of course the scouts made these visits under the cover of darkness, and whenever possible a very dark night was selected. They had a long India-rubber bag, which could be filled with air, and when slats were placed lengthwise and crosswise upon it this little boat would carry two men across the river.

About 10 o'clock at night the scouts would paddle silently across the Rapidan, and after reaching the opposite shore pull their light craft up on the bank, and go on about their business. Of course, they avoided the pickets as well as the camps of the enemy, and with revolver in hand made their way through the country as silently as possible.

But I shall confine myself to one eventful trip, from which the scout was fortunate in escaping with his life; and, lest I shall be charged with unduly coloring the matter, I shall endeavor to give the story as nearly as possible in the words of Anson B. Carney, who was for a long time employed as one of the scouts at Headquarters. Carney is now living at West Franklin, Bradford County, Pa., and he says that this adventure was the occasion of his first capture by the enemy. He thinks he then came nearer to being killed than at any other time in his life. Here is the story, substantially as Carney told it:

CARNEY. While a member of the company of scouts, and about the time I was making preparations to go into a Winter camp in the Fall of 1863, I was ordered to report at Army Headquarters. On arriving there I was informed that some rebel deserters had come into our lines and reported that a part of a brigade—or, perhaps, two or three brigades—of the enemy had left Gen. Lee's army and taken all their camping-outfit with them. The deserters said they knew this to be a fact, but they could not tell how many rebels had departed, neither could they give their destination.

I received orders to go out and find out if possible the truth or falsity of this report and bring back all the news I could gather regarding this movement. Judson Knight, the well-known scout, went with me, and crossing the Rappahannock at Kelly's Ford we marched on through the country till we reached a point above Falmouth. From there we cautiously worked our way in the direction of Chancellorsville, and not very far away from Gen. Lee's Headquarters at Spotsylvania we visited a Union man with whom we were acquainted. After telling him our business, we induced him to go south toward Richmond and find out for us all he could, as well as get us copies of late Richmond papers. I withhold his name, as he has some relatives living who might not wish to have all the facts known.[58]

When the Union man returned, he said that, as near as he could find out, two brigades had reinforced [Maj.] Gen. [J. E. B.] Stuart in the Valley, and were contemplating a raid over in Maryland for horses, forage and recruits. As it was important that either Knight or myself should get back to Gen. Meade's Headquarters as soon as possible, we drew cuts, and the lot fell to me.

I started that night about 10 o'clock, and having arrived near the Rappahannock River a little after daylight next morning. I concealed myself in the bushes all day. I tramped all the next night, and about daybreak reached the vicinity of Chitten's Mills, on the road from Harwood Church to Kelly's Ford. I thought I was near enough to the Union pickets to be out of danger, unless I should accidentally meet a rebel scout. Yet, I kept in the cover of the woods as much as possible, but while walking along a bridle-path and eating some chinquapins [chestnuts] I had gathered on the way, the first thing I knew I was looking down five carbine barrels, and the rebels shouted at me:

"Halt! Surrender! Unbuckle that belt! Don't touch that pistol!"

They took me right down a steep hill and away from the road, where they stripped me of all portions of my clothing that they thought better than theirs. Now, I had in the lining of my boot a paper on which I had sketched some plans that could be understood only by myself, and I also had copies of Richmond newspapers. I accounted for the Richmond papers by saying that I had been on a visit to a brother of mine who belonged to the 4th Pennsylvania Cavalry, and who was on picket, and that my brother had traded newspapers with rebel pickets over the river.

But unfortunately, the men who had captured me were rebel scouts, and as they did not want to return to their camp for a few days, and besides, as they did not wish to be bothered with guarding a prisoner, two of them said they were determined to shoot me then and there. Lucky for me, however, one of the scouts, by name Esom, who lived near Bealton Station, said that he would take charge of me and see that I was safely landed in Libby Prison.

All these men had been raised in that vicinity, and were well posted about all the roads and bridle-paths, and after debating awhile as to whether I should be killed, they took me to the house of a man with whom they were well-acquainted and called for something to eat. I began to think my time had come, because the old man and his daughter joined in with those of the scouts who thought I ought to be shot.

Esom pleaded my case as well as he could, but was overruled by the others, who condemned me to die as soon as they got what they wanted in the house—that is, something to eat.

In the meantime, the old man, Stratton, said that he would be my executioner, and that as he was too old to serve in the ranks, he could serve his country by killing a Yankee prisoner, and thus show his loyalty to the Confederate Government. Not only did Stratton say he wanted to shoot me, but his daughter said she wanted to be present when the shooting was done.

Of course, by this time I had made up my mind that this was a case of "root hog or die," and it can well be imagined that I did a great deal of rapid thinking. Well, they all sat down to their hoecake and mackerel, and I was told to take a back seat in a chair by the window. Of course, as I was condemned to be shot as soon as they had eaten, it was not thought best to waste any Confederate victuals on me. About this time I noticed a pail of water near the window and a gourd hanging on a nail above it, so I rose to my feet and said I wanted a drink of water.

I started for the pail, and at once jumped through the window, and then, of course, I struck out as fast as I could for the woods. They fired some bullets after me, but I kept on running, though one bullet made a flesh wound under my right arm. You can easily imagine that I had a hard time of it that night in the woods in my bare feet, but I succeeded in reaching the river and crossing it at Kelly's Ford. I traveled on until my feet became so sore that I stopped at the first house I came to, and made up my mind to risk the chances, because it was almost impossible for me to get any farther.

Good luck was on my side, for the man who lived in the house was a preacher, and he took me in and fed me. His name was James Brennan, and his wife, God bless her, made me a pair of cloth shoes that would be easy for my sore feet. These good people concealed me until they could get word to Gen. Buford. Mr. Brennan said that some of Gen. Buford's men used to come to his wheat stack nearly every day to get feed for their horses, and that he would watch for them and make report about me. He did so, and soon afterward I was taken to Headquarters in an ambulance, where I made a full report of all that I had discovered.

After I recovered so as to be round again a party of us went over to visit my old friend Stratton, the man who wanted the job of shooting me. This time circumstances had changed and Stratton was very friendly, but said he had nothing to eat. However, we did not believe him, so we hunted around and found plenty of victuals, and we also found his son-in-law, who belonged to the rebel army.

H. M. COBURN. Somehow or other his buildings all caught fire and burned down, and it remains a mystery to this day how those buildings caught fire, especially when so many people were about. James Brennan, if alive, still lives near Kelly's Ford, and his address is Culpeper, Culpeper County, Va.

# IV

# Between Gettysburg and the Wilderness

*EDITOR'S NOTE: The book excerpt that opens this chapter, which also appeared in* The National Tribune, *provoked Judson Knight to take great exception in the subsequent article to the "penny-a-liner" author's misrepresentation of the story of his friend, William J. Lee, in the unattributed account from the book* Heroic Deeds by Blue and Gray. *It is included to illustrate the level of fictionalization and inaccuracy that found its way into so much Civil War literature.*

The National Tribune
February 26, 1891

A Scout's Adventures

Experiences of Two Who Tried to Find Out Where the Enemy Was

"Blue and Gray"

UNKNOWN AUTHOR. IMMEDIATELY upon reporting to the Federal General above-named [This article does not mention this officer's name.], Mr. Lee was assigned to scouting duty. One of his adventures is worthy of record, though not strictly a part of the story of his work as a spy for the Union. His companion or partner was Judson Knight; each knew the other well; and each would have trusted the other with his life, his fortunes and his sacred honor.

It was the 20th of November, 1863, and the Federal force, under the command of Gen. Meade, was encamped at Mine Run. How large a body of the enemy was near them, and in what direction it was to be feared, were questions yet to be determined. In obedience to the higher authorities, a number of scouts were sent out, in small squads and pairs. Among the latter, who were of course expected to penetrate deeper into the unknown than the larger parties, were Lee and his friend Knight. In order to accomplish their purpose the better, they had donned Confederate uniforms. This, of course, would materially increase their danger in case of capture.[59]

It was late in the afternoon when they rode away from camp, and for several miles no adventure befell them. They had decided to make Orange Courthouse their goal, as the Confederate outposts were believed to be just beyond that point. By skillful management, aided by their gray uniforms, they hoped to get in the town such points as would enable them to judge of the enemy's force and exact location.

But when they were three miles away, or some half-dozen miles from their starting-point, Knight turned to Lee, "What is that on the hill yonder?"

"I've just been looking at it," returned the other, "and it looks to me mightily like a battery."

"There's more than a battery there," said Knight, shaking his head doubtfully, "It looks more like a brigade."

"I don't believe there's a brigade of rebs within 10 miles," answered Lee, testily, "but let's ride over."

Acting on this suggestion, they approached the point where the doubtful body of men was located. They were challenged by a picket. Lee recognized the voice as belonging to an old Richmond acquaintance.

"Why, Burton, don't you know me?" he asked, with great heartiness of manner.

Burton looked hard at him through the gathering dusk of the November afternoon.

"D____d if I do, unless it's Lee," replied the picket, who, it is hardly necessary to say, was not aware of the 4th Georgia's loss of a Sutler.

"Lee it is," returned the scout. "This is my friend, Mr. Knight, Mr. Burton, one of the honorable class of high privates."

"Same as myself," answered Burton, with a short laugh. "Happy to meet you, Mr. Knight."

The Federal muttered something which might have meant an acknowledgment of the introduction, and accepted the Confederate's proffered hand.

"Many of the boys about here, Burton?" inquired Lee, in an off-hand manner.

"Well, the regular picket-guard; the relief will be here in a few minutes. Hi, Jim! Did you know Lee was here?"

Thus summoned, the comrades of Burton gathered about the two Federals.

"Fourth Georgia, I s'pose, Mr. Knight?" asked Burton, by way of doing the polite, "Didn't know you were in the neighborhood."

"Yes, we've been here—that is, hanging around Meade—for some little time; we've heard of your being here, and Lee insisted on riding over to see some of his old friends.

"Did he? Well, I'm mighty glad to hear he remembered us so kindly. Sort o' makes a man feel good, these war times. Say, Lee, if you're so anxious to renew old acquaintances, there's plenty more on the road."

"Are there?" asked Lee, with genial interest; "and where may they be now?"

"Well, I reckon they're pretty near all of them at Orange Court-house by this time. Just about, I should say, for there comes the relief."

"But not all of my acquaintances, I suppose?" asked Lee. "Another regiment?"

While Burton and Knight had been talking, he had ascertained that this was the outpost of a regiment of artillery, and supposed that some infantry was coming to support it in case of an attack.[60]

"Another regiment! H___! It's old Pap Longstreet's whole corps."[61]

"You're joking."

"No, I'm not; it's so—ain't it, Brown?" turning to a comrade. "They've been getting in all the afternoon, and they're just about settling themselves to salt mule and chicory now. Have a chaw?"

A glance of quick intelligence passed between the two scouts, then, with the rapidity of thought, each sprang upon the back of the horse nearest to him, and spurred away. The astonished rebs grasped the situation in a moment.

"Spies! Spies! Yankee spies!" they yelled, and fired hastily after the fast-flying figures. "And then and there was hurrying to and fro," as the alarm was given, and the chase began.

The fugitives bent their heads down to their horses' necks, and gave the fleet animals the rein. The bullets whistled about their ears, but still they rode on unharmed; the leaden messengers of death tore up the earth under their horses' very feet; but fainter and fainter grew the yells behind them. Onward, still onward; and now they are out of range; now they approach the Federal lines, and at last are safe within them, astonishing Gen. Meade with the news of so large a force scarcely nine miles away.

* * *

*The National Tribune*
April 9, 1891
Judson Knight, Washington, D.C.

*The analytical heart of the Bureau of Military Information—seated left to right: its chief, Col. George H. Sharpe; its order-of-battle and interrogation expert, civilian John C. Babcock; an unidentified officer; and Capt. John McEntee, who supervised the scouts. The unidentified officer may be Lieut. Frederick L. Manning, an analyst and interrogator or Lieut. Alfred Tanner, a visitor from the 20th New York State Militia. LC-DIG-cwpb-03707.*

*Headquarters of the Bureau of Military Information, Army of the Potomac, in winter quarters at Brandy Station in 1864. Author's collection.*

*Select scouts of the BMI in winter quarters at Brandy Station 1864. Standing left to right: James Doughty, James Cammack, unknown, Henry W. Dodd, unknown, unknown. Seated: John M. Irby, Milton Cline, Dan Cole. On ground: Dan Plew, Milton Cline's son, W. J. Lee, unknown, James R. Wood, Sanford McGee, John W. Landegon. Alexander Gardner, Library of Congress, LC-B817-7032.*

*4-4. Thirty-five scouts, guides, and cooks of the BMI in winter quarters at Brandy Station 1864. These may have been close to the entire complement of the BMI other than clerks and officers at this time. All of these men were paid from a special secret service fund. Library of Congress, LC-B8171-7105.*

## A Scout's Adventures

### A Criticism of the Book *Heroic Deeds by Blue and Gray*

KNIGHT. IN AN article in your edition of Feb. 26 I read, "A Scout's Adventure," taken from a book called *Heroic Deeds by Blue and Gray*, and must say that I read the article with surprise. What kind of scouts must they have been who, after having established their status with the rebels, and being in conversation with them, to suddenly spring upon the backs of their horses and risk their lives from bullets, besides running the risk of Gen. Meade never getting the information that "Pap Longstreet's whole corps" were within swallowing distance. Why were they dismounted? There certainly was no necessity for it. And why did they not make some excuse to ride to some neighboring house to get feed for their horses and themselves and ride away slowly, like men who had some brains? Then the information about "Pap Longstreet" is more fishy, one of those pieces of news that certainly would have seriously disturbed Gen. Meade's digestion.

The story is without foundation in fact, as "Pap Longsreet" and his troops were in Tennessee at the time spoken of, and scouts who did not know it were unworthy of the name. Longstreet did not rejoin the Army of Northern Virginia until the Winter of 1863, in time for the Wilderness Campaign, and, if I am not very much mistaken, the most of them did not reach Lee's Army until the last of February or first of March, 1864.[62]

Other portions of the story that you did not publish are, if possible, more ridiculous than what you gave to one who knows all of the circumstances. Silver never lived four miles inside the Union lines in 1862 or 1863; he lived four miles inside the rebel lines, on the south side of the Rapidan, not far from where the battle of Chancellorsville was fought in May, 1863, and was living in the same place in the Spring of 1864 at the beginning of the Wilderness campaign under Gen. Grant.[63]

A few days before the opening of that campaign M[ilton]. G. Cline, who was then Chief of Scouts, a man named Chas. Forrestall, and myself went from the army headquarters, near Brandy Station, and staid several days in a tent which we had pitched in a swamp not far from Silver's house while he was getting news for us. When he brought us the news of the number of rations that were being issued at Orange Courthouse it was considered of enough importance for one man to go back and report the fact to headquarters. The duty fell to me.

When I left Silver's place that night he had a splendid farm—young peach and other orchards, good fences, Winter wheat two or three inches high, and everything flourishing. The next time I was at the place the Army of the Potomac had been on the south side of the river about a week and the Cavalry Corps had camped on his farm. The young fruit trees were all destroyed, not a rail left, nor a green blade of grass or growing grain was to be seen. It looked like a desert. I said to him, "Mr. Silver, how is this? Why did you not tell these people who you were, and that every one in authority at our headquarters knew you and could vouch for your loyalty?"

He replied, "I did tell them that, but no one would believe me, or at all events, they pretended not to believe anything I said."

Sheridan was on his raid toward Richmond at this time, and Silver told me the Chief Commissary or Quartermaster, Col._____, was going to leave there the next day, and said, "What I am to do after they go, I don't know. There will be nothing in the shape of provisions to be bought in this country. Every animal I had is killed; I can't make a crop now, and if I could, how are we to live in the mean time?"

I went and saw Col._____. At first I asked him if he could not have provisions enough to subsist the family for two or three months at least. He said there was no authority by which he could do so, and after I had given him a history of what I knew personally and what I had heard from others, he seemed to regret that he had no authority to act. At last a solution of the difficulty presented itself to my mind, and I asked the Colonel if he could not issue rations to me, as I was in command of a party of scouts that day, although I was not the chief. He said, "Yes, certainly I can; you make out a requisition on me and I will fill it. It's none of my business what you do with the rations after you get them." I drew ten days' rations for the men I had with me. The Colonel did not take the trouble to verify the number of men.

Five years ago next May, Patrick McEneany and I visited Silver. At first he did not remember anything about me, although he and his wife remembered McEneany, but had forgotten me until I told them of the rations. Then they remembered, and were very glad to see me.

I would like someone to tell me how Samuel J. Ruth,[64] who used to go to Winchester, Va., was to communicate with Silver, who lived near Fredericksburg. I certainly wish Ruth was living, as it would be very interesting to know how it was done. I am convinced in my own mind that some "penny-a-liner" has, at some time, heard Lee talking, and has given us this garbled statement as coming from him. Mr. Lee certainly would not state that he rode on horseback into our lines, when dozens of men are still living who know just how he did come.

When Gen. Lee found it advisable to evacuate the country between the Rapidan and the Rappahannock Rivers, Maj. Bridgford, Provost Marshal-General of the Army of Northern Virginia, told Lee (Wm. J., not the General) that they were going to leave that night, and for him to have his goods ready to load on the cars. *[EDITOR'S NOTE: Lee was a Union spy in the guise of a Confederate sutler at this time.]* Instead of doing so he took them to the premises of one Mr. Hogg, a cabinet-maker, from whom Lee had learned the trade before the war. When our troops took possession of Culpeper Court-house he came out and surrendered to them and was brought to army headquarters, where he saw for the first time Gen. George H. Sharpe, who was at that time Colonel of the 120th N.Y., and Deputy Provost-Marshal General of the Army of the Potomac. He had at Culpeper a quantity of plug tobacco, which was purchased from him by John C. Babcock, at that time Private Secretary to Col. Sharpe.[65]

On the Mine Run campaign one would think from reading your extract from "Blue and Gray," that Gen. Meade was a dullard and had been encamped at Mine Run for some time and had gone over there on a sort of "wild-goose chase," while the fact is he knew exactly where Gen. Lee's troops were. I saw a map in the possession of John C. Babcock that gave Lee's position not three days before we started on that campaign. Early and Hill's Corps were some distance apart, Early on the left guarding the fords from above Mitchell's down to Raccoon Ford, and perhaps below. The First Corps, Gen. French commanding,[66] crossed at Jacob's Ford and were to march to Robinson's Tavern, six miles south of the river. If Meade's program had been rapidly carried out Early would have been cut off from Hill and the Army of the Potomac would have fought the rebels in detail.[67]

A guide named Ebenezer McGee was furnished French and turned over by him to [Brig.] Gen. [Henry] Prince, who was in command of the division having the lead.[68] Soon after crossing to the south side of the river Prince pointed to a small road leading into the woods westward and said to McGee, "where does that road lead to?"

"I don't know," answered McGee, "probably to some little farm."

Gen. Prince then turned to some of his staff, saying, "A d_____d pretty guide they have sent us; one who doesn't know the country."

McGee then said to him, "General, I was sent to guide you to Robinson's Tavern; that road leads to it," pointing to the road they were on.

The troops were halted and Prince and his staff started off on the road that led into the woods westward, and some three hours later came back with a negro mounted on a mule for a guide, when the march was resumed. Not long after they were attacked by some of Early's troops, while the remainder hurried to the assistance of their comrades. Had not that delay occurred, for which there was no occasion, the troops that crossed at Germania Ford could have formed a junction with the First Corps at Robinson's Tavern and Gen. Meade's plans would not have been frustrated as they were.[69]

This is what really did happen. The morning that Meade's headquarters crossed the Rapidan at Germania Ford, Col. Sharpe, who is the Federal General referred to in the opening lines of the article in *The National Tribune* of Feb. 26, said to me, "You take Lee with you, and keep him with you." We had no horses. My own horse had a sore back, and I had left him with my servant to bring up our camp equipage. We had no horse that Lee could be mounted on, but I had an order to take any horses that we could find in the country, for Lee and myself.

When we had got about a mile south of the river we turned into a wood road leading westward, and soon came to the plantation of a widow Willis. The residence and barns, with the negro quarters, were nearly in the center of the open ground, which descended both from the east and the west sides toward the buildings. When we were about half way from the woods to Mrs. Willis's house a horseman came out of the woods on the west side at a gallop, and we halted and held our pistols in hand ready for use. After he had passed the house we could see he had a blue uniform, and as he came towards us we could see he wore the shoulder-straps of a Major. When he came up he eyed us sharply, as we were both in civilian suits. He said, "Who are you, men?" to which I replied, "We belong to Gen. Meade's headquarters."

"Well," said he, "you can't get through those woods, for there are too many rebs in there, as I have just tried to go through to the road from Jacob's Ford and came near being captured." He then spurred on and disappeared in the timber we had just left. He had not been out of sight long when some six or eight horsemen came in sight from the same place the major had come from. When they had got about half way from the woods to Mrs. Willis's house, they stopped. I said, "They are Johnnies."

"No," said Lee, "they are your own men." Then pointing out one he said, "That is Cline and that is McCord." Cline was our Chief Scout at the time, and McCord was from Battery H, 1st Ohio Artillery. There was some resemblance to both of the men named, but the others and the horses did not look right. We were too far apart to make sure of anything. Presently they turned and rode back into the woods on their side of the plantation, and separated, half going to the right and half to the left. They turned too soon to succeed in their little game, which was to go around the place and come around in our rear and capture us. We then turned back and went to the Germania plank road, going along with our troops, who were marching along it.

A mile or so south of where we joined the troops we came to a house that had been deserted by the family who lived there, whose name I found was Beal. Mr. Beal had been a Postmaster before the war. This I found out from documents that had been scattered on the floor. No doubt hundreds of our men had ransacked the place before we got there, as papers of all kinds were scattered around through the rooms, among which Lee began diligently searching. After a time I inquired what he was looking for. "Cotton bonds," said he.

"Suppose you should find any, what good would they be to you?"

"Oh," said he, "they will be paid."

I turned in and looked for cotton bonds also, but found none, after spending an hour or two. I discovered a shirt that looked as though it would fit, and said to Lee, "I have not worn a 'boiled shirt' for so long I am going to put this one on," which I proceeded to do.[70] Lee found a violin and sat down and played a tune or two as well as he could with one string gone. We then started ahead, he carrying the violin and I wearing the "boiled shirt." We eased our consciences by thinking that if we had not taken them others would.

After going a mile or so we struck into the woods to our right, where there was neither road nor path, and started in the direction of Robinson's Tavern. It was slow, tedious walking, and the day was hot, even if it was November. After we had gone about three miles we began to hear firing in what we thought must be in the vicinity of Robinson's Tavern. The farther we went the harder it became until it sounded like a regular battle. After we had gone probably three or four miles we came to a place in the woods that was comparatively free from underbrush, and I proposed to Lee to sit down and rest awhile, to which he assented. A large tree formed a good place to lean against.

We had sat there but a few minutes when a mounted Johnny came in sight about 100 yards to our right. He was evidently on a road of some kind, which brought him within about 60 yards of us. I whispered to Lee, "There is one horse for us, any way," and cocked my pistol so that it should not click, by holding the trigger, and was just going to order him to halt when he stopped of his own accord and dismounted. Surprise kept us quiet. Throwing his bridle over his arm, he walked about eight or 10 steps and stopped. He had stopped in front of ten or a dozen other Johnnies who were sitting on a log. How we had reached our seat without being seen by them I can't say. I immediately turned sideways and got my hands to the ground and traveled on hands and knees for a pine thicket a few feet in our rear. When we got a few feet into the thicket we ran upon an old sow with a large litter of pigs, all sound asleep. As soon as we reached them they woke not only themselves but all the echoes near. I had never realized until then how much noise could be made by a litter of pigs and their mother. We came upon them in a shape that, in all probability, the mother had never seen men in before, and she was correspondingly scared. She made a noise that could have been heard over a quarter of a mile. Being aware of the fact that the Johnnies were fond of fresh pork, I expected them to come and investigate.

As soon as we had crawled through the thicket we concluded to go back to the Germania plank road which we reached about 3 o'clock p.m. We then kept the road along which our troops were still passing until we came to where it crosses the old turnpike leading from Fredericksburg to Orange Court House. Army headquarters were on the hill to the right of the junction, where Gens. Grant and Meade were located the next May during the Wilderness fighting.

We were both hungry and tired, and went to the large brick house on the hill, southwest from the junction. A yellow flag was still flying from it, that had been placed there the previous May, when it had been used as a hospital at the time of the battle of Chancellorsville. A few of our soldiers were there on the same errand as we ourselves, trying to get something to eat. We soon found there was no chance to get anything. While we were expressing our disappointment a gentleman, also in citizen's dress, said, pointing to the Old Wilderness Tavern, "Gentlemen, you can get corn bread and bacon over there. I have just come from there." Upon my asking who he was, he said he was a correspondent of the New York *Times*. Then I asked if they had milk or butter. "No, nothing but corn bread and bacon, and they will charge you a dollar of that."

When we got within 50 yards of the house, we met two women, who asked where they should go to get a safeguard. Pointing to Gen. Patrick's flag on the hill,[71] I told them to go there, and added that we were just on our way to the house to see if we could get some supper. "Go right on and take a seat on the porch, and we will be back presently," they said.

Presently they returned, unlocked the door and invited us in. One of them went out to prepare our supper, while the other one went out on the porch to listen to the firing. After they had left the room, I got up and as I passed Lee said to him, "I am going out on the porch, and I am going to stay until that woman comes in. As soon as she does you tell her that we are Confederates." When I reached the porch she began trying to find out what I thought of the fight then going on. She used the words, "your army," and "our army," to which I made hardly any response, but acted moody and dejected. She finally got me to say the sound of the firing did seem nearer than it did an hour or two ago, which I well understood was caused by the air becoming more dense as it came nearer nightfall. She soon tired of my company and went into the house. She had not been inside above a minute when I heard her call out: "Betty, these are not Yankees, they are our men." I at once stepped into the room, and said in a tone of intense disgust, "Did you take us for Yankees?"

"Well," said she, apologetically, "when we first met you I thought you were a Southern man, but I thought this man was a Yankee."

"Well, madam, you made a great mistake; he is a sutler at Gen. Lee's headquarters and I am sutler of the 69th Ga." Betty came running in, and our hands were shaken and we were congratulated on our not being Yankees, and the whole program for supper was instantly changed. We soon sat down to a supper of fresh pork, hot biscuits, and butter, while coffee, sugar, and milk were plentiful. We learned that Mrs. Sims was the name of our hostess and that her husband belonged to Capt. Kincheloe's company of the Prince William County cavalry.[72]

After supper, which seemed to me to be about the best one I had ever eaten, we began inquiring how it happened they had coffee and sugar in apparent plenty. "That's nothing," said Mrs. Sims, as she disappeared into another room, from which she presently emerged loaded down with felt hats, gauntlet gloves, cavalry boots, cords, and plumes for officer's hats. "Why don't you ask how we get these?" On our expressing our surprise to see such quantities of those things, and a hint that we would be pleased to be enlightened, she told us that there was a "blind ford" on the Occoquan River called the Widow Sally Davis's Ford, and that the Yankees had never guarded it, as they did not know of its existence. That the widow Davis could go into Alexandria any time she wanted to and buy anything she desired, for there was a Yankee detective there named Smoot who vouched for her. She brought the things to her house, and after dark the men of Kinchloe's company went over and got them. It is needless to say the "Widow Sally Davis's Ford" was shortly thereafter guarded and a detective was out of a job.

Knowing, as I did, the nocturnal habits of such parties as our friend Kincheloe's gang I suggested to Lee that we had better be starting, as there was no telling where we would find headquarters, as they had undoubtedly moved since we had been at the house, and it was fully 8 p.m. Mrs. Sims showed us a bed, and said we could occupy it if we chose, and added, "I am sure my husband will be home some time during the night and will have some of his men with him and you can get away," to which I replied, "That is all true, no doubt, Mrs. Sims, and we are more than obliged to you, but we are on parole and if we should ever be captured again we would be hung, I am afraid."

"I had never thought of that. I suppose you had better go," she said.

We had very hard work to make her accept $2 for our supper, but she finally did. It must have been 9 p.m. when we got away. Headquarters had moved and we did not get there until about 11 p.m.

The next morning early we started on our search for horses. We soon reached Robinson's Tavern, where we came up with our skirmish line and kept along with them until we came to Mine Run. There our skirmishers had to halt, the rebels were working like beavers at throwing up earthworks. At the point where we first saw them they already had substantial works completed with several guns peeping out of embrasures. A large open field on the left of the road was occupied by two or three batteries of artillery as fast as they came up.

On our way to this point, which was the residence of a Col. Roe or Rowe, we passed "Johnson's Tannery." An icehouse, built in the way they were usually constructed in Virginia, by digging a hole in the ground and covering it with a roof, caught my eye and I looked into it. A large lot of blankets and bedquilts at the bottom looked to me as if it had been used the night before by some of the Confederates as a sleeping place. A ladder was in position and I went down to investigate. Hastily pulling over some of the top quilts I felt something stirring underneath them. Concluding it was some kind of an animal the rebels had left to play a trick on the Yanks with I worked very cautiously, and at last found an infant but a few months old. It was a very pretty child, but for something grown over the pupil of one eye, which projected so that the child could not shut the lids of that eye. I went to the house and saw a mulatto girl and asked her if she knew there was a white child in the icehouse. She said, "Why dat's my child." I asked where Johnson and his family were, and she said they had gone to Col. Rowe's.

Col. Rowe's house was taken by Col. [Samuel Sprigg "Red"] Carroll, of the 8th Ohio, as his headquarters. In talking with Maj.-Gen. Carroll some four or five years ago he told me that Rowe's cellar was filled with men, women, and children, both white and black, who had fled to his place as the safest place they could find.[73]

Lee and I stood in the open field near one of our batteries until it became evident to me that the batteries would soon open. My desire to stay there was not all great, as by crossing the road an equally good view could be had from behind some trees. I pointed out the advantages of the position to Lee, who did not appear to appreciate the difference in the position until a solid shot from one of the rebel guns fell in a group of 15 or 20 men within a few feet of where we stood. As luck would have it no one was hurt. I again mentioned the advisability of a "change of base," to which he assented.

We had just crossed the road when Gen. Meade rode up, and, looking around upon the troops, who had crowded up where they could see, he said, in crisp, curt tones, "What are you doing here? Those that have any business get to your places, and those that have none clear the road." They melted away like magic. We got good positions to observe the artillery duel that was evidently about to begin. Presently they opened from both sides, and at the second or third shot from one of our guns we saw a brass gun in the rebel works jump about three feet high. After a few shots both sides ceased firing, and we wandered out into the field and went down to some of the out buildings of Rowe's place. The rebel skirmishers fired upon every one they could see.

After staying around the outhouses awhile, I looked into Col. Rowe's barn through the cracks and discovered two horses. We then tore off boards enough to get in. On looking the horses over we found them to be two very sorry specimens of rebel artillery horses, still in harness from the day before. We stripped off the English harness, leaving the head stalls on. There was a beam that the horses could neither get over or under on the backside of the barn, so that the only way we could get them out was to take them out of the door, which opened toward the rebel skirmish-line. Mounting the horses inside the barn I suddenly swung one door open, and Lee got out as quickly as his old plug could be got to move, and I followed him as fast as my animal could travel. We passed along the south side of the barn until we reached the back of it, where we immediately took shelter.

The Johnnies fired a few shots, but did no damage either to us or the horses.

We had hardly dismounted when Col. Carroll's Quartermaster came up and took the horses from us. I told him that if the horses were good for anything he should not have them. As it was we would not make any fuss about them, for I would a great deal sooner let him have them than enter into explanations as to who we were, with a whole crowd of soldiers standing around that I did not want to know anything about us. This is all there was of anything resembling the "Blue and Gray" account and one must have a very robust imagination to make the two agree.

That night we went back to Johnson's Tannery, and found the Surgeon of my old regiment (2d N.J.), with his assistants, had possession of Johnson's house as a hospital. Lee and I were both invited by the boys to stay all night, which we did. Lee sold the violin, which he had stuck to for two days, and which had become a great nuisance to him. The next day I reported to Col. Sharpe where we had been and what we had done since crossing the Rapidan. When I came to getting the horses and how we lost them, he said, "We will have those horses if you want them."

"No, Colonel," said I, "they are not worth the making of an enemy of the Quartermaster."

# V

# The Kilpatrick-Dahlgren Raid

*EDITOR'S NOTE: Scout Anson Carney narrates his partici-
pation in that part of the raid against Richmond in February-
March 1864 led by Col. Ulrich Dahlgren. This 21-year-old hero
of Gettysburg lost his leg in the pursuit of Lee's Army after the
battle and was personally promoted by Lincoln from captain to
full colonel for his exploits. Dahlgren was the son of Admiral
John Dahlgren, a close Lincoln advisor and friend. The young
officer cut a dashing figure with his lithe, blond good looks, his
outstanding horsemanship, and his taste for special operations.
His involvement in the raid on Richmond was to ignite one of
the great controversies of the Civil War. Carney's articles, as
well as the article by scout John W. Landegon and contem-
porary letters by Captain John McEntee, the BMI's officer in
charge of scouts, and scout Joseph Humphreys, are heretofore
little known accounts of direct participants in this raid.*

*The National Tribune*
March 29, 1894
Anson B. Carney

### ADVENTURES OF ONE OF OUR SCOUTS ON THE KILPATRICK RAID

CARNEY. Like many soldiers in other branches of the service, the scouts attached to the Headquarters of the Army of the Potomac had to take the fortunes of army life just as they came along. We had, of course, certain seasons of rest, and then again we passed through adventures which were of a nature to try the stoutest heart. And not only have I passed through many scenes of trial and danger myself, but members of my family have also suffered.

I wish to give some account of my experience on Kilpatrick's raid to Richmond, the purpose of which was to make a dash on the city, liberate the Union prisoners at Belle Island and Libby Prison, and arm them from the armory in the city. If everything were successful so far, then it was hoped that they could fight their way out to where some of Gen. Butler's forces had been sent up from Fortress Monroe to assist them.

---

### THE KILPATRICK-DAHLGREN RAID

*The Kilpatrick-Dahlgren Raid (February 28–March 3, 1864) was an ambitious attempt by Union cavalrymen to assault the lightly defended Confederate capital at Richmond, Virginia, and free prisoners of war during the Civil War. The brainchild of the flamboyant Brigadier General H. Judson Kilpatrick, the raid turned into a fiasco when Kilpatrick's men were stopped northwest of the city and a supporting column, under the command of twenty-one-year-old Colonel Ulric Dahlgren, was routed to the east. Dahlgren was killed, and papers found on his body, which were subsequently published by the Richmond press, detailed plans to burn the city and assassinate Confederate president Jefferson Davis and his cabinet. Public opinion in both the North and the South was inflamed, and historians continue to debate the authority behind these so-called Dahlgren Papers. When she read of Dahlgren's corpse being mistreated, Elizabeth Van Lew, a Union spy in Richmond, used her contacts secretly to exhume the body and rebury it elsewhere.*

*Encyclopedia Virginia, http://www.encyclopediavirginia.org/Kilpatrick-Dahlgren_Raid#start_entry*

*The Kilpatrick Raid to Richmond. Edwin Forbes, Library of Congress, LC-USZ62-7037.*

The Kilpatrick-Dahlgren Raid (February 28–March 3, 1864) was an indeed an ambitious attempt by Judson Kilpatrick, the raid turned into a fiasco when Kilpatrick's men were stopped northwest of the city and a supporting column, under the command of twenty-one-year-old Colonel Ulric Dahlgren, was routed to the east. Dahlgren was killed, and papers found on his body, which were subsequently published by the Richmond press, detailed plans to burn the city and assassinate Confederate president Jefferson Davis and his cabinet. Public opinion in both the North and the South was inflamed, and historians continue to debate the authority behind these so-called Dahlgren Papers. When she read of Dahlgren's corpse being mistreated, Elizabeth Van Lew, a Union spy in Richmond, used her contacts secretly to exhume the body and rebury it elsewhere.

On the 28[74] of February 1864, 10 of our band of scouts at the Headquarters of the Army of the Potomac were ordered to report to Gen. Kilpatrick, at Stevensburg, Va.[74] We went there, and timed our departure from Stevensburg so that we should arrive at Ely's Ford on the Rapidan in a short time after dark.[75]

We halted in the woods, and the General sent [Martin] Hogan and myself, accompanied by a suitable detail, to cross the river as best we could, and capture the rebel pickets on the other side.[76]

After considerable scouting around, we concluded to make the attempt about half a mile above the ford, and started to cross the river, holding our ammunition and arms above our heads. Though part of the way the water came up to our armpits, we did not look

*Ulrich Dahlgren was jumped from captain to colonel personally by Lincoln for his brilliant and daring service at Gettysburg. He was bold and adventurous but was killed in the ill-starred raid on Richmond in March 1864, in which a number of the BMI scouts were wounded, captured, and killed. Author's collection.*

Brig. Gen. Judson Kilpatrick (1836–1881), commander, 3rd Division, Cavalry Corps, Army of the Potomac. He was known as "Kilcalvary" for the reckless disregard of the safety of his men and horses on the march and in battle. It is believed that the orders captured from Dahlgren's corpse for the murder of Jefferson Davis and his cabinet and the burning of Richmond originated from Kilpatrick in coordination with Secretary of War Edwin Stanton. He vociferously denied this, but he was openly referred to as a known liar by Carney's superior, Capt. John McEntee, who managed the BMI's scouting operations, Provost Marshall General Brig. Gen. Marsena Patrick, and the commander of the Army of the Potomac, Maj. George B. Meade. After the raid he was so unwelcomed in the eastern theater that he was transferred to Gen. Sherman's army in Georgia.

*Brig. Gen. Judson Kilpatrick commanded the 3rd Division of the Army of the Potomac's Cavalry Corps. He instigated the raid on Richmond, to the support of which Col. Sharpe contributed one third of all his scouts, ten of whom were killed, wounded, or captured. LC-DIG-cwpb-00983.*

back, but crossed the river all right, and then struck into a ravine between two rebel pickets, whose position we had accurately located before crossing.

In a few moments we were halted, and then we claimed to be the relief. We were told to advance and give the countersign. Hogan went forward. Shoving a pistol under the picket's nose, Hogan intimated that if he opened his mouth he would blow the top his head off.

We secured the whole picket-line in the same way, until we came to the reserve, which was quartered in an old house on the bank above the ford. We surrounded this reserve, and captured them without a shot.

We recrossed the Rapidan with our prisoners, and reported that the way was clear. Our prisoners were sent back to Brandy Station [Headquarters, Army of the Potomac at this time] and we advanced. Favored by the darkness of the night we were not noticed, although before daylight we passed within 30 rods of some rebel camps.

---

*Headquarters, Cavalry Expedition, February 29, 1864, 1 a.m.*

*To: Chief of Staff, Cavalry Corps*

*My advance captured the picket and reserve of the enemy at Ely's Ford, consisting of a captain, one lieutenant and 15 men. It was a complete surprise. No alarm has been given. The enemy does not anticipate our movement. My command is crossing in good order.*
*Brig. Gen. J. Kilpatrick*

The War of the Rebellion, A Compilation of the Official Records of the Union and Confederate Armies, Series 1, Vol. XXXIII, pp. 181–82.

---

Perhaps I may as well make a digression here, and I mention a circumstance that occurred about 2 a.m. One of our men accidentally discharged his carbine, which offended Col. Dahlgren so much that he made the man dismount and lead his horse until after daylight. I felt sorry for the man and interceded for him, but without avail, for the Colonel said that such carelessness ought not to be overlooked.

On our route toward Richmond we met several parties who came to investigate, and we took them right along with us. The next morning about 9 o'clock I was in advance, and saw that something unusual was going on at a brick house. I reported this, and was ordered to take 30 men and surround the house. The rebels were holding a court-martial in the house, and I captured the whole outfit, prisoners and all. This house was about 40 to 50 rods off the main highway, and when I returned to the column the General said:

"Carney, you have finished a good job. Good for you."

We kept the prisoners until the afternoon, and when we thought they were tired enough and far enough away from Lee's army to do us very little injury, we paroled them and let them go.

That afternoon my horse gave out, so I started ahead, and a little to one side of our route, to find another. Leaving my saddle in an ambulance and taking the bridle on my arm, I started for a house I saw about a mile to the left.

When I got near the house I noticed an old hovel of a barn, and upon entering I saw three horses. A fine bay mare took my fancy, so I slipped the bridle into her mouth and led her out. She seemed to be very wild, and bothered me some, as I had no saddle, and by this time three men and four or five women came out of the house. They were not looking for Yankees, and supposed that I was some Confederate ruffian who wanted to steal their property. One man yelled for his gun, and a woman went back into the house and brought out a shotgun. I wheeled, and got the mare between me and them, and I thought I could get out of their way by the time they reached the hovel.

As it was, however, I ran right into a trap. It happened that I was in a lane, and this lane only ran about 15 rods to a watering-trough, and then stopped. The pole fence was too high for the mare to jump. I did not dare to get off, because the mare was getting excited as well as myself. The man with the shotgun had not fired, and I therefore made up my mind that his old blunderbuss was not loaded. So I determined to face-about and charge him with my Colt's revolver. But about this time I thought I heard the report of cannon, for sure enough the gun was loaded, and in his excitement the old rebel fired both barrels at once.

I was unharmed, but some of the shot struck the mare, and she jumped out from under me almost like a flash of lightning. I hung onto the bridle-rein, and was determined to keep that mare or die. I was getting mad, so I raised my revolver and began to pump the lead at them, for the other men had approached behind the old man. They retreated to the hovel, and commenced to load the old gun. I led the mare off as rapidly as I could, and I soon saw the welcome heads and shoulders of Pat McEneany and Hogan, two of our scouts, coming up on the other side of the hill. They were brave boys, and they helped me out. It seems that they had heard the firing, and knowing that I was over there somewhere and might be in trouble, they had come as rapidly as possible to my assistance.

We soon joined the command, and that evening our forces captured a small wagon-train loaded with corn, on the way to Richmond. Our horses had a good supper and breakfast, as well as ourselves, for some of our company came across a barrel of peach brandy in the cellar of an old tavern; it was, of course, confiscated, and about one-half of the brandy found its way into canteens before the General knew it. He ordered two kegs from an ambulance to be filled, and it so happened that this circumstance was a great favor to me, the particulars of which I will explain later.

* * *

*The National Tribune*
April 5, 1894
Anson B. Carney

CARNEY. The next morning, March 2, we made an early start on our way to Richmond. The General told Col. Dahlgren to take 400 men and go off by way of Goochland to destroy some flour mills along the canal and also the locks. Dahlgren's command was composed of a squadron of my own regiment (5th U.S. Cav.), a squadron of Harris's Light Cavalry (2d N.Y.), and a squadron of the 5th Mich. Cav. Capt. [John] Mitchell, of the 2nd N.Y., and Capt. Hastings, of the 5th Mich. Cav., were in command under Dahlgren.

Our instructions were, after destroying the mills and canal, to cross the James River and go south of the city, where we were to watch for rockets as a signal, and then charge in from the south. This plan was knocked in the head by a negro guide, and we found out afterward that he was sent to us for the express purpose of leading us out of the way. He carried out his instructions well, for he delayed us several hours, and then it was too late for us to get south of Richmond.[77]

When Dahlgren saw what was done he said to me: "Carney, have that nigger hung alongside of the road within 15 minutes."

So I rode back to the ambulance, where I got a rope, and in about 10 minutes the negro was kicking in the air, having his hands tied behind his back with a handkerchief.[78]

After that we turned to the left and struck the Brooks turnpike. Then we turned our course up to the first line of the defenses of Richmond. There we waited about two hours for a signal from Gen. Kilpatrick, but received none. It was getting very hot for us about that time, for the rebel troops were pouring out from Richmond, and the militia began to crowd our rear. The Colonel ordered a charge, but we were repulsed and had to retreat.

In this fight about 100 of us were cut off and separated from Col. Dahlgren; indeed, I never saw the Colonel again, for he was killed

*The Reliable Contraband by Edwin Forbes. Judson Knight as well as Col. Sharpe asserted that they did not know of any case in which a slave betrayed a Union soldier behind enemy lines. Author's collection.*

either that night or the next morning. Capt. Hastings and Capt. Mitchell were with those who were separated from the main column, and they began to devise a plan to get out. We were in a tight place. We made a charge, cut our way out, and did not stop, but took to the fields till we came to another road near Hungary Station. There too we had to cut through another lot of rebels, and then we traveled on about a mile and turned off into the woods.

We were completely lost in the night, and knew that if we remained there during the night every mother's son of us would be candidate for Libby Prison. About this time Capt. Hastings said to me:

"Carney, you are an old scout; get us out of this scrape, if you can."

Of course I was as anxious to get out as the rest, so I told Capt. Hastings to have the men remain where they were until I returned. Every few moments we could hear the rebels passing back and forth in large squads along the turnpike. So I started out to reconnoiter, on foot, and when I heard anyone coming I would dodge quickly into the bushes along the road. I continued in this way for about one and a half miles, when I came near a house. I hunted around until I found the negro quarters, and knocked on the door. A negro opened it, and I was a long time in making him believe that I was a Yankee. After awhile I convinced him, and by promising to take him North with me he consented to guide us over the country to a road leading to the White House. I took him to where our men were and furnished him with a horse.

Then, with the negro and 10 men for an advance party, we started down the road on our perilous journey. After proceeding about half a mile we turned into a lane and crossed over the country for two miles, when we struck another road. The guide told us the names of the various roads and places, but I have forgotten them. After going on about a mile I heard some one at the side of the road call out:

"Halt! Who are you?"

Immediately shots were fired at us from each side of the road. The negro was close to me, and I heard a yell. That was the last of our unfortunate guide, and I guess about every one of our advance squad was hit in some way. I myself was shot through the body. I was almost paralyzed, but as my overcoat was strapped on the pommel of my saddle, I leaned my breast over that, and with my feet in the stirrups I did not fall off, but it seemed to me that I would never get my breath again.

After the firing the column that was behind wheeled about, and after going back a quarter of a mile turned off into the woods to hold a council of war. My faithful mare, that I had confiscated from the rebels, turned about too, and followed the rest of our men into the woods. She did this of her own accord, for I was so badly wounded that I had no control of myself whatever. Some of the boys helped me off, and I lay on the ground on my face till nearly daylight. About that time a couple of the boys helped me on the mare again. I kept drinking the peach brandy we had captured the day before, and that helped to keep up my strength.

We started at break of day, and at the first house we came to, we pressed another guide into service. Our men were scattered all over the country, and the roads were full of rebel squads picking them up. But, not withstanding this our little command kept well together, and when we came to a small band of rebels we charged right through them. This was quite often, for I think we made as many as 10 such charges that day. In the excitement of a charge and by the help of the peach brandy I was able to rise right up in my saddle and fire my revolver about as well as any of my companions.

As our horses were pretty well used up we hid in the woods that night until about midnight, when we started on our march again, and fortunately met Gen. Butler's colored troops about 10 o'clock. They had marched up from Fortress Monroe to help us, and met us near the White House.

I was put into an ambulance and taken to Yorktown. From there I went by steamer to the McClellan Hospital at Old Point Comfort, where I remained nearly two months. Before my wound was healed I left the hospital and joined Headquarters during the battle of Cold Harbor. As I was not strong enough to ride on horseback, Gen. Grant ordered me to Washington to operate from there on Gen. Early's line of communications. I would be conveyed down the Potomac to Acquia Creek and cross the country on foot to Madison Courthouse. After working Early's line of communications I would return about every week. After two months work there I went to headquarters at City Point. Of the two scouts sent on that raid I was the only one who got back, for the others were all killed or captured. My cousin, Phil Carney, was captured on the raid, but made his escape from Libby prison a few months later, and walked into camp one morning at City Point, having on a plug hat and looking comical enough. [*EDITOR'S NOTE: See Chapter 9 for a fuller account of this escape.*][79]

If Capt. Hastings is alive I would like to know if he remembers the horse I captured at the blacksmith's shop about two and half miles from Richmond and gave to the captain. It was a blooded mare.

\* \* \*

*The National Tribune*
May 31, 1894
J. W. Landegon, Danbury, Conn.

LANDEGON. [To the] Editor *National Tribune*: In your issues of March 29 and April 5 an article appeared, written by scout A. B. Carney, relative to the Kilpatrick-Dahlgren raid to Richmond, Feb. 29 to March 5, 1864. I think I was "in it," and desire to blow my own horn a little in reference to it, and also say a few words in reply to Comrade Carney.

Four days before starting on the trip I reached Gen. Kilpatrick's Headquarters at Stevensburg, Va., having been absent from the Army of the Potomac several weeks. I was told by Gen. Kilpatrick to get the scouts in shape to accompany him. The idea of releasing our prisoners confined in Richmond and vicinity was originated and planned by Kilpatrick, submitted and approved by the authorities at Washington, with Col. Dahlgren appointed second in command.

Four thousand cavalry, with artillery, were to do the work. The command was to move on Richmond in two columns—Kilpatrick from the north, Dahlgren to make a detour to the right, in order to attack from the south. Dahlgren's command numbered 500 picked men from Kilpatrick's (Third) Cavalry Division, with such subordinate officers as Lieut.-Col. Ed. Cook [Maj. Edwin Cooke], Capts. Mitchell, Hastings,

Col. Dahlgren was not Kilpatrick's overall second in command. The young colonel commanded only the smaller 500-man raiding party. The orders of the Commander, Cavalry Corps, Maj. Gen. Alfred Pleasanton, Army of the Potomac, to Kilpatrick merely stated that "Col. Ulric Dahlgren is authorized to accompany you, and will render valuable assistance from his knowledge of the country and well-known gallantry, intelligence, and energy."

Pleasanton to Kilpatrick, February 26, 1864

and others whose names I have forgotten, and a detail of 10 scouts from Gen. Meade's Headquarters.

Col. Dahlgren was to have the advance, capture the rebel pickets on the Rapidan River in the vicinity of Ely's Ford, proceed south to Spotsylvania Court House, here cut loose from the main column, move to the right, strike the Virginia Central Railroad at Frederick Hall Station, destroy railroad and telegraph communication, and, if prudent, attempt the capture of a large park of artillery encamped near there; then move to Goochland, cross the James River, thence down the south bank, recross the river just below Belle Isle at 9 a.m. March 2.

This accomplished, the prisoners on Belle Isle could join Dahlgren in Richmond and assist in forming a junction with Kilpatrick, who was to enter the city at the same time from the north by the Brook Pike, Kilpatrick to make known his presence by a report of artillery, the signal agreed upon by the two leaders.

The rebel pickets on the Rapidan were captured without firing a shot, and to Gen. Meade's scouts belong the credit.

This enabled the whole command to cross the stream and pass through and to the rear of Gen. Lee's army without being detected or alarming the enemy in any way, thereby greatly insuring the success of the movement.

Comrade Carney says Gen. Meade's scouts reported to Gen. Kilpatrick at Stevensburg. I think if the comrade will jog his memory a little it will tell him they reported to Col. Dahlgren. They were to go with him, and did, were in no way connected with the main column after crossing the Rapidan River. In fact after Dahlgren left the main column, just beyond Spotsylvania Courthouse, we knew nothing of him or any of his command until Capt. Mitchell reached us on the morning of the 4th.

Comrade Carney relates how some prisoners were captured near Frederick Hall, and the General said: "Carney, you have finished a good job. Good for you." "Humpty Dumpty on the wall," with Gen. Kilpatrick at least 15 miles away.[80]

Comrade Carney also says: "That evening our forces captured a small wagon-train loaded with corn on the way to Richmond. Our horses had a good supper and breakfast, as well as ourselves, for some of our company came across a barrel of peach brandy in the cellar of an old tavern." (Did they supper and breakfast on the brandy or the corn?) "It was of course confiscated, and about one-half of the brandy found its way into canteens before the General knew it. He ordered two kegs from an ambulance to be filled, and it so happened that this circumstance was a great favor to me, the particulars of which I will explain later."

Very handy to have an ambulance and kegs when wanted. "Humpty Dumpty got a fall." Comrade Carney—an ambulance—two kegs of brandy, with Kilpatrick 20 miles away.[81]

Comrade Carney then tells how they were lost; how a negro was picked up to guide them out of the wilderness; how the negro proved a traitor, leading them a long distance out of the way, delaying the command several hours, thereby knocking the plan in the head to enter Richmond from the south, etc.

It has always seemed strange to me that an officer of Col. Dahl-gren's ability should have been so misled. The route he was to take was not a difficult one to follow; and aside from this, one would suppose that some of Gen. Meade's scouts would have been selected to accompany him, on account of their knowledge of the country between the Rapidan and Richmond.

Comrade Carney states that they afterward found out the negro was sent them for the express purpose of misleading them. I do wonder how they found out that much. After Capt. Mitchell reached us the information I received from men who were with Col. Dahlgren led me to think then, as I do now, that the hanging of that poor black man was a cruel and cowardly murder. The negro was taken from the plantation where he lived; did not know the country; did not profess to know. Probably he had never been five miles from his house before. My experience with the Southern blacks during the war proved to me they were truly loyal to us, and were ever ready and willing to peril their lives to aid a Union soldier.

I believe Col. Dahlgren was a brave and able officer, and perhaps no other officer under the circumstances could have accomplished

*During the raid in which Col. Dahlgren was killed, scout Anson B. Carney was seriously wounded. Author's collection.*

the task assigned to him. I know he gave his life for his country; but we cannot forget that other brave soldiers of his command gave up their lives also, and that nearly 100 were captured and suffered many months the torture of prison-pens. Some were released by death. Col. Cook with others returned to us as physical wrecks. Cook was one of the officers placed in front of the Confederate works at Charleston during the bombardment. He lived but a short time after the war. Brave, gallant, genial Ed. Cook. He was beloved by all who knew him, particularly the members of his old regiment—the Harris Light Cavalry.

But why was Col. Dahlgren selected? I believe it was one of the many cases during the war where it was intended that the tail should wag the dog; that is, if the dog caught the rabbit. Does any soldier who knew or served under Gen. Kilpatrick believe, had the selection been left to him, he would have gone outside his old Third Cavalry Division for a leader?

Now to return to the main column. What did it accomplish? Not very much. After parting company with Col. Dahlgren it moved rapidly south by way of Beaver Dam Station. It did not get lost, hung no negro, but did arrive in front of Richmond on time, as planned. It opened fire with artillery, as planned, but received no answering signal from Col. Dahlgren. Before reaching this point a number of Johnnies were picked up, including the pickets on Brook Pike, by Kilpatrick's scouts (they being in the advance) without firing a shot, until the reserve pickets were encountered. At this time the scouts had been reinforced by a company of the 5th N.Y. Cav., and with the scouts they charged and captured some 30 to 40 prisoners, a few escaping within the rebel fortifications, and I dare say they quickly carried the news to "Jeff" that a "right smart heap o' Yanks" desired to pay him a visit.

The rebel authorities knew there were scouting parties out south of the Rapidan, but had no idea that an attempt would be made to enter Richmond. Our appearance at their gate was a complete surprise to them, and I have always thought the movement should have proved a success with or without the assistance of Col. Dahlgren. Up to this time Kilpatrick has resolutely and skillfully carried out the plan matured days before leaving Stevensburg. But now he was "not in it." He did not seem to be himself. I know he was feeling unwell before starting on the journey, and complained during the trip. I have always thought his illness the cause of the feeble effort made to enter Richmond.

Several hours were spent in reconnoitering the enemy's works. Three or four ineffective attempts were made to enter, not a soldier being killed or wounded. Finally, night approaching, the command fell back, moved to the left, crossed the Chickahominy and went into camp, the men tired, hungry, and disappointed, having had no sleep and but little rest for more than 48 hours. And to add to their discomfort a severe storm now set in—rain and hail and at times snow. It was now dark.

Soon after going into camp the General informed me he intended making another effort to release our prisoners. He desired that I enter Richmond, find out all I could, and return as soon as possible. Scout Charles McCluskey, Co. C., Harris Light Cavalry, accompanied me. I returned in about two hours with the information that nearly all the troops in Richmond had been sent to guard the city in the direction of upper James and Brook Pike, and that I had heard firing in that direction, which turned out to be Col. Dahlgren, he having arrived in said vicinity after dark, and that there remained only a small picket force on the Mechanicsville road, and they could be easily captured. A thousand men were now selected under Gen. Estes and Col. Preston, to make the attack, the main column to follow in supporting distance; but it was too late, the opportunity to release our prisoners had passed. Just as we were about to start the rebel Gen. [Wade] Hampton, with a large force furiously attacked our camp, and we were obliged to get. A running fight was now kept up for several hours. Finally the rebels were repulsed, gave up the chase, and at daylight we went into camp at Old Church. Here the command stayed all day, waiting for the detachments which had been sent out to learn, if possible, what had become of Col. Dahlgren. That night Capts. Mitchell and Hastings reached us, with about 100 of Dahlgren's command. Learning that Col. Dahlgren, with the remnants of his command, had crossed the Pamunkey and was moving in the direction of Yorktown, Kilpatrick then moved leisurely down the Peninsula and reached Gen. Butler's lines, having been five days on the march.

\* \* \*

*The National Tribune*
July 5, 1894
Anson B. Carney, Le Roy, Pa.

**Carney Protests**

CARNEY. On the 31st of May last your paper contained an article to which the name of J. W. Landegon was appended. In that article he says: "I desire to blow my own horn a little in reference to it, and also say a few words in reply to Comrade Carney."

Now, I will simply say that after I read his article I thought at first that it would not be worth while to make any reply whatever; but as some people think that "silence gives consent, or, at least a tacit approval, I have concluded to say a few words myself. And it seems to me almost a self-evident truth that after the lapse of so many years an old soldier cannot be expected to be exact in his memory of every single particular. If he did, he would be a man possessing a very remarkable memory indeed. I related my story as well as I could recollect it, and made no insinuations in regard to others. If I had mentioned the comrade's name or reflected upon him in any manner, there might have been some excuse for what he said about me.

As to his remarks about the peach brandy which he tries to make fun about, I am willing to leave the decision of the following question to any fair-minded man, whether citizen or old soldier. Suppose, for instance, that a notice appears in a newspaper about some club or society having a banquet, and stating that the spread consisted of roast beef, fried chicken, fried oysters, and a liberal allowance of champagne; would anyone ever go far enough out of his way to ask, sneeringly, whether that banquet consisted of the fried chicken, or whether it consisted of the champagne.

As to hanging the negro, any good soldier knows that the orders of a superior officer must be obeyed.

I think, like another comrade who recently expressed very much the same sentiment that I do in this sentence, that there is altogether too much inexcusable fault finding among comrades about trivial matters. I often see things that do not in all respects meet with my approval, yet I do not feel called upon to go out of my way to attack the statements.

I advise the comrade in future to cultivate a little more friendly spirit toward comrades who have made no reference to him whatever. He speaks as though he belonged to the scouts. I have taxed my memory and I cannot place him. There were, however, many scouts in the army, and because I cannot remember him that is no reason why I should say that he was not a scout. He admits that to the scouts at

Gen. Meade's Headquarters the credit was due of quietly and expeditiously capturing the rebel pickets, and I cannot see why he wants to try to make a very curious kind of fun by running off the track to tackle the statements about the peach brandy.

In my case the peach brandy served a very useful purpose, for it enabled me to bear up under the pain and inconvenience of a severe wound, and aided me in escaping from vindictive enemies who might have felt justified in taking my life.

## "Not Worth a _____"
## From the Scouts Who Were There

\* \* \*

*EDITOR'S NOTE: The following letter[82] was written by Capt. John McEntee, 20th N.Y. State Militia (80th NY Vols.) who was one of only three officers in the BMI and was generally in charge of scouting operations. He accompanied Kilpatrick on this expedition. This letter to Col. Sharpe seethes with indignation at the incompetence of the expedition and particularly lays blame on the BMI's Chief of Scouts, Milton Cline and considers Scout Andrew Humphreys to be "not worth a _____." Humphreys has, of course, a completely different opinion of himself, as shown in the section following McEntee's.*

HEADQUARTERS, 148th N.Y.VOL
YORKTOWN, VA. March 4, 1864

Col G. H. SHARPE,

Colonel: We arrived here this evening without any great loss of men in scout but the supposition here is that we have lost Col. Dahlgren and about one hundred fifty men including all of our men except Anson Carney who is here slightly wounded. I confidently hope that with all the guides Dahlgren had with him that he has worked his way out, but the officer commanding the part of his force which came in says that he was told that a colonel with one leg had been captured. Kline [Cline] is the man who is responsible for the loss of some of those men if they are lost. He disobeyed his orders in every particular. He went on ahead from Stevensburg and was to have reported to me at Ely's Ford. I told him expressly that Gen. Kilpatrick had no guide to Spotsylvania C.H. and that I wanted McGee to show him the road. He was told to have two men report to me to return from Chancellorsville and four to return from Spotsylvania C.H. The result was that when we arrived at Ely's Ford we were detained there about an hour and a half looking for a guide and finally found a negro in the command to pilot us. I did not see anything of Kline until we got three or four miles beyond Chancellorsville and then he only had two men with him having allowed the balance to go on with the Colonel whom I have not seen since. When we got to Spotsylvania Dahlgren was four hours ahead of us.

General Kilpatrick's force marched on without our crossing the north Anna at Thompson's Ford & the South Anna at the first bank above Elliot's about four miles from the RR bridge near Hanover Junction. At that point the Gen. sent a detachment of 450 men under Maj. Hall to go down and destroy the RR bridge and join him near Richmond as soon as possible after accomplishing the duty assigned him. Kilpatrick destroyed the depot at Beaver Dam, took up the track, burned the water tanks and stone houses and tore down the telegraphic wire, and captured about a dozen prisoners. We marched out, crossed the RR at Partons and destroyed the Depot there, struck the provost picket and went through the first line of defenses and when within about three miles of the city encountered the enemy in which the General considered a large force with too many guns and too strong a position for him to attack. He fired a few shots from his guns which were replied to from several directions along three lines of works but without the least effect. The firing was with blind ranges showing inefficiency of the gunners. The prisoners which he captured did not give intelligence of another new force having arrived in the city, in the city guard had just turned out! [Kirkpatrick] commenced the attack at one p.m. on Tuesday and prisoners and citizens who came out of the city on that morning stated that they had had rumors that we were coming but with no knowledge of our strength. The Tredegar Iron works were kept running until 6 p.m.

on Monday and is the regular hour for quitting work. The main difficulty with Kilpatrick and that the force which he had sent to the RR bridge over the Smith river had not returned nor had he heard any thing from them neither had he heard a word from Dahlgren who had been informed to communicate with him at 10 am on Tuesday. This reduced his force about 1,000 men and he thought that it would not answer for him to be detained there. He therefore commenced his retreat and marched down the road leading from Hanover C.H. to Mechanicsville about five miles from the latter places, destroying the RR bridge over the Chickahominy in his way. At the point mentioned he halted his forces for the night but about 12 o'clock his camp was attacked by a small force with one piece of artillery. He therefore got up and started for old town where he arrived before morning. From old town he marched by Tunstalls station to the White House where he thought by repairing the RR bridge he could effect a crossing. This he found impracticable as the bridge was in too bad condition. Yesterday we marched to Burnt Ordinary where we camped for the night and today about 4 p.m. we arrived here.

Dahlgren was quite as unsuccessful as Kilpatrick. He was deceived by the negro guide (whom report says he hung), could not effect a crossing at any point on the James River, and after trying up of twenty five miles above the city, intended to join Kilpatrick. He went down the Plank Road and had quite a skirmish with the enemy near the city but his force was too small to effect anything. On Tuesday night it being very dark and raining hard Dahlgren with his advance of 150 men got lost from his main column which joined us on Wednesday afternoon, 350 men strong under command of Capt Mitchell of the Harris Light [2nd N.Y. Cavalry]. Kilpatrick was followed up by the Maryland Battalion from Hanover Junction, and after considerable skirmishing with his rear guard he finally turned a squadron around and charged them after which we saw nothing of them. Capt Mitchell states that he was also detained by them for a time and he found no difficulty in charging through them then. My observation of the whole affair shows me that it is not the object of a cavalry raid to do any more fighting than is absolutely necessary but to do all the [words illegible] possible. As I was with Gen

Kilpatrick I do not wish to detract any from his credit, but I hardly think we will ever be able to take Richmond without some fighting. I consider the whole move a complete surprise to the enemy and the way through and there was no more troops in Richmond than we knew of before starting, but the failure of the commandants of two the detachments to report or communicate seemed to warrant the general in getting away with the remainder of his force. Humphries [Humphreys] is not worth a _____. He does not know a road in Virginia nor anything about the works above Richmond nor could he answer a question which the General asked him. He has been a perfect nuisance and a consummate boor to me. I have continually wished that he was in _____. I hope that they have not captured our men and think that some of them at least will work their way out.

I told the Times reporter who was with us not to publish a word about the loss of the men, and if he should do it he should be put out of the army. His name is Paul. I have been told by an officer here that Paul told him that Lieutenant Hogan [Hogan was a private], a scout, was killed, but there was no reliable information of that fact. Carney is wounded and he has the thing nuxed. He will probably remain here a few days to recruit the horses and [three words illegible] and to up to Banks or US ford or else take transports to Urbana and go up the neck. We have a few captured horses but probably not as many as we lost, stole all the chickens and all other eatables in the country which is about the entire result of the raid.

I do not make this as an official report but merely tell you very hurriedly part of what I saw and have heard.

I am with Manning who is all right and sends his kind regards to Gen Patrick yourself and Bab[cock].[83]

I will return to the Headquarters, Army of the Potomac, as soon as possible.

Very respectfully your obedient servant

J. McENTEE

P.S. Manning sends you a picture enclosed.

National Archives & Records Administration (NARA)
Joseph M. Humphreys

March 14, 1864

*EDITOR'S NOTE: Joseph E. Humphreys was one of the two original scouts in Col. Sharpe's BMI. He apparently accompanied Kilpatrick's part of the raid on Richmond, and describes his observations of the expedition in a personal letter to Sharpe.*[84]

## Colonel GEORGE H. SHARPE

Sir, I arrived at this place late last evening Sunday. I have turned over to the Cavalry department the horse & equipment etc drawn from them for my use on the expedition—the overcoat you purchased of one of the men I have is subject to your order—of the fifty dollars $50 you gave me I expended forty dollars $40. I think, Colonel, that Capt McEntee will corroborate the statement when I say we have demonstrated the fact that Richmond can be taken by a cavalry dash—aye![85] That we could have taken it, yet, Colonel, as I was judged worthy of taking a part in this affair, you will permit me to say that if I had been informed of the plan when it was being formed I would have asked that a hundred men be landed with me at port [name illegible] on the James River, & we would have worked our way up & made sure of cutting the Petersburg Rail Road & Telegraph in the event of Colonel Dahlgren's failure which, without egotism, let me say had I been with him I think it would have been a success—however the certain cutting of that Road & telegraph would have insured the success of the expedition anyhow the Road intact troops could be thrown from Petersburg into Richmond in from 1½ to 2 hours—so the General with the responsibilities resting on him did not deem it prudent not hearing from Colonel Dahlgren—though I am satisfied it could have been done & the city held. In a subsequent excursion into King & Queen County we found Mr. Wm. Chase of your department & another of our men who had escaped from prison & were hid away—Mr. Chase I think belongs to Captain McEntee's Regiment.

I very much fear that Mr. McGee has been killed though I hope he escaped into the woods & will make good his way though.[86] Please inform me whether Carney has arrived & how badly wounded. I helped him from his horse to the ambulance but had no opportunity of examining it close by; also how many others have come in & who of your department are missing and, Colonel, permit me further to say in regard to what you told me you heard I said to wit that "you used the government funds etc," but I not only never said it but never thought it & more that while certain parties were speaking disparagingly of you it was my earnest desire to see you Provost Marshal of the Army of the Potomac. All I ever knew of you was favourable etc. All that was unfavourable was what I heard from the other parties who have basely Lied!! & told as coming from me what they themselves desired to say. I will say, Colonel, to you that I know H. P. Clinton is no well wisher of yours & others there are not as open as they should be.[87]

With regard I am respectfully

JOSEPH M. HUMPHREYS
*Washington D.C.,*

# VI

# Wilderness to Cold Harbor

*EDITOR'S NOTE: Knight finds his old regiment and encounters a green cavalry regiment; makes observations of the gory consequences of war; shows how to collect information behind the lines and how helpful slaves were to Union scouts; and contends that he conducts the reconnaissance that caused Grant to move by the left flank at Spotsylvania.*

*The National Tribune*
March 9, 1893
Judson Knight, Washington, D.C.

KNIGHT. The day we left Brandy Station was as hot as it ought to have been in the middle of June, although it was only the 4th of May, 1864. While we were preparing to start, and I was writing the names of a number of men who had been sent to us as guides, I saw the most contemptible exhibition of meanness that it was ever my lot to witness. The scouts of the Army of the Potomac were mustered and paid in the Provost-Marshal-General's Department, and the Provost-Marshal-General was M. R. Patrick. While I believe Gen. Patrick was a good soldier and a fighter, having heard so from various members of his old brigade, both officers and enlisted men, he was the most tyrannical officer, to those he dared to be so to, of any officer I ever met in the army. There are hundreds still living who can verify this statement.[88]

*Brig. Gen. Marsena R. Patrick and Provost Marshal General of the Army of the Potomac throughout its existence. The BMI was one of his subordinate activities. He was a strict disciplinarian much disliked by the army's scouts under whose eye they worked. Nevertheless, he supported Col. Sharpe and the work of his bureau. Author's collection.*

*The temporary office of the Provost Marshal General, Army of the Potomac, at Acquia Creek, February 1863, at just about the date when the BMI was created as a subordinate activity. LC-B8184-10418.*

Our camp was at the lower end of a valley, at the upper end of which Gens. Meade and Grant had their Headquarters. Six or eight miles south of us, on high land, was Stevensburg, where Cavalry Head-quarters had been all Winter. Huge pillars of smoke were ascending to the clouds from the debris of their burning camps, and one small log house was burning in our camp. It had been set on fire by its owner, Dan Plew, of the 3rd Ind. Cav. Gen. Patrick rode down the valley and inquired who was responsible for the fire, and Plew told him he was. Patrick flew at him, and commenced beating him over his head with his riding-whip, and shouting in Stentorian tones, "Do you want to let the rebels know we are coming?" He then ordered him to his Head-quarters and had him taken along a prisoner for two or three days, when he was condescending enough to release him.

When we broke camp that morning Serg't Patrick McEneany and myself rode off together. Along in the afternoon we saw a short dis-tance ahead of us a solitary horseman. It was fearfully hot for so early in the season. Mack said to me: "That is Jack Coppin, Capt. Schuy-ler's servant; let's ride up and overtake him." On coming up to him, Mack said: "Have you anything?" "Nothing but a small flask here in the holster that belongs to Capt. Schuyler." "Let's have a look at it." Coppin took it out of the holster and handed it to Mack, who imme-diately elevated the bottom toward the sky, holding it in that position for a few seconds; then lowering it, he said, as he handed it to me: "It's first-class." While it did not seem hardly the thing to do, I could not resist the temptation, and the bottom of the flask went skyward.

When Coppin again received it he held it up so as to look between the interstices of the wickerwork to see how much the contents were lowered. It was equal to a comedy to see the expressions of incredulity, amazement, and horror flit across his face when he fully realized how much the contents of the flask had diminished during its two heavenward flights.

"Oh, wirra, wirra! The Captain will kill me, so he will," he exclaimed.

"Well, you might as well die for a sheep as a lamb; take a smather yourself," exclaimed the Sergeant. As I saw him alive and well several months afterward, it is fair to presume his Captain had not the sin of murder on his soul.

The next morning we crossed the Rapidan at Germanna Ford and started southward on the Germanna Plank Road. When about two and a half miles south of the river I rode into the woods on the west of the road about a half mile, and turned southward, trying to travel parallel with the plank road, but it was slow progress I could make through the scrub. As near as I can remember now it must have been about 10 o'clock in the morning when I heard the first shot fired, and about a half mile south and west of where I was.

Continuing on toward the sound of the first shot, it was not long before another and then another sounded until it might have been 11 a.m., the firing became so frequent and twigs began dropping in such close proximity that I turned my horse's head toward the Germanna Plank Road, coming out about noon near the junction of the plank road and the old turnpike leading from Fredericksburg to Orange Courthouse, where Army headquarters were shortly thereafter established on a hill west of the plank road and north of the turn pike, and where they remained during the three or four days fighting that took place there.

I shall not attempt to tell anything about the battles along different parts of the line, for I saw very little of the fights at various points, many of us being kept near Headquarters until needed for some special duty. Our quarters were in a building known as the Bone Mill, east of the plank road, not over 150 yards from Army Headquarters. On the second day I learned that my old regiment [2nd New Jersey Volunteers] and [New Jersey] brigade[89] were in line of battle not far from Headquarters, west of the plank road and toward Germanna Ford; so mounting my horse I started to find them, which I did in a short time, at the top of a hill, in the woods, behind a hastily-improvised breastwork. As I came up the hill toward them some of the boys discovered me, and began shouting: "Get off that horse; get off that horse." Riding him into a hollow close by, I dismounted and went up to where my old Company (H) was, and staid in the breastworks for a half hour or more, talking over the last three years. A great many of the boys were gone. The Captain of the company had gone out as Fourth Sergeant. His name was Henry Callan. Our old Orderly-Sergeant was First Lieutenant; De Witt, who went out as either a private or a Corporal, was Second Lieutenant. The regiment's time was nearly out. They were mustered in May, 1861, into the three year's service.

While I was there not a rebel could be seen in their front and seldom a bullet was heard whistling over head. The next time I met the boys was near Spotsylvania, and they told me I had not been gone 15 minutes when Capt. Callan was killed.

During the third day's fighting, during which there was heard scarcely anything but musketry, which was very heavy, an expedition to the rear of the rebel line was planned. I am not certain as to dates, for I have no memoranda and am writing from memory alone. It, however, was the day after the two divisions of the Sixth Corps were driven out of the woods. When that happened, and we all saw thousands of the Sixth Corps boys streaming to the rear across the open fields east of the plank road, it looked to me very much as though we might recross the Rapidan, and perhaps that night. I told the boys they had better be prepared to leave at a moment's notice. Seeing a crowd of Red Crosses[90] in the road between us and Army Headquarters, I rode down among them and almost immediately met Lieut. Col. [James N.] Duffy, of the 3d N.J. He had formerly been Captain of Co. C., 2d N.J., and was at this time on the staff of Gen. Wright, commanding the First Division of the Sixth Corps.[91] Being well acquainted with him I rode up and said: "Colonel, what is the matter?" His answer was: "I can't tell you. The first thing I knew I found every body going to the rear, and here we are." The next morning order had come out of chaos; the lines of the Sixth Corps were reformed with their right refused. Their line crossed the road within a few yards of the Bone Mill.

The expedition to the rebel rear consisted of three men. We had a deserter from the rebel army by the name of Morris, whose home was in plain sight from the north bank of the Rapidan, about half way between Germanna and a blind ford called Willis's. The idea was for McEneany and myself to take him and go down to Germanna Ford, cross the river and go up on the other side, cross at Willis's, and come back to Morris's house, where we would find ourselves in the rebel rear. We started out toward Germanna Ford, and when about half way to the river we saw a regiment of cavalry standing in line on the right side of the road, and inquired what regiment it was, and was told it was the 8th Ohio. A short while previous I had received a letter from a brother of mine in the Western army saying that a neighbor of his, Jas. Beach, was in the Army of the Potomac, in Co. C., 8th Ohio Cav., also saying he was a bugler. Telling Mack and Morris about it, I proposed to them to stop for a few minutes and find him. We rode along in rear of the regiment, and had just reached Beach, and I had asked his name, when an officer rode up and wanted to know what we were doing there. I told him I had come to see Mr. Beach, when he immediately asked Beach if he knew me, to which question he answered no.

"I want to know who and what you men are. You look to me more like spies than anything else," said the officer. It took some talking to keep from being arrested, but after showing the pass we had, and hearing what I had to say to Beach, he became satisfied. It did me good to see him so vigilant, and I have always entertained the greatest respect for him ever since. He was either Lieutenant-Colonel or Major of the regiment. Resuming our journey we had not gone far when we saw the 5th N.Y. Cav. drawn up in the line also on the east side of the plank road. I had got quite well acquainted with that regiment the year previous, and, among others, with Maj. [John] Hammond.[92] I was pleased to see him ride

down to the road wand ask where we were going. When I told him
he said: "You can't do it." Upon asking why, he said: "Come on
down to the ford and I will show you."

He rode down to the ford, and handing me a field-glass said:
"Watch that piece of woods over there a short time and you will see
the reason why you can't." I looked a while, and discovered at least
60 mounted men in the woods; how many more were there it would
be hard to say.

Hammond was the Colonel of the 5th N.Y. at the close of the war;
when I first knew him, in the spring and early part of the summer of
'63, he was Major. What his rank was at this time I don't remember.
He has been in Congress since the war. I, as well as hundreds of others,
used to listen to him singing "When this cruel war is over," and used to
think no man living could sing it as well. He was a good soldier, a fine
officer, and a splendid man, and had a good regiment, one that would
and did fight. Serg't Phelps, one of the Headquarters scouts, was from
the 5th N.Y. Cav., which is tantamount to saying he was a good one.

We could see that it would be of no use to cross until after dark,
so we rode back toward Headquarters until we came to a house that
belonged to man named Beall, where there was a good spring of cool
water. When we got there we found the 22d N.Y. Cav. drawn up in
line on the west side of the plank road.[93] A group of men from that
regiment were at the spring filling canteens. We got the loan of a cup
from one of them and all took a drink and then hobbled our horses
by tying the halters below the knee, and let them feed, while all three
of us sat down under large tree close to the spring. Presently one
man pulled off his cap and mopped his head with a bandanna. His
head was as bare as a billiard-ball, with the exception of a fringe
of hair that showed below his cap when he had it on. When he got
through and had put away his handkerchief, he gently remarked: "It's
a _____ shame we can't get into this." I gave Mack a nudge with
my elbow, to see if he had heard what had been said, and received one
in response that showed me that he had heard. Suddenly a volley of
about 50 carbine shots was fired from the top of a hill back of us at the
ground around the spring. Every shot was high, and no one was hurt.
Knowing a trick of my horse, "Old John," I looked around and he was

going up the hill as hard as he could run. He would whirl around and run at any sudden firing. I had to chase him half way up the hill before I could catch him. The other two horses had paid but little attention to it. We all mounted and rode over to the eastern side of the plank road to the top of a hill on that side about the same height as the one on the west side from which the firing had come. We were about 75 feet higher than where the 22d N.Y. Cav. were standing in line.

* * *

EDITOR'S NOTE: Knight picks up his tale of the 22nd New York Cavalry in the following article.

The National Tribune
March 23, 1893
Judson Knight, Washington, D.C.

KNIGHT. We had not been there over a half minute, when two mounted men rode out of the woods on the hill opposite us. When we first saw them we thought they were our own men. They came out on a gallop, and when they reached the brow of the hill one of them stopped while the other came on about half way down. He was opposite the right flank of the 22d N.Y. Cav. when he stopped his horse, raised himself in his stirrups, and looked to the right and left for a minute. There were no other troops in sight from where he stood. After he had apparently satisfied himself, he wheeled his horse and dashed up the hill again. When he reached his comrade he turned, and they both dashed into the woods. They were hardly out of sight before bang! bang! came the report of two guns, and immediately afterward two more, and then a third round. The shells passed over us 50 feet higher than our heads and burst a half mile in our rear.

By the time the second round was fired the 22d N.Y. Cav. were in motion toward Army Headquarters, which were about three miles away. About 100 yards to the left of where they stood was a broken-down bridge, and our teamsters had crossed the run to the left as you went south, and a slough some 50 feet across had been created, which was filled up with floating rails. The 22d N.Y. was a new regiment, and every man had his full equipments on. At least half of them were actually a little afraid of their horses. A green cavalry regiment is about as useless a set of men as can be got together. It was terrible to see them go through the slough. Many of them who had clung to their saddles until now dropped like over-ripe plums, and soon the slough was dotted here and there with rails and troopers.

They went down the road as fast as they could toward Headquarters. It finally struck us that they might spread a report that might make them think the rebels were massing on our right, for we had heard plenty of that kind of talk the night before. We finally concluded to go to Headquarters and let them know the truth of what had happened, but concluded not to go down the Plank Road, which was pretty well filled by the fugitives of the 22d N.Y. Cav., so we rode for the woods south of us, and a slight search revealed to us a path leading in the right direction, which we took, and in a short time we emerged from the woods in sight of the Bone Mill. Almost the first man we saw was our bald-headed friend who, back by the spring, thought it such a shame they not "get into it." The road was pretty well filled with cavalrymen, and we had to crowd a little to get through. Our friend had lost his cap in the race, and his head was glistening in the sun. We edged up close to him, and as we passed, although it was a rather small thing to do, I could not resist the temptation of saying: "You don't appear to be as anxious as you might be to get into it!" A mournful look was the only answer.

Upon reporting to Colonel George H. Sharpe the condition of things, and why we had not crossed the river, he took Mac and me to Gens. Grant and Meade, and we told them the story. Grant said to Meade: "Take their horses away and give them to better men, if they don't behave better." I am happy to add that their horses were not taken away, and they became a good regiment as soon as they acquired experience.

We immediately went back, and presently heard that Gen. Merritt was passing through the woods in our front, and it came with such detail that we did not believe it, knowing how such rumors start. So when the story was repeated to us by the cavalry (neither of us can remember the regiment) we told them to let us have 25 men and we would soon find how much truth there was to the report. The men were detailed, or volunteered, I think, and we went into the woods in front of where the Sixth Corps had been. We soon found a path, and in about half a mile came into a small cleared field of about three acres in extent. The fence on both the north and west sides was nearly hidden from sight by briers and bushes that in most places were higher than the fence. When we came into the field we eagerly scanned the signs of an enemy. We were riding by two's, Mac and myself in front, and when we got within about 50 yards of the fence we received a volley of about 40 shots that did no damage either to men or horses, being fired too high. The command to left-about was given, and every one turned his horse and we started to the rear on a walk, and went out of the field into the woods without being fired on again. When we returned to the regiment we informed them that Merritt had not got along as far as their front yet. We went again to Headquarters and reported that the bulk of the rebels, in our belief, had moved to the left, and the results showed that we were right.

**DESOLATION OF WAR**
During the fighting in the Wilderness, I set out with a party and went down to Fredericksburg. Some of our wounded had been taken prisoners the night before by mayor Slaughter and some of the citizens. Slaughter had got out of the way, and our errand was a bootless one. Our poor fellows had to go to prison, where some of them doubtless perished. On returning to Headquarters I went around by Mr. Silver's.[94] The "abomination of desolation" best expresses the scene. I had been there, as the reader of these reminiscences will remember, but a few days before, and never saw a nicer farm and growing crops, with young apple and peach orchards. Now it was like the desert of Sahara. Orchards, fences, growing crops all had disappeared from the face of the earth. I said to Silver: "Why did you not tell these people who and what you were?" Sheridan's cavalry had settled down on his place like a flight of Egyptian locusts. "I did, but no one would believe me; and it has seemed to me that they have treated me worse on account of what I told them than they would have done had I said nothing," said he.

I certainly felt sorry for the man. Continuing he said: "What am I going to do when these men that are here now go?" Sheridan had started on his raid toward Richmond, and the men Silver spoke of were of the Subsistence and Quartermaster Department. "How can my family live? There will be nothing to buy anywhere in this country. We would starve now, if it were not for the fact that these men divide with us."

I went and saw the officer who had charge; who he was I have forgotten. I told him who Silver was, and what he had done for us, the condition he was now in, and what he would be in when our people left, and asked him to furnish rations enough to keep the family for some time. His answer was that he was sorry he could not do it, but there was no law or regulation by which he could. After thinking the situation over, I asked if he could issue rations to me, and he said he could; also, that he would be pleased to do so. I made a requisition for a great many more men than I had with me for 10 days, and turned the things over to Silver.

About six years ago McEneany and myself went down to Fredericksburg and drove out to see him. He had forgotten many things, and that among others. His wife, however, remembered.

Returning to Headquarters, I concluded to go along in the rear of the line of battle south of the old turnpike, and was very glad I did, for before I had gone over half a mile I met a man named Wilson, who had one of his ankles shattered by a ball. He was being helped to the rear by two of his comrades. I had made his acquaintance the previous Winter, his regiment being stationed near Headquarters. I am not certain, but think it was the 77th N.Y. I dismounted and his comrades and myself got him into the saddle and took him to a field hospital. I have never seen or heard of him since that time. The next day I was sent to Belle Plain to meet the Christian and Sanitary Commissioners, if they had arrived.[95] I was alone on this trip. When I got into Fredericksburg one of the first sights was a soldier who had had his arm amputated at the shoulder joint, sitting on the steps of a house pouring water from a canteen on the wound. I stopped and talked to him a few moments, and found that he had made his way down there from the Wilderness alone. He was tired, but very cheerful and as full of pluck and patriotism as any man I ever saw. I dismounted and helped him on my horse and waded the river, leading the horse, and continued to lead him until we were about half way from Fredericksburg to Belle Plain, when I told him I must have the horse and go on. He had been urging me for some time to leave him to his own devices. His name and regiment are also forgotten, but he never will be while life lasts.

When I came within a mile of Belle Plain I met a skirmish-line of ladies and men belonging to the Sanitary Commission, who had landed and started to see if they could find any of our sick and wounded. I told them of the one-armed man who was making his way on foot, and several of the men started off to meet him. They had milk punch and various kinds of refreshments with them, and met him but a short distance, some two or three miles, from the landing.

On my return I found the 2d N.Y. Cav. in Fredericksburg, where they informed me they were going to do provost guard duty. As I was leaving the town I overtook a Lieutenant of whom I inquired the reason why his Colonel was under arrest, and was informed that it was because he did not give the order to retreat sooner. I told him I did not think the Colonel had been fairly used, because I had seen the whole affair, and could not see how it was possible for a regiment to retreat any sooner than it had.[96]

When we left that portion of the Wilderness where Headquarters had been for several days, we had a guide named Miller, whom we all had noticed poring over maps continually, until the boys had nick-named him "Miller's Map." It was a very dark night, and we had not gone far before the limb of a tree brushed the only hat I had from my head. As there were several hundred cavalrymen immediately behind I dared not dismount to try and find it, for fear of being ridden over, and I tied a white handkerchief around my head and rode on.

## GETTING HEADGEAR

For two more miles we rode between the lines of the two armies, and neither party fired. Miller or some one else finally discovered where we were about the time we came to where there was a long line of breastworks on fire, and we took another road. When we arrived at "Parker's Store" it was about midnight, and a halt was ordered and we bivouacked for the night. When my boy Henry came to take care of

"Old John," my horse, he saw the handkerchief on my head and said: "Have you lost your hat, Captain?"

"Yes, Henry; don't you think you can find some sutler's store open yet, and get me another. You know my size. Be sure and get one large enough." "All right; I will look around, and if there is a sutler open I will get you one."

Next morning, just after daylight, I awoke. A hat was leaning against my head, with one side of the brim on the ground. Raising up, I examined it and found a cord with acorns on each end, which came off as quickly as I could pull it off. The hat fitted exactly. When Henry came around I handed him a five-dollar greenback, and asked him if that would pay for it, and was told that was exactly what it cost. All sutlers had been sent to Washington before we left Brandy Station, and Henry knew it as well as I did.

After breakfast about 15 of us started out toward our left in the direction of Guiney's Station. We soon came to the 17th Pa. Cav. Maj. [George F.] McCabe was in command. He wanted to know where we were going.

*EDITOR'S NOTE: Knight here is mistaken; McCabe commanded the 13th Pa. Cavalry. The error will be corrected in all subsequent references.*[97]

We told him we were going out to drive in the rebel pickets until we came to the open country, and see if we could not learn something. McCabe said we ought to have more men, and we asked him to loan us some. He soon had 50 men detailed and we took them and all deployed in open order and started through the woods. We soon came upon the enemy's pickets, who rapidly fell back, and we advanced about five miles, when we came to the plantation of Dr. Boulware, about a mile and a half from Guiney's Station. It was a fine place; clover a foot high, which our horses reveled in. There was everything in profusion in the shape of food—flour, corn-meal, lard, butter, milk, fresh veal, an ice-house full of ice. The servants were more than glad to cook for us, and one of the first things we did was to have a square meal. The Confederate pickets had fallen back to a position across a ravine, and we took a position on a bluff just outside the woods, near

*Maj. George F. McCabe, 13th Pennsylvania Cavalry, was always ready to lend Knight some cavalry for special missions. Library of Congress, LC-DIG-cwpb-05349.*

the main road, a little east of the overseer's house. We soon learned that Dr. Boulware was a receiver of "taxes in kind," and had a large barn stored with fodder, shelled corn, etc., which all found its way to Army Headquarters, including the ice that was in the ice-house. When we sent McCabe's men back we sent him an invitation to come out and dine with us, which he did.

* * *

*The National Tribune*
March 30, 1893
Judson Knight, Washington, D.C.

KNIGHT. In my last article I spoke about returning the men loaned me by Maj. McCabe of the 13th Pa. Cav., to make a reconnaissance in which we captured plenty of good forage, and then inviting the Major to come over and dine with us and partake of some of the delicacies we had captured, which he did, he enjoying his square meal very much.

Soon after the Major left us I discovered a signal flag working about a mile and a half away, through an opening in the woods on the other side of the river, which some of the negroes told was the Mattapony. A man was sent in to Headquarters with the news that we were in a position where we could see a signal station, with a request that a Signal officer be sent out. Mrs. Boulware and the overseer were both very bitter, and Mrs. B. told me she hoped her brother would come back with force enough to kill the whole crowd of us, myself in particular. I asked her why he did not stay while he was there to which she deigned no answer. I had gone to the house to see about getting someone to cook something for the Signal officer when he came.

Mrs. Boulware's brother had been on picket at the house when we came to it. On my way back to where the boys were I stopped at the overseer's house to let him know we expected to have a meal prepared and the table set in his house. He was sitting in his front door, and as I came to the gate I distinctly heard him trying to get his dog on me. I opened the gate, and the dog, which was a large one and very fierce, came for me. I drew my pistol and fired. The dog concluded he had business in the house, to which he retired and crawled under the bed, where he died in a short time. I told the overseer that he was the one that ought to have been shot instead of the dog. When the Signal officer came he watched the signals until he said he had obtained a good deal of information in regard to the movement of troops. When I took him into the overseer's house to get a square meal, that gentleman was mild as new milk. When the Signal officer was starting back I told him we would like to stay here until the army moved; to which he replied: "I don't blame you. I would like to stay myself." When he returned to Headquarters, he gave a glowing report, and we received orders to stay where [we] were until further orders.

About 2 o'clock I saw a train come in from Richmond to Guiney's Station, and one of the negro men told me that it was the mail train, and it came every day at the same hour. We sent back word to Maj. McCabe that we wanted him to come out the next day with 100 men, at a certain hour, as we wanted to capture the train. He came. We were a little late to get the train, but did get the mail, and retired to Boulware's plantation, as the 9th Va. Cav. came over the Mattapony in too great numbers for us.

We went through the mail, and found a letter from a member of a flying artillery company attached to "Jeb" Stuart's Headquarters, to a young lady. If the writer had tried to give Gen. Grant the information of what Sheridan had done, and what success he had, it would have been impossible for him to have done any better. He told the young lady day and date where they had met the Yankees, and how they had got whipped; how his battery was lost, all owing to the cowardice of their cavalry, and wound up by advising her never to marry a cavalryman.

*EDITOR'S NOTE: This is an excellent example of the sort of document exploitation that Sharpe's BMI provided to Meade and Grant.*

Col. George H. Sharpe told me afterward that Grant asked how many scouts there were that had got the information, and said that he never had any information while he was in the West that would compare with what he had on that campaign.

*Lt. Gen. Ulysses S. Grant, shown here at Cold Harbor, quickly came to appreciate the combat multiplier represented by Col. Sharpe's Bureau of Military Information and especially its scouts with whom he frequently dealt. Library of Congress, LC-USZ61-903.*

We were ordered that night to fall in with the advance-guard next morning. One of Dr. Boulware's slaves told us that if we had got there one day sooner we would have captured a barrel of whiskey, instead of the two gallon demi-john which we did find in the ice-house. When the advance came out the next morning I was glad to find they were the 5th N.Y. Cav.

We fell in with the advance-guard of that regiment. A Sergeant was in command of it. I did not know his name at the time, and did not know who he was until 28 years afterward, and then learned his name in a very singular way.

We kept along the road with but little delay, the pickets of the 9th Va. Cav. falling back as we advanced, until we came to where a road led to the right from the one we were on. Part of the 9th Va. kept straight on toward Bowling Green, and a squad of them took the right-hand road, which led to Milford Station, on the Richmond & Fredericksburg Railroad. We followed the latter party. When we had gotten about 200 yards down the latter road the Confederates started on a gallop, and we soon heard the clatter of their horses' hoofs across a bridge. As soon as they crossed four of them halted and dismounted. One man caught all four horses by their bridles, one jumped behind a tree with a gun, while two ran back and stopped to pull the planks from the bridge.

I said to the Sergeant: "Do you see that red-headed fellow behind the tree taking aim? One of us is going to catch it."

"If they get those planks off they will play _____ with us," he replied, and yelled "Charge!" We both sprang forward, the gun rang out, and the Sergeant fell dead, I always thought. My horse leaped the opening in the bridge, and I saw two planks floating down the stream.

As soon as my horse struck the further bank I threw myself from his back, and down the stream, caught the plank and inside of five minutes we had the plank replaced. We hardly had this done before we were ordered back and took the other road, which led to Bowling Green.

A few months since an article headed "Almost a Personal Encounter" appeared in the columns of the *National Tribune*. It was written by a friend of mine, who is an ex-Confederate soldier. He importuned me one night to relate some of my experiences, and I related the incident of the bridge. He looked at me with astonishment for a few seconds, and then said:

"Do you know what cavalry was in your front that morning?"

"Yes," said I: "it was the 9th Va."

"Do you know I have heard that story from the other side. Byrd Lewis was Captain of the Westmoreland company in the 9th Va., and he told me the same story. I am going to bring him around and introduce you to each other."

He did so, and one or two questions from each convinced the other we were the same men who confronted each other that May morning of 1864, at the bridge across the Mattapony in Woodford's Lane, Caroline Co., Va. I expected to be the one shot, for the reason that I expected to be taken for a "pilot," as I was wearing a straw hat, and did not look much like a soldier. Lewis said he was sorry to know he had killed a man, and he had always had the impression that the one who jumped his horse across the opening was the one who was hurt, as he fell from his horse and a bush had prevented his seeing what occurred on the other side after he fired.

The article above mentioned called out a number of communications from comrades of the 5th N.Y. Cav. from which I learned the name of the Sergeant who fell by my side was Sartor, and I received a letter from his brother, who lived at Duke Center, Pa., who was too young to be in the army in 1864.

After being ordered back on to Bowling Green road, we rapidly hurried the few cavalry in our front, until we came near the village. When we came to an open gate on the right hand side of the road, a little over a quarter of a mile away, we could see people hurrying toward Milford Station on a road that ran past the end of the field where the gate was open. We turned into the field and galloped our horses to the road leading to Milford Station. A solid and high stone wall crowned a sharp rise in the ground, which made it impossible to jump our horses over it, and we had therefore to dismount and tear the wall down. Before we had this down a squad of the 9th Va., who were in our front when we turned into the field, came galloping down the road toward Milford and each one fired his pistol as he passed;

without exception every one of them fired high and neither man nor horse of our party was harmed.

As soon as the wall was sufficiently torn down we got our horses over into the road, which was close by. We captured a conscript officer

*Dan Cole, another excellent scout from the 3rd Indiana Cavalry. Author's collection.*

with all his papers, who bitterly bemoaned his fate, and wished he had not stopped to secure them.

As soon as we got into the village we inquired for Grey Boulware's place, and I advised Dan Plew and [Dan] Cole to look for the barrel of whiskey of which we had heard from one of Dr. Boulware's slaves.[98] I immediately went to the post office, which was kept in a store. No one was in at the time. I made a clean sweep of all newspapers and letters, but touched nothing else. Just as I was ready to leave a woman came in from a back room and said to me with much astonishment, which I could see was genuine: "Mister, what are you doing?"

"Helping to sort your mail," I said.

"You will assort your self into jail if you are not careful," said she.

"I reckon not. At all events, I'll risk it." She took me for one of the Confederates, I could plainly see.

*EDITOR'S NOTE: Knight's sweeping up of all the newspapers and mail is an example of the importance of the intelligence collection priority given to enemy documents by Col. Sharpe.*

When I returned to where the boys had started their search for the barrel they had found it and had it behind a barn belonging to Grey Boulware, which stood on the main street of the town. Two or three young negro men were looking on with a pleased expression. When I asked them if they could get any bottles, they wanted to know if they brought me three bottles I would fill another for them; to which I agreed. I rolled my three bottles in a blanket and strapped them to my saddle, intending to give them to the officers of Clark's Battery (B, 1st N.J. Arty), which I did the same day about noon in the lower end of Woodford's Lane, at Milford Station. For years afterward I used to hear from Lieut. Clark about that "villainous whiskey" I gave them; and the worst of it was, I could not deny that it was villainous.

We were in Bowling Green nearly 20 minutes before any of our troops came in. The cavalry, which was under command of [Brig.]

Gen. [Alfred Thomas Archimedes] Torbert, began passing through; I knew many of them, both officers and men, so I sat on my horse at the gate, and when any one came along that I knew was "all right," he got an invitation to go behind the barn and get his canteen filled.[99] The barrel was more than three-fourths gone when a young Lieutenant of the 5th N.Y. Cav. rode up to me and said: "The General has heard there is a barrel of whiskey down this way somewhere being dealt out to the men. Do you know anything about it? He has sent me with the Provost Guard to find and upset it."

"Yes, Lieutenant, I know all about it. Our boys have got it in the yard behind the barn. Go in and upset it, but fill your canteens first." The boys told me that not over three gills were spilled, and the Lieutenant reported to the General that he had found it and carried out his order, and everyone was happy.

We had a sharp little brush at Milford and took some rifle-pits manned with infantry. When Hancock arrived with his corps he was in Lee's rear several miles, and there was some lively work done by the Confederates during the night to get themselves out of the scrape they might have been in had we known the country as they did. This is given on the authority of a young De Jarnette, son of the Daniel De Jarnette who was a member of Congress before the war. De Jarnette was in the rebel army at that time.[100]

\* \* \*

*The National Tribune*
April 6, 1893
Judson Knight, Washington, D.C.

KNIGHT. In my last letter I stated that Hancock's Second Corps got several miles in the rear of Lee's army at Milford, where we had a sharp brush with the rebels.

The next day, or perhaps two days afterward, we found ourselves on the River Po. Just how we got there, or the day of the month, I have entirely forgotten. A party of scouts started out on the right, and after going about four or five miles we came to Tinsley's Mills. The water was not running over the dam; on the contrary, the planking of the

*Tinsely's Mill, toward which Sharpe sent Knight to discover any movement on the Confederate left at the battle of Spotsylvania. Edwin Forbes, Library of Congress, LC-USZ62-79165.*

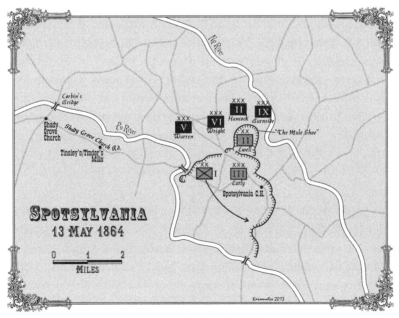

*Spotsylvania, May 13, 1864.*

dam was bare and dry for at least four feet. The house and mill were surrounded by shrubbery and trees so thickly that at a short distance it was almost impossible to see the buildings. The enemy seemed to be in force on the opposite side of the stream. We were about a mile below Corbin's Bridge.[101]

Tinsley's barn, which stood about 75 yards from the so-called river, and about 50 yards higher up the stream, offered a shelter for our horses of which we availed ourselves. Two or three of us dismounted and went into the barn and looked through the crack of the doors, from which we could see their works and pickets on the opposite side. We had not been there but a few minutes when a young lady made her appearance in the barn. It was amusing to hear her talk. I think she was about 17 years of age and pretty. She pretended to stand in great fear of the Yankees, and at the same time had placed herself in their power to prevent them from stealing. She naively informed us that was what she came to the barn for, and commenced walking around to see what she could save from our rapacious grasp. She at last selected a pair of cushions from a double-seated carriage and prepared to depart. Just before she opened the door I said to her: "Miss, I wish you to understand that you have deceived no one as to what you came here for. You were not afraid of being insulted. You knew perfectly well you were as safe with us as you would have been across the river among the 'chivalry.'[102] You have gratuitously insulted us for no earthly reason except to find out how many men we have in this party. This is why you have been walking up and down across the floor at the back of the barn. You know there are not many of us. Go and tell your friends to come over on the dam and we will give them all they want." She was scared then sure enough and left.

Soon after her leaving, we heard the clatter of horses' hoofs coming over the dam, but not many of them. A row of shrubbery extended from the house in a diagonal direction nearly to the barn. The two of us in the barn were on the watch, clearly. In a short time I discovered a cavalryman, dismounted, stealing along inside the shrubbery, and fired a shot at him, which turned him to the right-about in a great hurry.

Soon after, we heard horses recrossing on the dam and left the barn, the majority of the party going on up the river toward Corbin's Bridge.

When near the bridge the party suddenly ran into at least twice their number of rebel infantry; stragglers, footsore and weary. I will do them the justice of saying I don't believe there was a "coffee cooler" among the lot.[103] They surrendered easily and their guns were destroyed before they had any idea of the number of our party. When they came to realize that they had surrendered to a smaller force than themselves, their curses were loud and deep; the army in Flanders could not have beaten them.

*Coffee coolers, shirkers who could always be depended upon to miss anything dangerous. Edwin Forbes, author's collection.*

One man in particular, with a very handsome head of auburn hair called a Confederate regiment of cavalry who were in plain sight on the other side of Corbin's Bridge, everything but gentlemen and soldiers for not coming across the bridge and recapturing them. He shook his fist at them, and cursed until he appeared to realize how useless his rage was, when he suddenly cooled down and began looking at his captors. In a moment he exclaimed: "Well, if I have got to be a prisoner I know of no body of men on God's earth I would sooner be a prisoner of than you all."

He had recognized [Milton] Cline, [Dan] Plew, and [Dan] Cole. He had been captured by our party the year before in the Gettysburg campaign.

Several of the boys who were with the Headquarters scouts the year before were prisoners at this time themselves, or away wounded— A. B. Carney, in the latter category; [Martin] Hogan, [Jacob] Swisher, and others in Andersonville; Ebenezer McGee, dead.

The man who did this swearing was a Captain in a Mississippi regiment, and had nothing to wear, except what he had on. He was not turned over as a prisoner of war until we had made up a very fair outfit of underclothing, blankets, etc., for him. Before he left us he said: "boys, God bless you; I know you think you are right; we think the same. When this cruel war is over I want you all to come to Mississippi and see me."

I am sorry to have forgotten his name and address, for there is no man living I would be more pleased to see than he.

Col. George H. Sharpe, Deputy Provost-Marshal-General, told me the next day to take a man with me, go out and watch as long as I could see what was going on in that vicinity. The next morning, with a good field-glass, two of us went out and took our positions on a hill, down stream from Tinsley's Mill about 150 yards. There was a capital view of Corbin's Bridge and the other side of the stream, until you came as far down as Tinsley's Mill;[104] then the woods were so dense that little could be seen. We discovered that a large barn on a hill beyond Corbin's Bridge was used as a hospital. I think the man with me was James Hatton, but am not quite sure.[105] At all events, whoever he was, I asked him to go up the tree we were sitting under and take a look through the glass from there. I held his horse while he went up. When he was up so that his feet were about six feet higher than my head the angry hiss of a minie-ball, that passed about half way between my head and his foot, warned him to come down.

The first day out there was bare of incident, and our report that night was a meager one. Next day we went again and took our positions, the same as the day before. We had not been there long before a young and bright negro came and told us that his young Missis,

Miss Laura Tinsley, had told a friend of hers, that if the two Yankees who were on the hill the day before should come again the next day, they would not go back, as she had been to the woods in our rear and found there were no Yankees in them.

She was going to see or had seen the rebel cavalry, and was going to have six men go up a ravine to the woods and come in our rear, and either capture or kill us. The negro showed us a place they would have to pass before they could get into the ravine, and advised us to keep a close watch on that point.

*EDITOR'S NOTE: This is another example of what good and willing sources of intelligence slaves were and how they often saved scouts from death or capture.*

About 10 o'clock a.m. we saw one man for a few seconds as he crossed the place pointed out, and at short intervals there after, one man at a time dodged across the open space, until five or six of them had gone into the ravine. We gave them time enough to get about one-third of the way from the mill to the woods in our rear and then galloped our horse to the ravine and caught them where they could not get up to the side to us. A few pistol shots sent them whirling back toward the mill, and Miss Laura Tinsley's scheme had failed.

We staid until nearly sundown, and then returned to Headquarters with another meager report.

Col. Sharpe told me that he might want me to go out again the next day. Before starting the next morning my boy Henry said to me: "Why can't I take them niggers and go out foraging." We had as many as 50 or 60 colored men who had come to us, who were used as guides in the neighborhood where they belonged. Seldom one was found who was of any use over five miles from his home. As we were on short commons, nothing but hardtack, pork and coffee, I said to him: "All right, go ahead, but be very careful and do nothing that will get you into the tender mercies of Gen. Patrick, and don't run any risk of being captured, and get back before dark if possible."

\* \* \*

*The National Tribune*
April 20, 1893
Judson Knight, Washington, D.C.

KNIGHT. Spotsylvania Courthouse was the next snag we struck.[106] I was close enough to the front to see the charge that Hancock made at the time [May 12th] when Johnson's Division was captured and brought out of the Confederate works. One of our boys, I remember, was there, and perhaps more, but I distinctly recollect Serg't Wood was mixed up in the melee.[107]

*Some of the thousands of Confederate prisoners taken at the salient at Spotsylvania, some of whom Knight interrogated. Library of Congress, LC-USZC4-6469.*

When Johnson and his men were brought out and taken to the rear, among others guarding them was an Irishman rather older than the majority of soldiers, who had lost a finger. In less than an hour I saw him going to the front again, and said to him: "Most men with as great an excuse as you have would stay in the rear."

"Me comrades are ever yon, and I want to be with them," he said. I have often wished I knew what that man's fate was. All that I can remember is that he was in Hancock's command.

When the rebels rallied and drove our men back I saw soon afterward a regiment of troops from Herkimer County, N.Y., in which I felt great interest. It was Col. Upton's old regiment, the 121st N.Y.[108] A mist set in, which at last became a drizzling rain, and those boys stood up to their work like brave and gallant fellows as they were. I don't mean to say that the other regiments which were in that fight on the outside of the works that were taken from the rebels early in the morning did not do their full duty, but I felt more interested in those farmer boys than anyone else on the field. When they came out they could scarcely have been distinguished from negroes, their faces and hands had become so black by biting cartridges and getting the powder smeared on their wet faces and hands.[109]

In my last [article] I told of my boy Henry wanting to forage for our command, and, giving him certain instructions, after thoroughly convincing him that he must be careful in his treatment of citizens, and that he must control the negroes he had with him, I saw them start, with some misgivings as to what the result would be, and then started myself for another day's espionage in the vicinity of Tinsley's Mill and Corbin Bridge. In going out I kept off the roads and in the woods entirely. I had not gone far before I found a deserted field hospital of our own. There was a large lot of amputated limbs, piled up as much as four feet high, and one dead man who had been brought in on a stretcher. He was a Sergeant, and had evidently died before the Surgeons had an opportunity of operating on him.

Before going a mile beyond there an awful stench assailed me, and the further I went the worse it became. I could hardly get my horse along, it was so overpowering. At last I discovered the source from whence it came. A poor Confederate evidently had been wounded, and died. The corpse was in a fearful condition – swollen and blackened beyond recognition. I sat for a moment and looked at him, and "How sweet to die for one's country" came to my mind, "Not like that; excuse me," I thought to myself, and went on.

On arriving at the edge of the timber, before entering the open field, I gave the whole of the country in my front a thorough examination with my field-glass, and could see nothing that looked suspicious. The first thing to do was to ride direct from the woods and examine the ravine higher up than our friends, the enemy, had penetrated the day before. There were no horse tracks to be seen, and I rode directly to the top of the hill and took my position under the tree where the two of us had been the day before. Nothing of any moment took place until between 3 and 4 o'clock in the afternoon, when two regiments of cavalry came from behind the woods on the opposite side of the river and took a position as though they were going to dispute the crossing of the bridge.

They had hardly been in position five minutes when a long train of ambulances drove up and the wounded in the large barn before mentioned were transferred to them, and then disappeared toward the right of their line. Shortly after they were out of sight the cavalry followed in the same direction. I thought to myself they were preparing to evacuate entirely as soon as it was dark.

A little before dark the same negro man who had informed me the day before of the little surprise party that Miss Laura Tinsley had kindly prepared for me, came to where I was and gave me a map that he had found. The name of some Colonel of our forces was written on it, and the map itself was one that our Topographical Engineers had made of the vicinity, and was a very good one as far as it went. The man told me that he was over on the other side of the bridge and saw the wounded loaded into the ambulances and saw them move off toward the Courthouse; that what few men I could see were all that was left anywhere in sight, and they were going away as soon as it was dark.

When I got back that night to Headquarters it was quite dark, and Henry and the other contrabands had not returned and nearly all of our party were still out. A correspondent of the New York *Times* was sitting moodily by one of the fires that the boys had lighted. He eagerly inquired if we had anything to eat. Knowing that he did not mean army rations, I told him "Not a thing; but my man went out foraging this morning early, and if he has not got into trouble will be back before long. Your best chance is right here; you had better hang on a while."

Just then one of our boys said to me: "They are anxious to see you at Headquarters. They have sent over two or three times to see if you had got in. If I were in your place I'd go right over."

As it was about half a mile to Headquarters I mounted my horse and rode over. Our reports were always made to Col. Geo. H. Sharpe, in person, if he were present. When I reached his tent there was no one in but John C. Babcock, his Private Secretary.[110] He wanted to know how things were on the right. My answer was that there was nothing going on except that they were evacuating and moving off to our left. He immediately seized paper and pen and commenced writing. From where I sat I could see that he commenced thus: "Knight reports the enemy leaving their left." Then turning to me he said:

"This is one of the most important reports we have received during the campaign, and it is in direct conflict with reports received all day from officers along the lines. They report the enemy massing on our right, and the Second Corps [Maj. Gen. Hancock commanding] has been sent out there."

"Yes," said I; "I met them as I came in, and there is no use of their going, for I tell you the last one of them have left there before this."

Then by a series of cross-questions as to what made me think as I did, he learned every thing I had to tell. I showed him the map the contraband had given me—in fact left it with him, and fully committed myself to the report.

After leaving him I began wishing that I had not been quite as positive. I thought to myself, "Suppose these people fully realized what your presence there meant, and took that way of deceiving you. If they had troops where you could not see them, and should make an attack out there to-night, what will be thought of you." To make the thing short, I will state that no sleep visited my eyes that night.

When I returned from Headquarters to our camp everything was in status quo. No foragers had returned. The *Times* correspondent

---

*EDITOR'S NOTE:* A version of Knight's account is reflected in the following report by Sharpe.

*HEADQUARTERS ARMY OF THE POTOMAC,*

*May 13, 1864 - [6 p m.]*

*GENERAL: Knight reports he left Tinder's Mill on Po River 1 1/2 miles Corbin's Bridge at 3 p.m. Saw a small squad of rebel cavalry (15 men) on this side of the river at the mill. They recrossed on seeing our party. On other side of the Po, one-half mile below mill, on a*

*large clearing, were 75 to 100 cavalry horses grazing. No indications of other force. Not as much rebel cavalry up that way to-day as yesterday. Our men went 2 miles beyond, some of our cavalry picketing in that direction, and saw nothing except as above.*

*Respectfully,*

*GEORGE H. SHARPE,*
*Colonel, &c.*

*OR*, Vol. 36, Part 2, pp. 699

was despondent but not more so than I. I really liked Henry, and began to fear we would never see him again. At last we heard shouting at some distance which increased in volume until our contraband foragers emerged from the depths of the woods, and drove up into the circle of light emitted by our campfires. First came a covered spring wagon with a fine span of horses with silver-plated harness, then a mule and cart. Both wagon and car were loaded with chickens, ducks, pails of butter and honey, demijohns and jugs of milk, eggs, flour, cornmeal, lard, a Dutch oven in which biscuit could be baked, and various culinary utensils completed the outfit. As foragers, the contrabands had proved themselves a complete and glorious success.

The chickens and ducks were all plucked and ready for cooking when they brought them in. Hastily selecting some of the fowls, honey and butter, we sent them to Gen. Patrick with our compliments. We never heard of any complaints, although all hands had many misgivings when we saw the profuse supply unloaded.

The *Times* correspondent was a most grateful man and when we sought our blankets about midnight, all hands were very happy. I lay awake listening for the sound of cannonading on our right, which never came, and in the morning I found the Second Corps had been brought back, and it, as well as all the rest of the army, were moving to the left.

In the Fall of 1864 I saw John C. Babcock, who took my report when I came in from Tinsley's Mill. He did not remember anything of the report, but hunted up some old photographed maps of the vicinity of Corbin's Bridge. One had to hold them up to the light and look through them from the back.[111] While I make no claims to having put down the rebellion, I have always had an idea that my report that night had something to do with the army moving by the left flank at that time.[112]

When we left Spotsylvania Courthouse I don't remember anything of the roads or appearance of the country until we came to the

*EDITOR'S NOTE:* The following official correspondence addresses the realization that Lee was moving his army on May 13, 1864, from Spotsylvania.

*HEADQUARTERS ARMY OF THE POTOMAC,*
*May 13, 1864 - 8 [a.m.]*
*General HUMPHREYS:*

*Twenty prisoners brought in this a.m. were taken partly on the enemy's skirmish line but mostly in its rear, asleep in houses. They only know that their line has fallen back; don't know where. Their rations were out last night and were to have been issued last evening; but neither to those who were on the skirmish line nor to those who were with or near the main body of the troops were any rations issued. The prisoners represent four divisions: Anderson's, Rhode's, Early's, and Wilcox's.*

*Very respectfully,*

*GEORGE H. SHARPE,*
*Colonel, &c.*

*OR,* Vol. 36, Part II, p. 699
*HEADQUARTERS ARMIES OF THE UNITED STATES,*

*May 13, 1864 - 8.40 a. m.*
*Major-General MEADE:*
*From the dispatch just shown me by Captain Meade, I do not infer the enemy are making a stand, but simply covering a*

*retreat, which must necessarily have been slow with such roads and so dark a night as they had last night. I think it advisable to push with at least three good divisions to see beyond doubt what they are doing.*

*Respectfully,*

*U. S. GRANT,*
*Lieutenant-General.*

OR, Vol. 36, Part II, p. 698

Grant Moves the Army

*SPECIAL ORDER.- HDQRS ARMY OF THE POTOMAC,*

*May 13, 1864 - 5.45 p. m.*

*The following movements of troops are ordered for to-night: Major-General Warren, commanding Fifth Corps, will move immediately after dark and will proceed in rear of the army, pass to the left of the Ninth Corps, and make his dispositions assault the enemy on the road from Gate to Spotsylvania Court-House. Brigadier-General Wright, commanding Sixth Corps, will move in like manner at the same time, if roads can be found; if not, after the Fifth Corps and take position on the left of the Fifth Corps, and make his dispositions to attack on the road from Massaponax Church to Spotsylvania Court-House. These attacks will be made at 4 o'clock if practicable. Major-General Hancock will make his dispositions for attacking in his front, but will not do so till ordered, though he will in the mean time assume a threatening attitude. The trains, Artillery Reserve, &c., will be moved to Salem Church and vicinity. The telegraph wire will be taken up from Fifth Corps headquarters and will be extended from the Ninth Corps headquarters to the headquarters of the Fifth to-morrow. The chief engineer will furnish all information in his power, detail officers and guides if they can be procured, and take measures to repair or make roads for the artillery. The artillery of the corps should move by a route exterior to that on which the troops move.*

*By command of Major-General Meade:*

*S. WILLIAMS,*
*Assistant Adjutant-General.*

*OR*, Vol. 36, Part II, p. 700.

*There was no fighting on the 13th, further than a little skir-mishing between Mott's division and the enemy. I was afraid that Lee might be moving out, and I did not want him to go without my knowing it. The indications were that he was moving, but it was found that he was only taking his new position back from the salient that had been captured....*

*The night of the 13th Warren and Wright were moved by the ear to the left of Burnside. The night was very dark and it rained heavily, the roads were so bad that the troops had to cut trees and corduroy the road a part of the way, to get through. It was midnight before they got to the point where they were to halt, and daylight before the troops could be organized to advance to their position in line. They gained their position in line, however without any fighting....This brought our line east of the Court House and running north and south facing west.*

U.S. Grant, *Personal Memoirs of U. S. Grant, Selected Letters 1839-1865* (New York: The Library of America, 1990), pp. 556-57.

*EDITOR'S NOTE:* As much as Knight believed his report had been the cause of Grant's deciding to move the army to the left, the special order putting the army into motion was dated at 5:45 p.m., but Sharpe's summary of his scouting report was dated at 6:00 p.m. If anything, it was Sharpe's report of that morning that may have made Grant apprehensive that Lee was beginning to move, as he indicated in his memoirs, as well as the cause of dispatching Knight for a special reconnaissance.

Pamunkey River near old Hanovertown, where we crossed and head-quarters were established on a farm called Gold Hill, from which place Jas. Hatton and myself started to carry dispatches to Yorktown, an account of which was published in the *National Tribune* [*See Chapter 8*] but a few weeks ago.

After coming back from that trip I found Headquarters at Cold Harbor. I shall not attempt to give any description of the fighting at

*Judson Knight maintained that the intelligence he gathered caused the Army of the Potomac to maneuver from Spotsylvania to Cold Harbor. Here the army crosses the Pamunkey River toward Cold Harbor. Edwin Forbes, Library of Congress, LC-DIG-ppmsca-20698.*

this point, but will confine myself to the operations of the scouts. The reader of these reminiscences must not suppose that what is told in these sketches is a tenth part of what was done by the scouts.

I can remember that Cline and Phelps had made a perilous trip to Washington with dispatches. [Anson B.] Gus Carney and one other had tried by another route to get through a duplicate set; then they tried to go from the Wilderness by land, and failed. Cline and [Charles A.] Phelps made their way to the Potomac River, constructed a raft and got across to the Maryland side, where the river was several miles in width; got aboard a schooner where they had smallpox. They had to draw their pistols and threaten to use them before they could make the crew get under way.

On another occasion, when a few miles farther down the Wilderness, a large party of the boys went into the "Northern Neck," as a stretch of country lying between the Potomac and Rappahannock Rivers is called, and captured a signal station. A Lieutenant who had charge of the station was put in [the] charge of one of the new hands, called Honesty, who had been an Orderly for the Provost-Marshal-General. The Lieutenant had not been thoroughly searched. He had a small revolver concealed, and at a favorable opportunity shot Honesty in the back and made his escape. Honesty died in a few hours.

Sometimes the boys would go out single, some in pairs, and often eight or 10 together. At times they were away for days, and sometimes only for a few hours so that no one man can begin to tell all of the adventures that befell them.

At Cold Harbor I met a citizen who was sent to our quarters with orders for us to take care of him. He was with us, I should think, three days, then he came over from Gen. Grant's and Gen. Meade's headquarters and said to me: "Good-by; I am going to leave you."

"Well, sir, good-by. Where are you going?"

"To Philadelphia."

He then told me that Grant and Meade had not made him take the oath of allegiance; and when I asked him the reason, he said it was not expected from him, so that the Confederates should have no excuse, if they heard of it, for confiscating his property. Before I got through talking with him, I learned he was from Richmond; that his name was John N. Van Lew; that his family were from Philadelphia, originally; that his father had been a successful hardware merchant in Richmond for many years previous to the war; also, that he was in the same business; that his mother and sister were both living on Church Hill; that the family were known as Union people; also, that the rebel Provost-Marshal-General Winder was boarding at their house, and that they gave him his board as an equivalent for the protection he afforded the family.[113] As soon as he told me he was from Richmond I began importuning him to join our party, and he inquired what we were. As soon as I told him he declined, saying that the life would not suit him. I went with him two or three miles toward the White House using all the arguments I could think of in order to try and induce him to stay, but failed.[114]

\* \* \*

*EDITOR'S NOTE: Scout Anson Carney's account in a Bradford County, Pennsylvania, memoir addresses the near capture of Grant and Meade at Spotsylvania as well as the use of scouts in prisoner interrogation.*[115]

*Our Boys in Blue: Heroic Deeds, Sketches and Reminiscences of Bradford County Soldiers in the Civil War*, Vol. 1, 1899, by
C. F. Heverely

CARNEY. In the Spring of 1864 General Grant took up his headquarters with the Army of the Potomac. His objective point was Lee's army and not Richmond, and he kept pounding away at the Army of Northern Virginia until its military power was destroyed. Grant was well informed, through his band of scouts, as to Lee's army, for our roster of that force was sufficiently complete for all practical purposes. For some reason which I cannot explain, former commanders were inclined to over-estimate the strength of the enemy, but General Grant had a fair knowledge of the force opposed to him and overcame it both by moving by the left flank and by hard, continuous fighting.[115]

On May 4, 1864, we crossed the Rapidan. When our soldiers saw the pontoon bridges taken up behind them, they felt instinctively that they now had a commander who would lead them to victory. I need not pause to describe the terrific encounters between the opposing armies in the Wilderness. I well remember one incident of that advance. While moving by the left flank late at night about May 7th, General Grant and General Meade, accompanied by a small force of cavalry, headquarters' scouts, etc., passed between the rebel and Union lines. A scout was leading us, and in some way he missed the road. Suddenly we saw the rebel camp fires in the distance, and in that gloomy wilderness their lights reflected upon the surrounding trees made the scene remind one of descriptions of the Valley of the Shadow of Death; such indeed it was a little after. About an hour later battle raged along these lines. Our guide had, however, led us to the left into a bridle path and soon we were on the main road headed for the left of the army. In General Grant's memoirs reference is made to this ride.

---

### How Grant and Meade Were Almost Captured

*Meade and I rode in advance. We passed but a little way beyond our left when the road forked we looked to see, if we could, which road Sheridan had taken with his cavalry during the day. It seemed to be the right-hand one, and accordingly we took it. We had not gone far, however, when Colonel C. B. Comstock, of my staff, with the instinct of the engineer, suspecting that we were on a road that would lead us into the lines of the enemy, if he, too should be moving dashed by at rapid gallop and all alone. In a few minutes he returned and reported that Lee was moving, and that the road we were on would bring us into his lines, in a short distance. We returned to the forks of the road, left a man to indicate the right road to the head of Warren's column when it should come up, and continued our way to Todd's Tavern, where we arrived by midnight.*

U. S. Grant, *Personal Memoirs of U.S. Grant, Selected Letters 1839-1865* (New York: The Library of America, 1990), p. 439.

---

Early on May 12th, '64, a salient [the Mule Shoe] angle near the rebel centre was assaulted by General Hancock and others, and 4,000 rebs were captured. It was at the time reported that General Lee was a short distance in the rear and barely escaped capture, but this report I have never verified. We were near Spotsylvania and the prisoners were marched into a large open field, being soon after sent to the rear under a strong guard. Half an hour or so later I was ordered to ride after them in haste and secure information if possible with regard to the correctness of a rumor that the enemy had destroyed or burned a large portion of our wagon train. I rode rapidly to the rear. The prisoners had been halted on a hill for a brief rest. I made known my orders to the proper officer in charge. I questioned several of the Johnnies and found there was no truth in the rumor, I returned and reported. But our officers were uneasy, and believed there was something in the rumor, and presently another member of the bureau was dispatched after the prisoners on the same errand. When he returned he corroborated my report.

# VII

# Sheridan's Dispatches

*EDITOR'S NOTE: The following two accounts of the same operation by Judson Knight and William J. Lee, Sheridan's chief of scouts, complement each other and provide a fuller account of their mission given by Grant to see if Lee was being reinforced from the south after the battle of Spotsylvania.*

The National Tribune

April 10, 1890

Judson Knight, Washington, D.C.

## A Scouting Experience

## Virginia Revisited After 25 Years

## Part I—1864

KNIGHT. ABOUT THE middle of May, 1864, immediately after the battle of Spotsylvania Courthouse, Gen. Grant, wishing to ascertain whether Gen. Lee was being reinforced by troops from the South, dispatched a party of 13 scouts, including myself, in search of desired information.

Making a wide detour to the left, to get around Lee's right flank, we stopped on our way at the house of Daniel DeJarnett, where Mrs. DeJarnett and a young lady from Spotsylvania met us as we rode

*Judson Knight leads his scouts after the battle of Spotsylvania in search of Sheridan and his Cavalry Corps. Edwin Forbes, author's collection.*

up. Mrs. DeJarnett, in reply to our inquiry for provisions for ourselves and our horses, said, "When soldiers want anything, they want it and must have it," and directed "Uncle John" to supply our wants. During his absence on this foraging expedition, the ladies evidently began to entertain some doubt as to which side we belonged to, and Mrs. DeJarnett inquired: "Are you Yankees?"

"Yes," I answered.

"Well, you are the first Yankees we have seen, and if they are all like you I shall never be afraid of them again."

She then wanted to know whether all the Yankees had horses as good as ours, and I assured her that ours were fair specimens of a Yankee's mount.

We took our provisions uncooked, and offered pay for them, which the lady declined. As we were riding out of the yard she called me back, saying, "If you and your men will each accept a bottle of wine, we have some old port that has been in the cellar 20 years, and you are welcome to it." The invitation was, of course, accepted, and when

"Uncle John" had brought the wine, we knocked off the necks of the bottles, and drank the good health of the ladies without dismounting.

A few miles further on we met a contraband, from whom we learned of a "blind ford," so called to distinguish it from a public one, as there was no public road leading to it. After crossing this ford, two of us, J. W. Landegon and myself, proceeded on our way as far as Penola (then known by the odoriferous name of Pole Cat), leaving the rest of the men under cover of the trees that lined the bank of the Mattapony River.[127]

Landegon was attired in a full Confederate uniform that he had obtained on the preceding day at Milford Station, while I wore a wheat-straw hat and a coat that had once been blue, but had now turned almost purple.

On the top of a hill about half a mile distant, we descried a mounted man whom we took for a videt [cavalry picket], and started forward to interview him. Before we reached him, however, he raised an umbrella, which action satisfied us that he was no soldier, but a planter watching his servants at work in a cornfield. Turning to the left, we saw a man and a woman coming from a house situated in a grove of fine trees into the field through which we were riding. Greeting them with the customary salutations, I asked: "Have you seen any soldiers lately?"

The woman—who, by the way, was only about 18 years old—answered, "I never saw so many men in my life as were here yesterday."

"Who were they?"

"Col. _____'s command."

"Where were they from?"

"Charleston."

"How many do you think there were?"

"Oh! I can't tell; I never saw so many men at one time in my life; they reached from those bars clear up to that gate, in four ranks."

The space indicated by her reply would contain a brigade of our regiments. This being the information for which we had come around to the rear of Lee's army, we felt that we had obtained it very easily. I could readily see from the appearance of the place that these people could furnish us with food for ourselves and our horses, and as the lady made some remark about Yankees, which she would not have made if she had known that we belonged to that hated race, I deemed it best to spare her feelings by telling her the truth, before the rest of the party came up, when she would have known it anyway. I could also see that she was a lady, and therefore said:

"We are Yankees."

She evidently did not believe this, and replied, "You are about as much Yankees as we are."

Feeling it necessary to undeceive her, I looked her sternly in the eye and said, "We are."

I never realized until that moment, when she turned deathly pale, stepped back a pace or two, throwing both hands above her head, exclaimed in such a beseeching voice, "Oh! Don't hurt us!" how much we were feared.

I answered reassuringly, "Why do you think we want to hurt you? We are not making war on women."

This remark only partially calmed her fears, for they did not include her husband, and she pleaded, "Oh! Don't take the Doctor!"

I replied, "We don't want to harm either you or the Doctor. He is at home, minding his own business; he is not in the army, and we have no intention of interfering with him."

Turning to the Doctor, I continued, "Doctor, we have some men down there in the woods, and we want food for them and for our horses. Can you supply it? Understand, we do not want it gratis; we will pay for everything we get."

Upon his replying in the affirmative, Landegon waved his hand-kerchief and the men dashed out from cover and came tearing across the level land on a gallop. The sight of the blue-coats was evidently too much for the nerves of our hosts, for after one frightened glance, they took to their heels and scuttled off to the house. However, they soon regained their confidence, and provided an excellent meal. When it came to the point of settling accounts, we learned that the Doctor, who, by the way, was a very boyish looking doctor, expected to be paid in Confederate money. We told him we had nothing but greenbacks, but he objected to them, saying he could not use them, and that it was against the law to deal in them in any shape or form.

I knew this to be true, and said to him, "It will only be two or three days when you can use all the greenbacks you can get hold of."

"How so?"

"Our army will be all around you in less than three days."

"How is that; ain't we whipping you all the time?"

"That is what your papers say, but we are coming right along just the same."

After telling him the relative value of greenbacks and gold, we paid him and prepared to start. He then asked me to give him a "protection paper." I told him that such a document would be of no service to him unless it was signed by the Provost Marshal-General of the Army. He still urged his request, however, and I gave him a paper asking all Union officers and soldiers to treat Dr. Dew and his property with respect and consideration, as he had given me very valuable information, and I signed it as a scout of Gen. Meade's headquarters.

We had not gone over a mile when we ran into a party of the 9th Va. Cav., (although we did not know at the time who they were). Landegon was wounded in the shoulder, and one horse was killed. We took Landegon back to Dr. Dew's house, promising to call for him in three days; at which time, however, we found ourselves 12 miles beyond Penola.

Two of us rode back, and were met at the gate by Mrs. Dew, who seemed very much flustered, and exclaimed, "Mr. Knight, I was never so glad to see anyone as I am to see you. Since you were here the other day, there have been thousands of your men all over our place, but they have all treated us with the nicest respect as soon as they saw the paper you gave us until, these men came that are here now. I can't understand them."

I could see no one, and asked her what she meant. She said, "They are all back of the house, and are killing all our chickens and ducks."

At the rear of the house I found about 15 of the 3d N.J. Cav. (Butterflies), their saddles loaded down with the doctor's poultry.[118] I asked the Doctor what was up and he said they had killed the last fowl they had. I told him to set a price on them, and not to be afraid to say what they were worth.

He said, "I wanted to keep them."

"Well, Doctor," said I, "they are dead now. Say what they are worth."

"I think," he said, "about $12."

I rode up to a Second Lieutenant and said to him, "Officers are not allowed to maraud through the country as you are doing. You will have to pay the Doctor $12."

He answered in German, and I asked him to speak English. He replied again in German, when I said, "If you don't pay I will see that your shoulder-straps come off, your sword broken, and you kicked out of the army in disgrace."

"Who are you?"

"None of your business; you will find I am perfectly able to carry out my threats, if you don't pay."

He looked me over, straw hat and purple coat, and spoke to his men. In a few minutes they paid, but I have always thought if the price had been a dollar or two more, they could not have raised it. Landegon had been removed on the previous day by a member of his company of the 6th N.Y. Cav. I did not see him again until 1873, on my way to Minnesota. After he got well he went South with Kilpatrick, and was his Chief of Scouts, and an excellent one he made.

## Part II—1889
Some time during the month of March or early April 1889, I received a letter from Dr. P. A. Dew, who lives some 30 miles this side of Richmond, in which he stated that he would like to hear from my "wounded friend." After some delay, I sent him the address of John W. Landegon, of Coles & Landegon, Exchange Hotel, Port Jervis, Orange Co., N.Y., and soon afterward, I received an invitation from Dr. and Mrs. Dew to come and see them.

About four months ago I went as far as Fredericksburg with the intention of making them a visit, but gave it up, after going a few miles toward Belle Plain, to see an old friend named Silver. McEneany, one of my old scouts, and I, were caught in a rain storm, and finally returned to Washington without going to Penola. This time I told the Doctor I would come toward the end of May, but in the meantime a terrific storm destroyed the railroad from Fredericksburg to Richmond, and it was not until the middle of June that travel was resumed.

I reached Penola on the 20th of June, and was met at the depot by a young man, who asked, "Are you Mr. Knight?"

I said, "Yes, and I suppose your name is Dew."

He said it was, and added, "I was not thought of, I daresay, when you were here before." He insisted on carrying my valise, and said, "Father is at the house. Mother has been in Richmond several days, but we expect her home to-night. They will both be mighty glad to see you, and we were all very much disappointed at your not coming four years ago."

When we reached the house, the Doctor met me and shook hands and said, pointing to the stump of a tree, "That is the place where you left the man that was wounded." Dr. Dew is a smaller man than I had always thought him, and his whiskers are tinged with gray. His family consisted of two sons and four daughters. Phil., the young man who met me at the depot, is 22. Gertrude 11, and Lucy about five; these were the only ones at home. Lucy was one of the shyest little beings I ever saw. It was a long time before she could be induced to speak, and when she did, she appeared to recognize her own temerity and scudded off behind the house, peeping around the corner to see what would happen.

I could scarcely realize that 25 years had passed since my visit in 1864. I remained with the Doctor one day, and he gave me the address of his wife in Richmond. I called in the morning, but the family was out. I left my name and stated that I came from Penola, and that I would return at 4 p.m. When Mrs. Dew came home the colored girl told her that a gentleman named Knight, from Caroline County, had called. Mrs. Dew said, "I don't know anyone by that name in Caroline; I'll bet it's my Yankee friend from Washington."

When I rang the door-bell at 4 p.m. she came to the door herself. Neither of us recognized the other, but we could surmise each other's identity, and she asked, "Are you my friend, Mr. Knight?"

"I am, if you are Mrs. Dew."

She showed me into the parlor, and introduced me to her sister and her two daughters, who received me almost like a hero. The sister subsequently produced some well-preserved Confederate bills, which they insisted on my keeping as a relic. I had brought a couple of dolls for Gerty and Lucy, which were duly admired and pronounced the perfection of dolls. As the family intended to return to Penola, they were compelled to leave me alone in the parlor, while they made their preparations for departure.

Presently the door-bell rang, and as the girl opened the door, I heard a feminine voice whisper, "Is he here?"

"Yes, he is in the parlor, alone."

"Well, I am going in to see him," and a young lady came in and said, "Are you Mrs. Dew's Yankee friend?"

"I am," I said.

Whereupon she caught me by both hands and said, "I have heard of you all my life, and have always wanted to see you and tell you that I think you are a splendid man. If everyone had been like you, things would have been so much better."

The family returned to Penola in the evening and I called on Miss Van Lew, who is living with her niece. She said that none of her old friends ever called on her, and I also ascertained that all of my old Richmond friends are dead but one, and him I did not see. I append two letters, one from the Doctor and the other from his daughter, Gertrude.

Penola Station, Caroline Co., Va., Nov. 10, 1885
Mr. Judson Knight

Dear Sir: Yours received. Certainly I remember the party of scouts who came through in 1864; a surprise my wife and myself will ever remember. We were much divided, but liberally divided ham and eggs. We would be glad to have you call on us again. We will talk over old times.

With best regards, yours truly, P. A. Dew

Penola Station, Caroline Co., Va., July 2, 1889

Mr. Knight,

Dear Friend: I must write and thank you for the beautiful dolls you so kindly sent to my little sister and myself. We both enjoy playing with them so much. We were really sorry you did not come back Monday, as you promised; but mama told us why you could not. We hope you will not make it long before you come again. Papa, mamma and brother Philip desire to be remembered to you. I must subscribe myself your little friend.

Gertrude Dew

\* \* \*

*EDITOR'S NOTE: The following account by Sheridan's chief of scouts, J. W. Landegon, is of the same operation Knight relates above. Landegon was highly regarded by Sheridan and subsequently by Kilpatrick for whom he worked in the last year of the war. That Landegon respects Knight is a high compliment. It was a friendship that would continue long after the war.*

*In order to complete Landegon's narrative and fill in the gaps, elements from his accounts in William Gilmore Beymer's* Scouts and Spies of the Civil War *have been interspersed with those of his from the following* National Tribune *article. Where appropriate Beymer's third person narratives are included.*[119]

The National Tribune
July 24, 1890
J.W. Landegon, Danbury, Conn.

A Scouting Experience
Sheridan's Chief of Scouts is Wounded, but Escapes Captors

LANDEGON. An article in the *National Tribune* of April 10, entitled "A Scouting Experience," by Mr. Judson Knight, recently came to my notice. The fact that I am mentioned in that article as one of the party, and that that was my last scouting experience in Virginia, leads me to address you on that subject.

At that time I was Chief of Scouts for Gen. Sheridan. On the 8th day of May, 1864, Sheridan received orders to cut loose from the Army of the Potomac, to make a raid in the rear of Gen. Lee's army, to destroy his railroads, military supplies and communication with Richmond. It was thought the rebel cavalry would follow, thereby freeing us from a raid they were about to make in the rear of our army.

*EDITOR'S NOTE: It is worth pausing for Landegon's description of his relationship with Sheridan that appears in the book* On Hazardous Duty *(1912).*

LANDEGON. I mind one report I made. My first report to General Sheridan. I'd been out for three days somewhere in the enemy's lines, I don't remember where, or why and when I came in to report to the General. I thought it would be my last report. "Well," he says, "what did you find?" "Nothin'," I answered just that. "By Gee!" he yelled, and he jumped up from his chair. "That's the best report I ever heard a scout make!" I thought he was mad and just making fun of me, and I stood still and didn't say anything. He walked close up to me. "Do you know why I think so much of that 'nothin'' of yours? It's because you didn't think you had to make up a lot of lies for fear I'd think you hadn't been working. If you saw 'nothin'' in three days, that means there was nothing to see, and that's the one thing I wanted to know!"

I remembered that little talk of General Sheridan's, and it helped me all the rest of the war. I never exaggerated anything, and soon they got to count on what I said.[120]

LANDEGON [*National Tribune*]. On May 8th we moved to the left, passed between and then to the rear of Gen. Lee's army, the latter, as expected, in hot pursuit, fighting our rear-guard continually; but we kept on going just the same. At Beaver Dam Station, on the Virginia Central Railroad, we destroyed about 10 miles of tracks, several locomotives, many cars, and also a large amount of military supplies that had been sent there for the Confederate army. We recaptured about 400 of our men that had been taken at the Wilderness and were on their way to Libby Prison. Our appearance caused great

*Scout Landegon delivered the best reconnaissance report Sheridan said he ever heard. Alfred R. Waud, Library of Congress, LC-USZ61-1096.*

consternation, and Lee doubtless felt some uneasiness to know that a large cavalry force was in his rear.

On the afternoon of the 10th, we had reached Ground Squirrel Bridge, on the South Anna River, where the command halted for a short rest and to feed our horses. At this time Gen. Sheridan desired to send a dispatch back to the Commander of the Army of the Potomac. Disguised as a Confederate officer, I selected Patrick Myers, one of my scouts, to accompany me, he also in Confederate uniform, and to appear as my Orderly.

LANDEGON [*Scouts and Spies*]. After we left General Sheridan at Ground Squirrel Bridge, on the South Anna this was Sheridan's raid around Lee in May, '64. Patrick Myers, my best scout, and I rode around the flank of the Confederate cavalry where they were fighting with our rear guard. They had been fighting the rear guard ever since we had got in the rear of Lee's lines on the 9th. This day I'm telling you of was late afternoon of the 10th the day before Yellow Tavern, where Jeb Stuart fell, six miles from Richmond. We missed that fight.

The country was so rough that, to make time, we swung into the road behind the Confederate cavalry, and ordered the stragglers forward to their regiments. Y' see, I was in the full uniform of a Confederate officer, and Patrick Myers was my orderly; we kept hurrying the stragglers forward, and all the time we were getting farther to the rear. It was the best fun I ever had![121]

BEYMER [*Scouts and Spies*]. They stopped at dark at a farm-house and asked for something to eat. The owner of the house was too old to go to war; he gave them a good meal, and gladly assented to put them up for as much of the night as they could remain. After the meal they all sat about the table talking. In some way they misunderstood their host, something he said; they believed him to be a Union sympathizer who, because of their gray uniforms, dared not come out and say that he was against the South.

"We're not Confederates," one of them blurted out; "we are Union soldiers." The old man rose from his chair.

"Ye lied to me," he said.

They both sprang, startled, to their feet at his sudden movement, and it must have been a dramatic moment as they faced each other across the lamp-lit table the scouts with their hands on their revolvers, the white-bearded old man majestic in his indignation.

"I've given you food and offered you bed: and you have lied to me! You yourselves say that you have been telling me lies all the evenin'! I wouldn't have you sleep in my barn. It isn't which side you're on; ye lied to me!"

He drove them from his house by the sheer weight of his scorn. They sulkily rode away; but in the stillness of the night they heard a horse, hard ridden, leave the farmhouse, and they rode aside into the woods and waited. Presently a troop of Confederate cavalry swept by on the road they had just been on.[121]

BEYMER [*Scouts and Spies*]. It was night of the next day—the 11th—when they got through the Confederate pickets and struck the Mattapony River some miles below the Army of the Potomac. They stripped, and put their clothes on a bit of board, which they pushed before them as they swam the river; it was storming fiercely; in the dark the rain lashed the river into pale foam.[122]

LANDEGON [*National Tribune*]. We got through all O.K., and reached our lines on the evening of the 11th, without our horses, having abandoned them in order to get through the real picket-lines with less risk of detection. We were made prisoners by our men. I informed them who we were, and desired to be taken to army headquarters. We were sent under guard to Gen. Grant's headquarters. Col. Forsyth, Sheridan's Chief of Staff, had told me that should I reach Grant first, to give him the dispatch and other information that I would be able to get while passing through Lee's army. Gen. Grant was very glad to see me. I gave him the message and other information I had obtained on the trip, and was complimented by the greatest soldier the world ever knew. [*EDITOR'S NOTE: Below is the content of the dispatch.*]

*HEADQUARTERS, CAVALRY CORPS,*
*ARMY OF THE POTOMAC, May 10, 1864.*
*MAJ.-GEN. GEORGE G. MEADE,*

*Commanding Army of the Potomac.*
*GENERAL:*
   *I turned the enemy's right and got into their rear. Did not meet sufficient of cavalry to stop me. Destroyed from eight to ten miles of Orange Railroad, two locomotives, three trains, and a large amount of supplies. The enemy were making a depot of supplies at Beaver Dam. Since I got into their rear there has been great excitement among the inhabitants and with the army. The citizens report that Lee is beaten. Their cavalry has attempted to annoy my rear and flank, but have been run off. I expect to fight their cavalry south of the South Anna River. I have no forage. Started with half rations for one day, and have found none yet. Have recaptured five hundred men, two colonels.*
   *I am, General, very respectfully, Your obedient servant,*
   *P. H. SHERIDAN,*
   *Major-General, Commanding.*

*OR*, Part 2, Vol. XXXVI, p. 616.

He returned the dispatch to me and told one of his staff to go with me to Gen. Meade's headquarters, only a few hundred yards distant. Gen. Meade expressed himself as very much pleased with Sheridan's success, and said, "Now we will give those fellows no rest."

*Maj. Gen. George G. Meade, commander of the Army of the Potomac, often dealt personally with Col. Sharpe's scouts, accounts of which Judson Knight retells. Author's collection.*

We were then placed in Gen. Sharpe's charge, who provided us with dry clothing, etc. We had reached therein a very hard rain. Sharpe at this time was Deputy Provost Marshal-General, and had charge of the secret service of the army. He told me to call at his tent the next morning. I called. He asked me if I could return to Sheridan. I asked him where he thought I would be likely to find Sheridan. He laughed, said that I ought to know best, as I had seen him last, and they had no knowledge of him other than I had given. I told Sharpe where I had left Sheridan, but in what direction he would go I did not know, because unaware of his orders or plans. That was why I asked the question. I told Sharpe that I would return. He told me to remain where he could put his hand on me when wanted, as he would probably have work for me in a few hours. Three or four days later I was again sent for. Sharpe then told me it would not be necessary for me to make the return trip, as Gen. Sheridan had reached Gen. Butler's lines; that it would be several days before Sheridan would be again with the Army of the Potomac; that I could in the meantime go to the wagon-train and rest, or that I could remain with Gen. Meade's scouts, subject to his (Sharpe's) orders only. I told him I would remain, and did. It is thus made clear how I came to be with Gen. Meade's scouts on the trip that Judson Knight speaks of.

Now to return to Judson Knight's narrative. I remember the trip very well, and also having a talk with Gen. Sharpe before starting in reference to it. He said that the Second Corps would move rapidly 20 or 25 miles south in the direction of Richmond, hoping by so doing that Lee would leave his intrenchments to attack it; that the rest of the army would immediately follow and attack Lee before he had time to intrench; that we were to go in the direction to be taken by the Second Corps, only farther to the left and south. He also informed me that Gen. Sheridan was about to start, or had started, to return to the Army of the Potomac; that he looked for Sheridan to return in that direction that we were to take; that if we did not run across Sheridan before the scouts decided to return, he desired that I should continue on south in search of Sheridan; and when the latter was found to inform him of the contemplated movements of Meade's army.

I also remember stopping at the house of Daniel DeJarnett, having wine which was very good. I am not so sure whether we were invited to partake of the wine or not. Knight says the lady called him back and said, "If you and your men will each accept a bottle of old port that has been in the cellar for years, you are welcome to it." I hope Knight's memory is not at fault in reference to the invitation.

Some miles further on we discovered then a few horsemen in advance of us. They did not wait to be interviewed. They kept a safe distance ahead. We came to the conclusion that if we continued to follow them we would be warmly received later on, and as the scouts had proceeded farther south than ordered, we changed our course to the right and back in the direction to be taken by the Second Corps, and succeeded in doing so by the way of the blind ford that Knight speaks of.

After leaving the ford Knight and myself, the rest of the scouts remaining under cover, discovered a horseman on the high ground in the distance, also several other persons, whom we took to be infantry pickets, but who turned out to be, as Knight says, a planter on horseback, watching his servants at work in a cornfield. We felt sure that they were soldiers until within a short distance of them, but whether Confederate or Union, we could not guess. We thought they might be the Second Corps, who had established their picket-lines. At all events we had to know for a certainty, and found out as Knight relates.

Knight then speaks of our interview with Dr. Dew and his wife. I don't know whether Knight lied to them more than I did or not. I think he did, for he was good in that line. (I should add, however, that he possessed other and higher qualities of the successful scout beside glibness.)

BEYMER [*Scouts and Spies*]. They turned to ride back to their men, awaiting them on the river's bank, when there suddenly came out of a lane a man and a girl, who stared at them in surprise.

"Have you seen any troops come by?" the scouts asked, politely. It was the girl who answered.

"Oh, yes! More than I ever saw before at one time! South Carolina soldiers. How many? Why, they would reach from there to there!" The space indicated a brigade of four regiments. It was the information they had come out to gain; Knight was elated at the ease with which it had been obtained.

"We're Yankees!" he suddenly said. The girl looked at Landegon's gray uniform, at Knight's wheat-straw hat, his coat—purpled by the rain and sun; she laughed.

"About as much Yankees as we are!" she said.

"We are Yankees!" they sternly told her. Her eyes grew wide with fear.

"You shall not—I—you will not take the Doctor—my husband?" she pleaded.

They reassured her—they would only take dinner, and pay for it, they said. But she still was very much afraid. Landegon waved a handkerchief, and the rest of the scouts came up at a gallop from the river. Young Doctor Dew and his wife fled in terror. The scouts shouted with laughter, and trotted after them to the house, where presently they had dinner. Trivial little details, these, but I dare say such things stick in a man's mind, if he is shot that day.[123]

LANDEGON [*National Tribune*]. After Knight had told Mrs. Dew that we were Yankees, and I had signaled the rest of the scouts to come up, Knight made arrangements for food for men and horses. I did not have the cheek to remain after lying to such nice people, and consequently was not in on the ham and eggs the Doctor speaks of in his letter to Knight. Myers and I proceeded onto the railroad station, about a half a mile farther on, to wait there till the scouts were through eating, and to talk about our trip farther south in search of Gen. Sheridan.

The scouts joined us in about an hour. Just as they were leaving in the direction of our army, a few Johnnies came in on a road leading southward and fired upon us. As Myers and myself were going in that direction in search of Sheridan, and as Meade's scouts had accomplished the object of the trip, we all thought a little fight would be in order. I think we were all quite full—I don't mean of Mrs. DeJarnett's old wine, but of fight, and we gave the rebels chase. It was a very nice chase for about half a mile. We found more rebs, and then things again changed—in fact I think we returned quite as fast as we went.

I had received a pistol-shot wound in the right shoulder just as I had drawn bead on the reb who shot me. We were but a few feet apart. His shot paralyzed my arm and shoulder, causing me to drop my pistol. I then used my spurs to the best advantage. I hope he survived the war. How I would like to meet him, take his hand and say, "Well, Johnny, old boy, you crippled me quite badly; but I freely forgive you, for had you not got the drop on me, I would in all probability have killed you."

*EDITOR'S NOTE: Beymer provides a more detailed and dramatic account of the action in which Knight and his men took part and in which Landegon was wounded.*

BEYMER [*Scouts and Spies*]. They rode to Penola Station, not more than a mile away, and there lay the parting of the ways: Landegon and Myers must start south to find Sheridan, Knight and his scouts go back to the army of Grant and Meade.

A small band of Confederates dashed out of a crossroad, fired a bravado volley at them, and galloped away.

"Let's have a fight!" one of the scouts yelled, "before you fellows leave." In a moment they were riding hard after the Confederates, shouting and yelling like frolicking boys.

Landegon says he had the best horse of them all. As a brave man and a modest should, he lays it to the horse; I lay it to the man who rode. He drew farther and farther ahead; the road grew choked with dust that rose all about them like smoke-filled fog. The fleeing Confederates had been reinforced, had turned, and were coming back. In the dust Landegon flashed full tilt into them before he found what he had done. Horses reared and backed and shied; there was a tangle and confusion that sent up blind clouds in which no man knew friend from foe. Landegon whirled his horse about and fired a revolver in a man's face, and then some one shot him, and his paralyzed hand dropped his pistol, and the whole thing grew confused. He knows that one man followed him, shooting at him at every bound; and when his revolver was empty, the man rose in his stirrups and threw the pistol whirling over and over, and it struck him, barrel end on; it seemed to break his spine.[124]

LANDEGON [*National Tribune*]. Two of the scouts started with me in the direction of our lines, while the rest of the scouts remained at the railroad station to hold the enemy in check until I could get some distance in the rear. We had proceeded but a short distance when I became very weak, and the scouts had to assist me to remain in the saddle. The next I remember is finding myself in Dr. Dew's yard, lying on the grass under a shade tree, the Doctor and his wife doing all they could for me. The Doctor had succeeded in stopping the flow of blood, thereby saving my life. His wife bathed my face and temples with cold water. The scouts were all gone. I thought that they should have managed in some way to have taken me with them, as they well knew that if found, even though badly wounded, I would be hung—the penalty paid by spies.[125]

Nearly two years previous I came very near going by that route—the rope—and I well remembered how I felt about it. I thought some other route would suit me so much better. Having often heard the remark that some people would kick were they to be hung, I found myself no exception to the rule. My first enlistment, to be retrospective, was in the infantry [1st Connecticut Volunteer Infantry], and for the period of three months. Soon after we had reached the front, I gained some notoriety very cheaply, and as a consequence was detailed by Gen. Tyler as a scout at his headquarters.

Later in battle [First Bull Run] our troops were badly defeated and forced to retreat. On the part of the battlefield where I was at the close of the fight, I did not see much cause to hurry. I could see the Confederates on the hills in the distance. It seemed to me that they did not care to overtake us, but contented themselves by hurrying our departure by the use of their artillery. Some distance back I came to a church which during the battle had been used as a hospital. There I found much hurry and confusion. A number of cavalry horses were tied to the fence. An officer, I think a Surgeon, said, "Take them, or the rebels soon will." I selected a horse, and after fastening my gun securely to the saddle by means of the straps connected thereto, I mounted and proceeded to the rear.

I had gone but a very short distance when I heard firing in that direction, and a moment later I met a number of our men returning.

The rebel cavalry, it seems, had made a dash on the troops in advance of us near a certain bridge, and in the hurry and confusion that it caused the passageway across the bridge became blocked. All was confusion, our men running in all directions. I thought that I could not proceed on horseback, so abandoning the horse I did not wait even to unfasten the gun, but proceeded across a field back in the direction of the church, and to the right of it, and into a piece of woods, hunting for a place to hide. I climbed up a very high tree, intending to remain there till dark.

At this time I had a great dread of being captured; I thought I would rather be killed; but after I had climbed to the top of the tree and looked down, away down, I then quickly changed my mind. I thought I would much rather be taken prisoner, and said to myself that I had no show to be taken, for should the enemy find me the temptation to see me tumble would be so great that they would surely load me with lead, and then, oh! What a distance to fall after being shot to death. Thus we are always hard to please.

To return to the Doctor and his wife, they assured me that should the Confederates find me on their premises, they would not harm me; but I knew very well to the contrary, and that their pleadings would not avail. Mrs. Dew suggested that portions of my Confederate uniform that had been removed from my person be secreted; also, spy papers suggestive of my being a spy. She told a servant to bury them in the back yard. I was told that the scouts would return in two or three days with an ambulance for my removal. I thought it strange that they should wait so long. I afterwards learned that they expected me to "croak." I did not think I would be there when they returned. In fact, I expected the enemy would find me, and I knew it would be all up with me.

The Doctor's residence was some distance from the main road, a lane leading up to the house. I have often thought its being so located was the cause of the rebels not finding me. The Doctor wanted me to go to bed in the house. I wanted to remain where I was, in the yard. We compromised the matter by my resting on a lounge in the hall leading from the main entrance and promising to go regularly to bed next morning. I had reasons for not going to bed. My person and clothing were covered with blood, and I wished to save the Doctor and his lady all the trouble I could, and I also desired to be in a position to escape from the premises in the event of the enemy approaching, my strength permitting. I was very weak, and my wound gave me much pain. I did not sleep any during the night, expecting at any moment a visit from the enemy.

*EDITOR'S NOTE: Landegon was not taking lightly the likelihood of being hanged if captured. He had come very close to that end earlier in the war, as shown in Chapter 3.*

LANDEGON [*National Tribune*]. I think it was between 3 and 4 o'clock next morning when I was sure I heard the tramp of horses approaching. I thought I was a gone Yank; I attempted at once to leave, but found that I was so weak that I could not, and became reconciled to face the music. I soon heard someone approaching the house and could distinctly hear what I thought to be the clank of a saber striking the ground. The noise proved to be caused by a pair of large Mexican spurs worn by the person approaching. The next moment someone knocked very hard upon the door three or four times in quick succession. He seemed to be in a big hurry to gain admittance. Before the Doctor had time to dress and open the door, he had given it a very hard kick, the door flying open, and demanded to know if anyone lived in this house.

"Yes, Jack, I live here," I said.

Imagine my surprise and pleasure to recognize the voice of Jack Williams, one of my scouts.[126] He was with the advance of Gen. Sheridan's cavalry on their return to the Army of the Potomac, he acting as guide. Uncertain about the way, Jack had stopped at the house to make inquiries about the roads, etc. He was much astonished at finding me, and thought I had failed to reach Meade with the dispatch from Sheridan. I informed him how I came to be there, what Sharpe said about the movements to be made by the infantry, and that I thought the Second Corps was not more than three or four miles distant, which information proved correct. After learning from Dr. Dew about the roads, he left me, saying that as soon as he gave the information to the officer in command of the cavalry and saw the command started in the right direction for our lines, he would return and devise some way for taking me with him. He returned in about an hour's time and took breakfast with the Doctor. He then borrowed a horse, harness, wagon and pillows for my removal. I think they were never returned.

We reached our infantry in safety, found the army on the move south. We learned that Gen. Sheridan was some miles farther on, having reached our lines during the night, and was again with the Army of the Potomac. We wanted to reach him as soon as possible, but found it very difficult to proceed, as we had to go in the same direction that the infantry was marching, and on the same road. The weather was very hot, the roads very dusty, and we found the infantry very unwilling to give way and let us pass. They could not see why so much pains should be taken with a wounded rebel, which they took me to be. They said the rebs would not do as much for us. After having driven a mile or more, covering our troops with dust as we proceeded, and being loudly cursed and threatened for so doing, we gave up the attempt to reach Sheridan in that manner.

Williams left me at a farmhouse, and made me as comfortable as possible under a shade-tree. He then went in search of Sheridan to secure an ambulance. While waiting his return a Surgeon belonging to an infantry command removed the ball from my shoulder, which gave me great relief. Williams returned in a few hours with an ambulance, which enabled me to reach Sheridan on the same evening, May 24, having thus been absent from the afternoon of the 11th inst. The same night, with other wounded, I was sent to Port Royal, and from there to Washington, and a few days later to the hospital at Portsmouth Grove, R.I.

Before leaving Sheridan I was given a paper stating that I was a scout at his headquarters, was wounded, and should be allowed to return to him as soon as I was able. Much against the Surgeon's advice, and before I had recovered, I returned to the front. My wound still gave me much trouble. I reached City Point the day following Sheridan's departure to take command of the troops operating in the Shenandoah Valley. Some of his staff had remained to superintend the transfer of headquarters, etc. One of the staff informed me that during my absence some of the scouts had behaved badly; that they had been dismissed and returned to their respective regiments. In two of the men that were bounced I had much confidence, Williams and Myers. The latter had been with me for nearly two years. I did not blame Sheridan—probably he had good cause for so doing; but I will confess it may have had the effect of impairing my appetite to resume scouting in Virginia. My wound seemed to get worse, and since my term of enlistment would expire in three or four weeks, I decided to go to Washington and there remain till about that time.

I next saw Sheridan a day or two before my term of enlistment expired. I found him a few miles west of Harper's Ferry. He said he was very glad I had returned; that he had lots of work for me to do. I informed him I was done scouting in Virginia, and had come to so inform him. He seemed greatly surprised, and I think very angry; said something about deserting in the face of the enemy, and turned away from me. But I had my mind made up as far as scouting for the present was concerned, and nothing could induce me to remain. I had been on detached duty as a scout for more than three years, having first been employed by Gen. Tyler before the first battle of Bull Run. I had been with other Generals and previous to being with Sheridan had been Chief of Scouts for Gen. Kilpatrick for nearly two years.

Some time after my discharge I received a letter from Gen. Kilpatrick, who at the time was in command of Gen. Sherman's cavalry. He requested me to come South, which I did, and was employed by him as a citizen scout till the close of the war. Knight says that after I got well I went South with Kilpatrick, and became his Chief of Scouts. Capt. T. F. Northrup served as such while Kilpatrick was with Sherman. Northrup and myself had served together in Virginia. I had early in the war given him his first lessons in scouting. He became a much better scout than his teacher, and I think he was one of the best soldiers I ever knew. He was also a splendid horseman, but could not ride a stolen colt.

In conclusion I would say a word more in reference to Dr. Dew. I had intended, year after year since the war, to make him a visit, but did not. I had never heard from him until last April or May, 1889. Judson Knight had given him my post office address, and I was very glad to hear from him. In the letter he informed me that during the war he had suffered the loss of a great deal of property, which was taken for the use of the U.S. Army, and said that he ought to be compensated by the Government. And it does seem to me, taking everything into consideration, that he should be paid. He was a non-combatant, a physician, peacefully following his profession, and, as I remember, was at the time in poor health. As regards his loyalty I don't know, but I do know he was loyal to me, a wounded Union soldier. Why did he not hand me over to the Confederates? He would have found favor with them had he done so.

# VIII

# Adventures in the Swamps of the Pamunkey River

*EDITOR'S NOTE: Knight is given a mission directly by Assistant Secretary of War Charles A. Dana, after the battle of Spotsylvania, to carry dispatches to the nearest telegraph station which was at Yorktown on the Peninsula. It took him on a harrowing journey across Rebel controlled territory through the swamps of the Pamunkey River.*

The National Tribune
January 12, 1893
Judson Knight, Washington, D.C.

KNIGHT. AFTER THE fighting at Spotsylvania Courthouse was over, I cannot remember how the country looked, or what roads we took until we approached the Pamunkey River. In my mind's eye I can see the road for about a mile leading across a river bottom, filled with doughboys, as the infantry were called, who had been halted to let Army Headquarters pass. They had been marching in column of fours, and had separated, so that two were on the right and two on the left of the road. After Headquarters came a motley group of servants, all mounted, which appeared to excite the ire of the infantry. The day was hot, and they had had a long march that morning. As a general thing the scouts were not with headquarters when on the march; only a lot of so called guides, most of them negroes, although there were quite a number of white men and boys, Virginians by birth. The negroes were guides in some cases.[128]

After crossing the Pamunkey, Headquarters were established on a farm called Gold Hill. Soon after we had settled down, I mounted my horse and took a ride westwardly to see what the topography of the country was like. Just as I came to the first place west of Gold Hill, Gen. Grant and a number of his staff came out of a house; as I passed them Grant was saying: "I told her that I considered our losses about equal. As we had all the time been the attacking party, we had lost more in killed and wounded, but we had taken many more prisoners than Lee had." Afterward I learned Mrs. Newton was the name of the lady he was speaking of.

About 10 a.m. on the next day, an Orderly from Gen. M. R. Patrick, the Provost Marshal-General of the Army of the Potomac, came over to our camp, and said to me: "Gen. Patrick wants to see you." On reporting to him, he said: "Mr. Dana wants to see you." Mr. Dana was Assistant Secretary of War, and had been at Headquarters of the Army from the opening of the Wilderness campaign.

When I reached Headquarters, I asked for Mr. Dana. Gen. Rawlings pointed to him, and he (Dana) said: "I am Mr. Dana." Gen. Grant and Col. Rufus Ingalls, Chief Quartermaster of the Army, were also in the tent. I said to him: "Gen. Patrick ordered me to report to you."

"You are a scout. We want to send dispatches to Yorktown. That is the nearest point we can reach a telegraph."

Yorktown was about 70 miles away, and the country between in full possession of the enemy. I am free to confess that there was no craving on my part for the job. All that I knew of the country was what an infantryman serving with his regiment that landed at West Point, at the junction of the Pamunkey and York Rivers, would naturally learn in going from there to New Kent Courthouse; from thence to Cumberland Landing; from there to Gaine's farm; from Gaine's farm to Mechanicsville; from thence to Fair Oaks and Harrison's Landing, by way of Savage Station, White Oak Swamp, and Malvern Hill. Two years had elapsed since. I thought over our guides, and the different scouts; not a man of them knew a thing of the country, and told Mr. Dana that there was not a horse in our party in fit condition to make such a trip, and said my own horse had a sore back—in fact, they all had. Gen. Grant, I could see, was listening to our conversation. When I mentioned the condition of the horses in our party, he said: "Ingalls, haven't you got fresh horses in the corral?" "Yes," said he. Then he said to me: "When you get through here, I will go with you to the corral, and show you what I have."

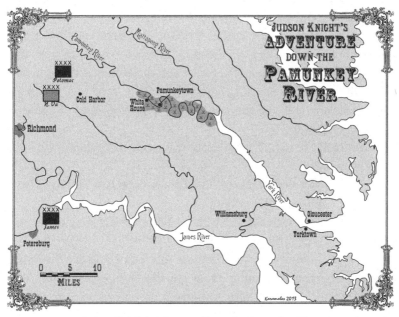

*Judson Knight's Adventure Down the Pamunkey River.*

That settled it, and I could see there was no way to get out of it, and might as well put on a cheerful air as any other. Mr. Dana then showed me a lot of dispatches, and marked them, saying, "This is to be telegraphed, and this is to be mailed," until he had all but three marked. Then he showed me those, saying as he did so: "If you are caught with these, you will be hung." I did not believe anything of the kind, and came near telling him that his telling me that would not make me one particle more diligent in endeavoring to get through without being captured. My impression was then, as it is now, that he thought I was a detailed soldier, and that if he could scare me into thinking I was in danger of losing my life by being captured with those documents, I would try harder to get through with them otherwise. He was careful not to tell me that a lieutenant with 16 men had been sent with the same dispatches the night before, and had returned with only half his men the same morning.

He wanted to know how many men I would take with me, and I said one. When Col. Ingalls saw that he had got through with me, he jumped from his seat, saying: "Come with me, now, and I will show you what horses I have."

On our arrival at the corral, I picked the largest and strongest looking horse there. The Colonel said: "That is a rough rider you have got there." I told him I knew it, but he had the bottom, I thought, and also remarked that I was not a lightweight. "No," said he, "that is so. He will serve you if you can stand the jolting. What kind of a man is the one going with you?"

"No better living. He will never leave one in the lurch. He is as good as gold."

"That is not what I mean," said the Colonel, smilingly. "How large is he? What will he weigh?"

"Why, he is a little fellow; won't weigh over 115 pounds."

"Let me pick him a horse," said the Colonel.

In a few minutes he selected one that one could see with half an eye, if he knew anything about a horse, would be an easy one to ride; then telling a negro to deliver the horses to any place I directed, he said to me: "Let me see the pass Rawlings gave you." After looking at it for a moment, he said, "Strange that some people never appear to think. Now, I am going to tell you something that may be of service to you, and I hope it will. We expect [Maj. Gen. William Farrar] Baldy Smith with the Eighteenth Corps [Army of the James] to land at the White House soon.[129] My advice to you is to go by the way of the White House. You may find him there. You have three dispatches for him in your bundle. If you should find him show him this."

*White House Landing, 1864. Library of Congress, LC-USZ62-60570.*

He was busy writing on the back of the pass, and when he handed it to me he had written an order on any Quartermaster in the United States service to furnish us with a steamboat, horses, or any transportation in their power, and to "facilitate these men in the discharge of their duty" by any means in their power, and a request to all Captains of gunboats to do the same. When I had read it I thanked him for his thoughtfulness and ready appreciation of the difficulties in the way of the accomplishment of our mission, which might be very much easier for [Jim] Hatton and myself by his forethought. Then, his way of doing it was so friendly.

How it became so well known Hatton and I were going to try and reach Yorktown we never found out; but in some way it became noised around that we were going, and several people came to us asking that we should carry letters for them; among others, Col. Collis, at the time commanding a regiment of zouaves [light infantry in the French Army, volunteers during the Civil War] attached to Headquarters as a guard, soon afterward promoted Brigadier-General, asked me to carry a letter for him directed to his wife, who had not heard from him in some weeks.[130] He never forgot it, and more than a quarter of a century afterward did not forget what he at that time considered a great favor.

After getting the horses we hastily swallowed not a "plate of soup," but our dinner, and started. About two or three miles from Headquarters we had to halt to let the Fifth Corps pass. Many of them had gone by when we came to the road they were marching on. The very last man in the corps was Joe Beggs, an old friend of mine. Capt. McDonagh, who was killed at Mine Run in the Fall of 1863, had told me before his death that Joe was in the army. He and myself had boarded in the same house before the war, and I had been on the lookout for Joe for months. It was a very hot day, and in addition to this regular load of blankets, cartridge-box, haversack, musket, etc., Joe had a camp kettle slung on his musket. He was hot, covered with dust, and tired. After the natural greetings of old chums who had not seen each other since the war began, I said: "Joe, will you have a drink of whiskey?"

"Will a duck swim? Have you got any?"

"Yes, but it is hot."

"That don't matter, so it is not boiling."

Unslinging a canteen from the saddle, I passed it over to him, apologizing at the same time for its being so hot. When he handed it back he said, "You have saved my life. I will have to hurry now to catch up; good-bye," and he was off.

Hatton and I crossed the road, and after going about two miles farther we came to a cavalry videt in the road. After showing our pass Hatton asked him what his regiment was, and the answer showed he was one of the Michigan Cavalry Brigade. I said: "Where is [Brig.] Gen. [George Armstrong] Custer?" He pointed into the woods on the left of the road, and answered: "In there, where you see that group of horsemen." As I had known Custer very well in 1861, while I was at Gen. Kearny's Headquarters where he was for a time Acting Assistant Adjutant-General, and at the same time commanding a company of the 2d Cav., of which he was Second Lieutenant, this was the first time I had a chance to see him since September, 1861, and I availed myself of it. He did not know me until I asked if he remembered Serg't Knight, at Kearny's Headquarters. There was no nonsense about Custer. I could see he was pleased to see me. After asking a number of questions, he said: "Where are you going?" I told him to Yorktown, and he replied, "I should not care to take such a trip," and said he hoped we would get through all right, wished us "bon voyage," and we parted. I never saw him afterward to speak with, and

only once at all, after the fall of Richmond, when his command had
started for Washington.

After leaving Gen. Custer we made good time and saw no one to
interfere with us until we came to a place called _____, which
was the name of an estate. The house stood on a high hill commanding a view of the road for some distance, both above and below it.
Here we met a Pamunkey Indian.[131] We stopped him to see what we
could learn about the situation of affairs. He told us that someone was
always on the watch from the house on the hill; also, that there was
a line of couriers from the White House to Richmond. In answer to a
question he said the couriers belonged to Col. Shingler's command,
and he believed Col. Shingler was from South Carolina.[132] He also
told us that he had just come up the road from where it crossed the
railroad leading from the White House to Richmond, and that there
was stationed there from 15 to 20 men; he had not counted them, but
was sure that there were at least 15 of them. We could not turn back
from hearsay.

As we went along, we found that we both had the same impression in regard to the Indian's truthfulness. Neither of us had a doubt
but what he had told the truth as far as he knew it. About two miles
from where we met the Indian we came upon the cavalry he had told
us of. There was but one man who was mounted, but I counted 16
horses, including his. The remainder of the men were lying around
under trees, endeavoring to keep cool. As soon as they saw us halt,
they commenced getting up and running to their horses. We saw that
it would be but a short time before they would be after us, so we
started back at a gallop, which we kept up until we passed the place
where we had met the Indian. As we were ascending a small hill I
noticed the ground was of such a nature that the tracks of our horses
could not be seen without very close observation. Small pines were
on both sides of the road, which was narrow at that point. We turned
out of the road and led our horses into the pines about 100 yards and
waited. In a few minutes about eight or 10 of our Confederate friends
came dashing up the road and went right on past. It was very nearly
dark when they passed, and we knew that they would come back soon
as wise as they went. We came back within a few feet of the road

and waited. It was nearly 9 o'clock when we heard them returning. We caught our horses by the nose to keep them from whinnying, or, as our Confederate friends called it, nickering. They were not in as great a hurry going back as they had been in coming, and were very much chagrined that they had not succeeded in overtaking us and were wondering who and what we were. It was finally decided that we were couriers, for one fellow said he had noticed the "big man" had a bundle in front of him that he felt certain was dispatches. He settled the matter by saying: "You need not say they were deserters, either from the Yankees or our army. They are couriers, and they have not gone far. They will be trying to get past us to-night, and if we keep a good lookout we will stand a chance to see them again." They little imagined we were then so close that we could hear every word they were saying.

After they had passed out of hearing we came out into the road and held a consultation. Jim said to me: "What shall we do now?" After thinking the situation over for a time I said: "Jim, you had better take the horses and go back. You will be able to reach our lines early in the morning."

"Well, what will you do!"

"The best thing to do will be for you to do as I say; take the horses and return. I will go down to the Pamunkey River and swim over, then work my way down to Pamunkeytown and get one of the Indians to land me on the south side of the York River, and depend on finding a horse in some stable and confiscating him, and then go on, provided I see nothing of Smith in the mean time. You know, there is a chance of meeting him at the White House. I am sure that I don't know this country well enough to attempt to flank those fellows down there as 'Tunstall's' in the dark."[133]

Said Jim: "What will they think of me at Headquarters, to come back and leave you alone, when we have not gone more—in fact, less—than one-third of the way? I hate to say it, old boy."

I argued with him some time, and finally he agreed to go back. I said to him, "The Pamunkey can't be more than two or three miles over there," pointing in a northeast direction. "I can perhaps reach the Indian village by daylight, and get to the south side of the York early in the morning, always provided Baldy Smith don't arrive in time to save going there. You can tell them at Headquarters that I said to you that they could rest easy about the dispatches being delivered, and you can tell them where and when you left me."

By this time it was about 10 o'clock at night. He wanted me to take the canteen, which I refused on account of its weight, although we had reduced that by some ounces, and parted. I plunged into the pines upon the other side of the road, and Jim started off on a gallop in the direction from which we had come.

When I started for the river I felt certain I would find it about two miles off. It was very slow time I made through the pines, which at that point must have been quite a mile through. When at last I came to a clearing I was not far from a house, so near that the dogs heard me, and I was escorted to the boundary of that plantation by curs of every degree, and they kept up a continual yelping as long as I was on the place. They stopped at a point I supposed to be the boundary of what they considered their bailiwick, and the chorus was immediately taken up by another set, who welcomed me to the hospitalities of their place. In this way I was escorted from one place to another, and several times was in danger of being bitten. It was only by the exhibition of "eternal vigilance" that I escaped it. The river was much farther off than I had anticipated, a bend in it that I knew nothing of causing me a much longer walk than I had expected. At last the river was before me and I hunted for a fence; one was soon found, from which I selected about a dozen suitable rails, which I placed in the water, keeping one end on the bank, then undressing, placed my dispatches and letters on them, my pistol on clothes on the end of the rails on shore, my top of the whole outfit, and taking the belt went down in the water and strapped the rails together tightly; then going to the end of the rails in the water bore down my weight on them until I had the raft afloat.

In a short time I had crossed the river, and nothing wet, with the exception of the belt. Resuming my clothes, and taking the dispatches under one arm, I started inland to find a road leading down stream. It was much farther than I anticipated; should think it nearly two miles before coming to one. When I at last found it I started down stream and walked fast. I had no idea that it was over three miles above Pamunkeytown.

*Tasked with taking dispatches from General Grant to Yorktown, Judson Knight was hunted through the swamps by Confederate cavalry and eventually slipped down the Pamunkey River shown here. William McIvaine, Library of Congress, LC-USZC4-6694.*

After going about a mile daylight overtook me, but I kept on for a short distance, when I heard a hello in my rear. Looking back I saw four horsemen coming along the road, and as they were evidently Johnnies, there was not the slightest desire on my part for an interview.

As good luck would have it, I discovered there was a swamp only a short distance ahead that extended for some distance toward the river. Immediately I sprang for the fence, which was a high one, "staked and ridered." As soon as they saw me climbing the fence, they started into a gallop and came for me. They were walking their horses when they first yelled at me. If they had said nothing they might have come close enough to me before I discovered them to have captured me before it would have been possible for me to get away from them. Evidently they had expected me to stop and wait for them to come up with me. When the long drawn-out "O-h-h-h-h, thar!" first struck on my ears, I felt under many obligations to them for their warning, which I would not have gotten, most likely, had it not been from the disinclination that all Confederate cavalrymen showed to exerting their horses except when obliged to. The reason probably was, that the horse he rode was private property.[134]

Before they got the fence torn down I was in the swamp. The first jump took me into water and mud above my knees. The surface water was clear, and the whole surface of the swamp was dotted over with small hummocks of bushes, with long grass growing in the soil among the roots. I passed several of the hummocks, as being, not only too small for my purposes, but not far enough from the shore. About 50 yards in I came to one which appeared to me to be the most suitable of any in sight. Passing along to the farther end, I crawled in among the bushes, so as to lie with my head toward the shore. As I crawled in three large water moccasins crawled out and wiggled their way through the water to another hummock and disappeared among the bushes and grass. I had got myself very comfortably settled, and knew that there was no motion among the tops of the bushes that could betray my hiding place, when I heard the sound of the horses' hoofs on the ground as they rode up to the spot where I had entered the swamp. From my covert I could not see them, and consequently knew they could not see me, so that I nearly laughed aloud, when I heard a voice saying, "Come out hyar. I see you. If you don't come I will fire."

At intervals of a few seconds the same voice would repeat the command to "Come out hyar," and breathe dire threats of vengeance if I did not. I was near enough to hear everything they said while they spoke in their ordinary tone of voices, but it was always the same voice that invited me to "Come out hyar," from which I came to the conclusion that my very persistent friend, who after each invitation would lie like Ananias by saying, "I see you."[135]

He finally became very profane and cursed "like a trooper." Had it not been for the dispatches there were times when I would have returned his "curses in kind, like the Confederate tax," and dared them to come in and take me out; and should they attempt it, had no fears as to the result, for I knew they could only come, at the most, two abreast, and I was good with a pistol at 60 yards for the size of a man's palm of the hand every shot.

I know they were up to 9 a.m. right on the shore of the swamp; then all noises ceased for nearly an hour. All of a sudden the same voice sang out: "Do you see anything of him?" "No," came back the answer from some place east of me at considerable distance. I could judge that they had sent three of their number around on the borders of the swamp east of me to see if I had come out, which I felt certain they could easily tell, for a look at the water in the vicinity of the hummock I was on looked roily yet. I heard them shouting to each other occasionally, until about 3 p.m., after which hour everything was silent.

* * *

*The National Tribune*
*January 19, 1893*
*Judson Knight, Washington, D.C.*

KNIGHT. BEING IN fear of some kind of an ambush, it struck me forcibly that the best thing to do was to keep quiet until dark. I had lain still all day, so as not to move the tops of the bushes, and came to the conclusion to still continue the same tactics, although it would have been a great relief to me to change my position, for it seemed to me as though every bone and muscle in my person was aching, so that it appeared as if I never would get over it. Added to this was hunger and thirst. I tried to dip up some water with my hands, but could not quite reach it, and would not move for fear they were watching and would see the tops of the bushes shake and give me away.

It was a terribly long afternoon, but at last the sun went down, and very soon afterward I emerged from my hiding place and very carefully made my way out to the solid land, coming to it with my head held as low as possible, and sweeping the circumference of a half-circle, to see if I could discover anything that looked like my Confederate friends or horses between myself and the sky. After looking and listening for sometime, I could neither see nor hear anything suspicious, and so emerged from the swamp. As soon as I reached the solid ground I took off my boots and emptied them of the water that had been there all day. Thinking what I should do myself if the position was reversed, and I the hunter instead of the hunted, I concluded not [to] go to Pamunkeytown by the road, but make my way to the river, and in case that no boat could be confiscated, swim to the other side and make my way down to the White House as best I could.

I soon found the river, and it was much nearer the road than where I had crossed the night before, owing to a bend in the stream at the place where I came to it. On reaching the river I discovered three men doing something on shore, and leaving my dispatches hidden in a safe place I "fetched a traverse and snaked my way" up to where I could hear what they were saying and see what they were doing. A short observation showed me they were negroes, hanging up a seine on stakes along the shore. I soon satisfied myself there were no white men among them and walked right up to them saying: "Good evening, boys; what luck?"

They showed me two sturgeon they had caught, one of which was the largest I ever saw. After speaking of the size as being something uncommon, I said: "Boys, have you seen any of our soldiers around to-day?"

A tall mulatto, who appeared to have charge of things said: "Yes; Lieut. Rodgers and three men swam their horses across here three times this evening; they went over first, then came back gain, and just before dark went over again."

"Can you tell me where they are now?"

"Just at dark they were over there," pointing with his hand, "by the old mill."

"I wish I had been there before they crossed the last time; I should have been glad to have met them. Do you know of any more of our men on this side of the river?"

"Look yere, maussa; you aint one of our men, you aint."

"I aint?" Well, tell me what I am, if I aint."

"You's a Yankee, you is."

"What makes you think so?"

"Oh, you don't talk like our folks does."

Up to that time I had imagined I was playing the part of a Confederate rather successfully, and to be detected by this fellow so easily made me ashamed. I had played the part of a Confederate surgeon only the previous Winter, and knew that there was no suspicion on the part of several families of white people of my being anything than what I represented myself to be. It lowered me several pegs in my own estimation. The thought instantly came to me, You had better own up; these people will tell you more if they see you trust them. So I said:

"Suppose I were a Yankee, would you betray me?"

"No, sah."

"Well, boys, you are right; I am a Yankee, and a very hungry one, too. Can you get me something to eat? I have plenty of money and will pay you well for anything you do for me."

"Don't want no pay, maussa. I will go right away and get you something," said the mulatto.

When he left I walked into the bushes, from which I had listened to their conversation, and the two who were left began asking all kinds of questions, one of which I remember well. They wanted to know if, when we got hold of any negroes, we cut off one of their arms. I told them no, of course, and asked why they asked such a question as that. They said the white folks told them so.

Much sooner than I expected, the mulatto came back, bringing with him two pones of hot corn bread, a large pitcher of buttermilk, and some of the fattest, rankest bacon I ever saw. Buttermilk I always detested; bacon, even the best of it, never was a favorite; but I got away with everything—buttermilk and all. After eating, I began inquiring in my turn, and found that I was about eight miles above the White House; that no Yankees had come there that day, they felt certain, as they would have heard the steamers' whistles; for they had been on the river all day. In looking at their boats, I found one about 10 feet long, made of five pieces of boards. The bow was about four inches wide, stern, 14 inches; sides and bottom made of half-inch stuff; bow and stern pieces of inch boards. In the center, the boat was about 20 inches wide. When I found the mulatto knew the channel of the river, I offered him $10 to take me down and land me at Pamunkeytown. Before getting through I offered $50, but soon discovered that money was no inducement to him. While friendly to me personally, and Yankees in general, and he hoped they would be successful, he thought more of himself than anything else. He also knew that Lieut. Rodgers and his three men were on the south side of the river; how many more might be there he could not tell. He also knew that in rowing he would make considerable unavoidable noise,

*"Suppose I were a Yankee, would you betray me?" was the question Knight posed to a slave he encountered on the Pamunkey. The man's reply was, "No, sah." And he didn't.*
*Edwin Forbes, Library of Congress, LC-USZ61-1353.*

and that a pistol-shot, even, fired from the shore, would kill, provided it hit, and his belief was that he would be killed if he went. He would sell the small boat and throw in a paddle for $5. He also had something that he had found on the south side of the river in 1862, after

McClellan had gone from there. "There was glass in both ends, and there was two of them fastened together, side by side," he said, and that if I would wait he would "go to the house and get it." He went and brought back field glasses, that, as near as I could judge after dark, was a tolerably good one, and I gave him $5 for that. I then made him the offer of $50 again to go down the river with me, and told him that I had lost all of that day, and that was the reason why I would give him that amount.

Said he: "You is the man that Lieut. Rodgers run in the swamp this morning soon after sun up. Well, sir, Lieut. Rodgers cussed like the debil for bein' a d_____d fool for to holler at you. Shore you carry dispatches, and he say he have you shore befoh you get two miles from dis place."

When there was no further use in endeavoring to overcome the timidity of the mulatto, I stepped into the boat, and seating myself in the stern, I began using the paddle, and soon discovered the tide was against me, and that progress was altogether too slow to reach Pamunkeytown or the White House in any reasonable time. The idea came to my mind to run in close to shore and use the paddle as a "settling pole." When I put it in practice it worked to be a charm. By using the blade so that I could draw it edgewise through the water, I soon found that I was going faster than I could walk, and making no noise that could be heard even at a short distance. Keeping along the north shore for a mile or more I found a bayou, and concluded, as I knew nothing of the channel, to follow the shore even if it did increase the distance considerably, believing that in this case "the longest way around is the shortest way home."

I had just got into the channel again, and was close in shore, under an almost perpendicular bluff, when I heard voices on shore that sounded above me. Looking upward I discovered silhouetted against the sky, a man and a woman on the top of the bluff. Scarcely had I discovered them when a stone thrown, no doubt, by the man, as large as he could conveniently hold, struck the water not a foot from the boat, barely missing it. Had it struck the boat it would have gone through the bottom like a shot, and stopped my trip by water. An instant's thought satisfied me that I had not been seen, which was confirmed immediately by the voice of the woman saying: "What a splash!" Giving several vigorous shoves with the paddle, I was soon out of reach of any more "dornicks," should the notion take the stranger to make another splash.[136]

There were plenty of bayous, which I followed the same configuration of until I felt certain that the distance to the White House could not be over four miles, when the sweetest music that ever struck mortal ears was plainly borne to mine. It was the shrill, and, at the same time, hoarse whistle of a steamer. I was making good progress when the sound first came to my ears, but when I heard it and knew, as I did, that Baldy Smith must have arrived at the White House, new vigor was imparted to my muscles, and the cockle shell I was in fairly flew.

Before going over a mile from where I was when the first whistle sounded five or six more were heard, which did not cause me to lessen my exertions. At last the whistling became almost continuous. I knew that there was a large house on the south side of the river, one mile above the White House, called Eltham. When I got there I concluded to land and sneak around to the negro quarters and wake one of them, and get him to guide me through the fields to the landing. Crossing the river and running my boat ashore, I stepped out and listened a moment, and could near no noise of any kind, except the cries of insects. Following a path that was plainly to be seen by the white sand where the grass had been trodden out by constant use, I passed around to the rear of the mansion and knocked on the door of one of the quarters. Immediately came a coarse, low growl from a dog that was somewhere outside, whether fastened or loose I could not tell. I got no response to my first rap and tried it again. This time a louder growl, and one that very plainly showed me the dog was a large one, came from the same direction as the first. After thinking the matter over a moment, it struck me that the most sensible thing to do would be to go back to the river and resume the boat, cross over to the north bank, and escape being fired at by our own pickets, which I imagined would be close to the shore immediately below Eltham. I had nearly reached the shore when a startled voice rang out, "Halt! Who goes there!"

"Who are you?" said I.

"Who are you?" said the challenger.

"Do you belong to the Union army?" said I.

What the answer was I don't remember, but I do know that it was such as convinced me I was parleying with a Northern man, and I said, "It is all right; I can tell you are a Union soldier."

Without saying this was true or not, he insisted on knowing who I was, and I told my mission. While the sentry and myself had been trying to ascertain each other's status, men had been rising from the ground all around me; three or four rose within a yard of me, and when I declared that I was carrying dispatches from Gen. Grant, one man, who had risen from the ground within two feet of me, said, "I will take this," and put his hand on the paddle which I was holding, with the blade resting on the ground. It looked to him in the darkness to be a gun. They huddled around me, and wanted to know how I got there. I answered that I had come down the river; which did not satisfy them at all.

"How did you come here, right where you are standing now?"

"As I told you before, I came down the river in a boat, and landed at the foot of this path; came up this path, and went to the rear of the house yonder to see if I could find a negro to guide me through the fields to the landing. When I knocked on the door, I heard a dog in the yard growl; the more I knocked the worse he growled. I did not know how many Johnnies might be around, for they were always prowling around just on the outskirts of any of our forces. In 1862, when we landed here under McClellan, two or three pickets were found the next morning with their throats cut, within a mile of this place. Knowing their nocturnal habits, and having a lively desire to keep my hide whole, I concluded to go back to my boat and resume my journey by water."

It took some time to make them believe that I had passed through them and they had not heard me, but it was more astonishing to think I had not heard anything of them. I took them down to the boat and got the dispatches, which were rolled up in my coat in the bow. When they saw the boat they began to believe me. The Lieutenant in charge said he would have to keep me until morning. There was not a match in the party, and there was no way of verifying my story until daylight.

\* \* \*

*The National Tribune*
*January 26, 1893*
*Judson Knight, Washington, D.C.*

KNIGHT. THE TENSION on my nerves, which had been considerably strained for the last 24 hours, had become relaxed, and I felt
more like having fun than anything else. When the Lieutenant said he
would have to keep me until morning, it put a stop to all funny business as far as I was concerned, and I told him it was his duty to either
send or take me to Gen. Smith at once, and I also said that he would
be very apt to get blamed for not doing it. A Sergeant in the party settled it when he said: "Yes, Lieutenant, you will get into trouble if you
don't take him to Gen. Smith at once."

*Maj. Gen. W. F. "Baldy" gave Knight every assistance to get his dispatches to*
*Yorktown. Library of Congress, LC-B811-2436.*

A guard was detailed, who surrounded me, and we set off across
the fields. I don't know how often we were tripped up by the running
blackberry or dewberry vines, but as near as I remember every one
of our party were down more than once before we made the mile that
separated us from the "White House." On our arrival Smith's tent had
been pitched, and he had just lain down, when the Lieutenant went
in, and told him who I said I was, and he ordered him to bring me in

immediately. When I came in he said: "Who are you?" After telling him, his next question was: "When did you leave Gen. Grant?" Upon answering this his next was: "When did you leave his Headquarters?"

"At noon yesterday."

"What have you been doing since?"

I gave him an outline of my experience, and said I came out of the swamp since dark. "I heard the first whistle about four miles up the river. Here are the dispatches for you; the remainder go to York-town; please to look at this," handing him Col. Ingall's order on Quartermasters.

"Capt._____," roared he. Capt._____ came into the tent. "Give this man the fastest boat you have got, and don't wait to unload anything."

Then to me: "I trust the remainder of your trip will be much pleasanter than the first part. Good-night."

In a few minutes—not to exceed 10, I think—I was sound asleep on the steamer, and remained so until we reached Yorktown. The steamer landed me and went back immediately. Going first to the telegraph office I delivered the dispatches that had to be telegraphed; then to the post office and got rid of the remainder, together with the letters. The next thing in order was to find an eating-house, where I ordered a breakfast regardless of expense. After breakfast I concluded to replenish my wardrobe. Socks, drawers, and shirt had suffered in the swamp, and they were replaced by new ones. The shirt was gorgeous, French cashmere. I could not burden myself with anything except what I could wear, consequently only one article of a kind was purchased, with the exception of paper collars. They were something that one had to make some sacrifice for, and I laid in a supply of at least a dozen of "Gray's patent molded collar."

After going to a barber shop and getting my hair cut and a shave, I made my appearance in the streets of Yorktown. My wide-brimmed straw hat and purple coat made me a conspicuous object, even without the extra adornments. I had mounted, and I was immediately surrounded by a crowd of both soldiers and officers all eager for news. Somehow they had learned from the telegraph office that one of Grant's Headquarters scouts was in town, and they picked me out immediately as the man. No certain news for some time had they heard, and I was literally besieged. It happened that I had seen most of the fighting at Spotsylvania Courthouse; had seen Johnson's Division when they were taken out of the works, and could give a pretty good description of the operations in that neighborhood for several days which culminated in the fight of the12th of May, 1864. I entertained them to the best of my ability for over an hour. I never saw men in my life so eager for news.

I was really glad about 2 p.m. when the Quartermaster came and told me he had signaled a steamer going up the river to run in. She came and I went aboard the steamer *Wyoming,* Capt. Lyttleton S. Cropper, of Havre De Grace, Md. Capt. Cropper was as whole-souled, genial a man as I ever met, and his boat, which had double engines, was fitted up as a hospital boat. When Capt. Cropper learned who I was, there was nothing on board too good for me. My name, as well as all of the scouts at Headquarters, was entered on his log-book, and a signal was agreed upon by which he would know any of the boys who might signal him from the shore, and he requested me to inform them that he would always be pleased to have any of them come on board and make themselves known to him at any time.

Some did go aboard of the *Wyoming* later, but who they were I have forgotten now, but I can remember they were loud in their praises of Capt. Cropper. There was a number of soldiers on board who were detailed as guards and nurses, under the charge of a Surgeon, whose name has escaped my memory. I met the Surgeon afterward, several months subsequent to the close of the war, and one of the men who was detailed, and serving board on that trip. His name was Jones, and he belonged in the town of Marcy, N.Y.

The next day, early in the morning, I found the *Wyoming* fast to the wharf at the White House, and found that the Eighteenth Corps had gone forward the day before. Leaving the boat, I started on foot up toward Tunstall's Station. By the time I had gone three or four miles I came upon one of our cavalrymen, and from him learned that Gen. Gregg was not far away. Gen. Gregg was a man I was very anxious to see, and I took a good many steps in various directions, as I was told by several cavalrymen where they thought he could be seen.

At last I found him. Showing him my pass, to let him know who I was, I asked him to loan me a horse, and to tell me where the Army Headquarters were to be found.

"See here," said he, "I have loaned you scouts horses before, and never saw them again."

"Well, General, you never loaned me one, did you?"

"No, I never did, and don't think I ever will. You people get a horse, and that is the last of him."

I could see by the twinkle in his eyes that he intended to let me have one and pressed the request saying: "You acknowledge you never let me have one. How is it possible for you to say you will never see him again. I will promise that he shall be returned as soon as it is possible to do so—in four or five days at the farthest."

"Well, I suppose I will have to try you. Now, if I don't get this horse back, it is the last time a scout ever gets one from me."

Calling a man, he ordered him to furnish me with a certain horse that I thought to myself would be small loss if he should never see again. On asking him where I would be apt to find Army Headquarters, he replied that he had no idea, but the night before they were at Old Church Tavern, which was several miles off.

I saw no one that could give me the desired information until I arrived at the tavern. The landlord was surly, and would scarcely give me a civil answer, until my patience became exhausted, when I asked him which of two roads both in sight (I had come in on a third one) they took when they left his place that morning, at the same time intimating that a civil and quick reply would be condu- cive to his well being. He very graciously pointed to the road that he said they had taken. I followed that road into the woods probably four miles, when shell began tearing through the tree-tops, and the farther I went the worse it got until I became satisfied the landlord had lied.

I remembered seeing a road about two miles back, leading to the left, and concluded to go back and try it. I had not gone far before I saw an infantry regiment come out of the woods and take the same direction on the same road that I was on. My horse soon overtook them, and turned out of the road of his own accord, and commenced passing them. We had passed over half the regiment before anyone bestowed more than a casual glance at us. At last a young fellow took a good look at the whole outfit, left the ranks, and ran toward the head of the regiment. Just before I came up I saw him speak to the Colonel. When I attempted to pass, the Colonel stopped me, and wanted to know who and what I was. I rode along by his side and showed him my pass, which was written on a printed form; explained to him that I had just got back to the army, and was looking for Headquarters. The young soldier meanwhile was on the other side of the Colonel, and as soon as he discovered that his Colonel was satisfied with my explanation, he attempted to sneak back to his company. I saw the move and stopped him, and said: "I want to have a few words with you, young man." A half-sullen look came to his face as I began. I thanked him for what he had done, and told both him and the Colonel that I was frequently disgusted with the way men could go through the army without being stopped by anyone; that it appeared to me sometimes that they did not care whether a man was spy or not, nor whether he found out what was going on, and went direct to the enemy and reported. I also told them that frequently I had heard other scouts make the same complaint, and I said: "Now, my young friend, I am glad to see that one man, at least, in this regiment cared enough to put himself to some trouble to find out whether I was a friend or enemy." The sullen look had disappeared; he had expected a cursing, which I am sorry to say was what a private soldier got more than was good for him.

I found Headquarters in the course of a couple hours after leaving that regiment, which was an Ohio one. The battle of Cold Harbor was fought the next day, I think; if not on that day, within a couple or three days, at all events. How long the army stopped here after the 4th of June I can't remember. My old regiment (2d N.J.) went home from Cold Harbor, and a day or two afterward one of the guards at the "bull-pen,"[137] a member of the 20th N.Y.,[138] came to me and said: "There is a man in the bull-pen who says he belongs to your old regiment, and wants to see you."

*The Bull Pen, as the prisoner of war stockade was called at the Headquarters, Provost Marshal General, Army of the Potomac. Alfred R. Waud, LC-DIG-ppmsca-21194*

I went back with him, when a young fellow who was on the inside of the line of guards pressed forward as far as the guard would let him, and said: "Don't you know me, Sergeant?"

I took a good look at him, and answered: "No; I can't say that I do."

He said: "Sergeant, I used to belong to your old regiment."

"What company were you in?"

"G, and yours was H."

"Yes; that is right. So you were in Capt. Close's Company. How did you get in here? The regiment has gone home, and I can't see how you should be in the bull-pen."

He then told me that he was in one of the Wilderness fights, and was wounded; had been sent to Washington to a hospital, and as soon as he could leave it applied to be sent to his regiment; had come down the Potomac to Port Royal, and had helped to guard a wagon-train from there to Army Headquarters; when he got there his regiment was gone. His story had not been believed, and he had brought up in the pen. After listening to his story he said:

"You remember me now, don't you, Sergeant?"

I could not recollect him, and said so. Tears came into his eyes as I turned away and walked to Col. Sharpe's tent, who at that time was Deputy Provost-Marshal-General of the Army of the Potomac.[139] I went in and told the story to Sharpe, and when I got through he said: "Do you remember him?"

"Hardly; but I know he tells the truth."

"Well, said he, "it is a shame, and we will have him out."

He then wrote an order to turn the boy over to me, and told me to go and get him. When he came the Colonel questioned him a few minutes, gave him an order for transportation and the paper he would need to keep him out of trouble with military authorities, and turned him loose. He was one of the most grateful boys I ever saw. He was not over 21 years old, and lived in Bloomfield, N.J. His name has escaped my memory. Within a few days I got a chance to send the borrowed horse to Gen. Gregg, and did so.

# IX

# Petersburg

*EDITOR'S NOTE: Judson Knight and his fellow scout Anson B. Carney were both eyewitnesses to the failure of the Union commanders to seize Petersburg when it was essentially defenseless, a state they discovered by personal reconnaissance and prisoner interrogation.*

*The National Tribune*
April 27, 1893
Judson Knight, Washington, D.C.

KNIGHT. IN MY last article, I spoke of endeavoring to get John N. Van Lew to become a scout, following him several miles on the road to the White House and using every means to accomplish this end, but failing signally. When we parted, he said to me: "I will tell you something that may be of value to you. If you can ever get into communication with my mother or sister, they are in a position where they might furnish you with valuable information. Their names are both Elizabeth N. Van Lew." I walked with him several miles and urged him to stay with us, for patriotism if nothing else, but did not succeed.

At some point during this campaign, after leaving Spotsylvania Courthouse, a colored man named [Richard] Johnson came into our lines. He was a preacher, and belonged to Maj. Thos. Doswell of Hanover County, Va., the father of the present Maj. Doswell, of the same

County. When he came to us he had a running mare that would have been white had she not been covered with small red spots. I think the name of the mare was Nina. According to Johnson's account she had never lost a race. Johnson said he was a preacher. He certainly knew more of the country and made a better guide than any colored man that I ever saw while with Headquarters of the Army of the Potomac.[140]

Milton G. Cline was my immediate predecessor as Chief of Scouts at the Army of the Potomac Headquarters. He was a Sergeant in the 3d Ind. Cav. The mare was purchased from Johnson by Serg't Cline for $400. It soon became nosed around Headquarters that Nina was a celebrated racer, and it was decided that it was hardly the right thing for an enlisted man to have so valuable a piece of horseflesh; so that [Brig] Gen. M. R. Patrick, Provost-Marshal-General made Johnson give Cline his money back, and the mare fell into the hands of Col. [Rufus] Ingalls, Chief Quartermaster of the Army. I never knew positively, but my private opinion has always been that Johnson was $400 out on that transaction.

The Summer after the close of the war I was introduced to Maj. Thomas Doswell one day in Richmond, Va.[141] After a short conversation with him I asked if he had ever owned a negro preacher who ran away from him in 1864, taking with him a running mare called Nina. He expressed much surprise that I should know of them, and said he would like to know what had become of the mare; the preacher, of course, was beyond his reach; still he spoke kindly of him, but said he was a much better groom than an expounder of the gospel. I told him where his mare was, and heard through a granddaughter of his that he had recovered her.

During this campaign at some point, I think, at the North Anna River, Anson B. Carney rejoined us after an absence of three months. Carney was one of the eight Headquarters Scouts who went on the Kilpatrick and Dahlgren raid, and was riding by his side when the volley was fired that ended Dahlgren's life. One of the balls struck Carney and passed through his body. He was supposed to be dead and left lying on the ground, and came to his senses after a while and managed to get a stray horse and made his escape.

A cousin of his, Phil Carney, was captured at this time, taken to Richmond, successfully played sick, was put into the Shockoe Hospital, where he and a young cavalryman, who was one of the raiding party, managed to secure Confederate uniforms, and one day when the doctors made their rounds through the hospital, Phil stuck a pen behind his ear, picked up one of the hospital books, and he and his friend walked a short distance behind the doctors. When they came to the guard at the door the young cavalryman asked Phil how many Yankees there were in the hospital, to which he made some kind of a reply that satisfied the guard, and they walked out. They both reached our lines and rejoined their commands.[142]

## HEADQUARTERS ARMY OF THE POTOMAC, OFFICE OF PROVOST-MARSHALL-GENERAL,

*June 25, 1864.*

*General HUMPHREYS:*

*Phil. Carney, one of our men who was captured in Colonel Dahlgren's expedition, and Charles McCormick, of the First Michigan Cavalry, taken April 8, 1864, near Falmouth, escaped from Richmond last Monday, about 9 o'clock in the morning, went through the Chickahominy Swamp to the White House, and arrived here this morning. They were employed as nurses in General Hospital No. 21, in Richmond, to attend to the Union soldiers there [wounded], and on the night of the 19th instant, an order having been received to send to the front every man capable of bearing arms, the sergeants in charge of the wards, and the guards about the hospitals belonging to the army, were relieved by militia [boys scarcely able to bear the guns], and the next morning Carney and McCormick, having got on Confederate jackets, pretended to be clerks, took up the books as if they were such, and passed the guards. The troops who were thus relieved, it was understood, were sent to attack our forces at White House. At that time, and immediately previous, there were no troops in Richmond or in the fortifications about it, except the small number which the above order withdrew. There were of our men then in Richmond about 900 sick and wounded and about*

> *200 well men, and a week before 1,000 had been sent to Americus, Ga. Carney says that there are three bridges between Fort Darling and Richmond. He was so told by a Union man there. He claims that there are a number of such, and that it is not difficult to find them out. Hogan is still in irons. Dykes and Jake Swisher have been sent to Georgia.*
>
> *Very respectfully,*
>
> *GEORGE H. SHARPE,*
> *Colonel, &c.*
>
> *OR*, Vol. XL, Part 2, pp. 403-4

An account of my trip to Yorktown with dispatches, which was published a few weeks ago, shows that from near old Hanovertown to Cold Harbor I was absent from the army; just how many days I can't say. Soon after the day the charge was made against the enemy's works where it had been said we lost 10,000 men in 10 minutes, a number of our so-called guides were sent away to Washington. Most of them I have never heard from since. Three or four I have met since the war closed.

When the army left Cold Harbor we marched to the James River, where a pontoon bridge had been laid across that river below Wilcox's Landing. The first time I ever saw the berries of the mulberry tree was here. There were several very large and tall trees that must have been at least 160 years old. I, among several others, climbed one of the trees and ate a good many of the berries. They were longer and about the size of large blackberries and much sweeter.

When Headquarters crossed the river quite a force had proceeded us. The bridge was protected by several monitors, both above and below. When we struck the south shore a battery of Regular artillery was in a field on the right side of the road. Standing on a barrel was one of the soldiers belonging to the battery, so close to the road that everyone who crossed the bridge could not help seeing him, with a board suspended across his breast on which was painted, "Thief." It was the worst form of punishment I ever saw in the army.

As soon as we crossed the river a number of us went ahead to see what the country was like. Not one of us had ever been on that side

of the river before. We soon came to a burning building. Why it had
been set on fire I never knew. I took the first road we came to heading south from the road the troops were on, who were on their way to
Petersburg under command of [Maj.] Gen. [Gouveneur K.] Warren.
About a half mile through the woods I came to a clearing. I jumped
my horse over the fence and soon discovered that four or five infantrymen and a drummer boy had proceeded me. They evidently had not
arrived many minutes ahead of me. A log house, inhabited by a large
family, who were grouped in and around the doorway, with fright,
horror, and despair depicted on their faces, were looking at the antics
of the drummer, who was evidently determined to make an attack
on a row of beehives but a short distance in front of the house. He
advanced gallantly, closely followed by the infantrymen. I had hardly
time to take in the situation before the drummer made a rush and upset
a straw hive, and immediately dropped upon his knees and began tearing out the comb, while his support began a frantic dance and the
family made a rush to get inside as the bees sailed out for revenge. I
staid not upon the order of my going, but went. That scene has always
been one of the most prominent of the many very comical ones I saw
during the war. I would like to know who the drummer-boy was.

*Stealing beehives. Author's collection.*

About 4 p.m. we came out on the high ground to the east and in full view of Petersburg. No Confederate troops were to be seen, and the outer line of works captured by [Brig.] Gen. [Augustus Valentine] Kautz [commanding the cavalry division of the Army of the James] a day or two before were standing there unmanned. The troops in the advance were halted and bivouacked for the night. It could not have been over two and a half miles from the heart of the city. A little before dark, Cline and I rode down the Prince George Courthouse road, through the works that had been captured by Kautz, very nearly to the top of the hill. Some gasworks were just to the right of us. A few shots, not over a dozen altogether, were fired at us. Cline said to me if we had a hundred men we could go in and do what we pleased. My belief was that we could, but next morning it was too late.

## U. S. GRANT'S EXPLANATION OF THE FAILURE TO SEIZE PETERSBURG

*I then, on the 14th [June] took a steamer and ran up to Bermuda Hundred to see General Butler for the purpose of directing a movement against Petersburg, while our troops of the Army of the Potomac were crossing [the James River].*

*I had sent General W. F. Smith back from Cold Harbor by the way of the White House, thence on steamers to City Point for the purpose of giving General Butler more troops with which to accomplish this result. General Butler was ordered to send Smith with his troops reinforced, as far as that could be conveniently done, from other parts of the Army of the James. He gave Smith about six thousand reinforcements, including some twenty-five hundred cavalry under Kautz, and about thirty-five hundred colored infantry under Hinks.*

*The distance which Smith had to move to reach the enemy's lines was about six miles, and the Confederate advance line of works was but two miles outside Petersburg. Smith was to move under cover of night, up close to the enemy's works, and assault as soon as he could after daylight. I believed then, and still believe, that Petersburg could have been easily captured at this time. It only had about 2,500 men in the defenses besides some irregular troops, consisting of citizens and employees in the city who took up arms in case of emergency. Smith started, as proposed, but his advance encountered a rebel force intrenched between City Point their lines outside of Petersburg. This position he carried, with some loss to the enemy; but there was so much delay that it was daylight before his troops really got off from there.*

U. S. Grant, *Ulysses S. Grant: Personal Memoirs of U. S. Grant, Selected Letters 1839-1865* (New York: Library of America, 1990), p. 509.

> EDITOR'S NOTE. Smith was too mindful of the debacle at Cold Harbor and undertook exhaustive reconnaissance that ate up the clock. His hand was also stayed by the rumor that Lee's army was momentarily about to arrive. He simply lost his nerve instead of pressing every effort to bounce into an essentially undefended city. He was relieved on July 19th.

During the night a portion of Lee's army had arrived and everyone knows how long it was before we went into Petersburg. We were now in a part of Virginia where none of us had ever been, and the first thing we set about was to learn all we could about the country. About the second day after our arrival several parties started, some going east and south, while I started with a party towards to the southwest. I can only recall one man for certain who was with me, and that was Frank McCord. After we crossed the Norfolk & Petersburg Railroad we kept on until we came to the Jerusalem Plank road, which led directly south from Petersburg. When about a quarter of a mile from the Plank road we came to a handsome house, painted white with green blinds, wide verandas—a very comfortable and homelike looking place. Just before reaching the house one of the boys rode under a shed and found a large [two words intelligible] filled with manufactured tobacco of the kind used to be called nail-rod. We took a few plugs and went on.

An old negro met us as we passed the house and handed me a letter, saying as he did so, "Is you Col. Spear?" I told him I was not Col. Spear, and he advised me to read the letter anyway, which I did, and found that the owner of the house knew the Colonel, and had left this letter for him asking that his property might be protected, and asking him to take possession of the house and make it his headquarters. After reading I handed the letter back to the darky, and told him that I did not know when Col. Spear would be along. On our way back to camp that night we helped ourselves to several pounds of tobacco apiece. The old negro major-domo of the premise did not see us get it.

The next day we came out again and extended our rambles in various directions, without finding any Confederate troops outside the city of Petersburg. Before leaving camp we had provided ourselves with sacks, so that we could carry about 10 pounds apiece of the tobacco. The major-domo saw us this time, and came down to the shed and threatened us with the vengeance of his master. He said his master would raise hades with us. Poor old fellow, he thought his master was all-powerful, and could do with us about what he pleased.

One day, in going out, I recollect stopping opposite a narrow road through the pines, about in the rear of where Fort Hell was afterward built. We could see the enemy's works through the opening in the pines. They were nearly a mile away. After looking a moment, I made the remark that it would not do for us to stay there long, as the Johnnies would think we were a group of officers and fire on us. Frank McCord made a jesting remark about my being afraid. He had hardly uttered the words when a ball fired from the rebel works struck the ground about 30 feet from him, ricocheted and bounded over his horse, passing about a foot in front of his breast, and went on with an angry whizzz! McCord was a detailed man, by order of Secretary Stanton, from Battery H. 1st Ohio L.A [Light Artillery]. Wood Dodd was another one from the same battery.[143]

* * *

*EDITOR'S NOTE: Scout Anson Carney's account in a Bradford County, Pennsylvania, memoir supports Knight's assertion that more celerity on the part of the Union forces would have bounced them into Petersburg against minimal opposition.[144]*

CARNEY. One day General [Benjamin] Butler [commanding the Army of the James] had taken 200 prisoners near Petersburg. I had a long ride that day, and upon coming into camp looked forward to a comfortable supper and a good rest. I was called to headquarters, however. Here I received a verbal order [almost surely from Col. Sharpe], something like this: "General Butler has captured some prisoners near Petersburg. Now, Carney, get on your horse and gallop all the way there and all the way back, even if you kill your horse and see that you don't get gobbled up, for I want you to get back and let me know what troops have been fighting General Butler to-day; also, whether General Lee's army has arrived there."

I rode rapidly away, some shells passing high over my head enroute. I found the prisoners in a sheep pen guarded by colored troops. Explaining my orders to the proper officer, I jumped over the

*Fort Mahone, known as Fort Damnation, one of the major forts in the defenses of Petersburg, after its capture on April 18. Knight found the defenses nearly empty when Grant stole a march on Lee to strike at the city, but the Union commanders hesitated while Confederate reinforcements rushed to man them. Library of Congress, LC-B811-3211.*

fence and commenced talking to the rebs something after this fashion: "Well, Johnny, you had quite a skirmish to-day?"

"Yes, we did; and when Uncle Bob [General Robert E. Lee] gets here he will pay back for it."[145]

"Hasn't he got to Petersburg yet?"

"No, but he is coming."

"What regiment do you belong to?" The regiment was named and then I passed on to another prisoner. In this way I ascertained that only rebel General Kershaw's brigade had been fighting Butler's troops, but that this brigade would soon be re-inforced from Lee's army. I returned to headquarters with the information. It was thought by many officers at headquarters at the time, that if the information had been obtained a little earlier, Petersburg might have been captured that day.

*The National Tribune*
May 4, 1893
Judson Knight, Washington, D.C.

KNIGHT. AFTER WE had been in front of Petersburg for a week or two, although we had been busy and had done some hard work, it seemed to me that it was time something tangible should result from our service. Both armies were extending their lines to the left. There was no reason that all of us should stay in camp every night, and I concluded to make a night-trip and see if I could learn anything of importance. I left Headquarters in time to cross the Jerusalem Plank road before dark, saying nothing to anyone of my intention, and not even asking for a pass to get out of our own lines. It placed me in exactly the same position a rebel scout would have been in had he been inside our lines and wanted to get out.

Striking out to the left and rear from Headquarters where I knew I would find no troops, I placed such distance between myself and our lines that I felt safe in changing my course to the west and crossed the Jerusalem Plank road in the dark on the farm of Mr. James. As I crossed one of the fields I saw a number of men and a force belonging to [Judson] Clark's 2d N.J. Battery. I kept on through the woods after leaving James' farm, until I was quite sure that I was beyond our left flank, and then turned directly north toward Petersburg, until I could see that but a short distance ahead was cleared ground; then I looked for a pine thicket and crawled under the lower branches and slept till daylight. As soon as I could find a good place to stow myself away where I could get a good view I did so, and the Confederate works already built and those in the process of construction south and west from Petersburg were in plain sight.

As soon as they had finished breakfast large working parties, consisting much to my surprise, of white men, came out and went to work with a will that astonished me. Time passed very monotonously, after watching them for an hour or two. About 11 a.m. came a slight change in the program. Quite a large body of troops came out under arms, and I began to think I was going to witness a brigade drill. More soldiers came, until I felt certain I was to witness the evolution of a division. Still more soldiers came, and after a very few maneuvers arms were stacked and they settled down with apparently nothing to do but lie on the ground and kick up their heels, as plenty of them were doing.

They were quiet so long that I became convinced they were not there for any purpose of drill. It finally dawned on my benighted brain that it was just possible they might contemplate making an attack on our left flank. The longer I thought of it the more it seemed probable that this was just what they were ordered out there for, and I began to get uneasy. I knew I could not begin to reach Headquarters in time if the attack was to come off that evening.

I had also an experience of reporting to people who did not know me; besides, I had no credentials with me, and had always been careful to make as few acquaintances as possible. I felt certain that if I was to go and report to the first troops I came across I was sure to be insulted, if not arrested as a possible spy for the rebels, for I had just that kind of experience many times. There was but one way for me to do to make what I partly knew and partly surmised of use, and that was to make my way to Clark's battery and let them know. They were about four miles away and first I had to make my way to the rear by a process William Gilmore Sims called "snaking" [low-crawling].[146] I dared not to raise my feet until I had gotten some distance to the rear. After I rose up from the ground I still made my way south, until I felt certain I could get through to Clark's battery without seeing any other troops.

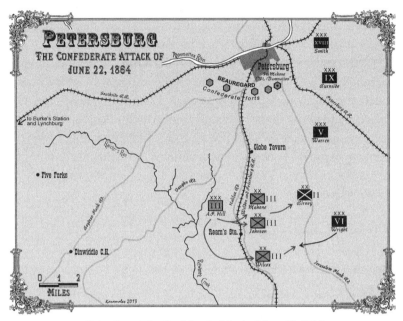

*Petersburg: The Confederate Attack of June 22, 1864.*

When I reached Clark's quarters he said to me, "What's the news?" His brother, Lieut. Clark, had previously extended up an invitation to partake of some liquid refreshments. As soon as that had been attended to I told the Captain that an attack was going to be made that afternoon or early the next morning. The words were no sooner uttered than I was politely informed by a man, who wore the eagle of a Colonel on his shoulder straps, that I was much more scared than hurt and he did it in so offensive manner that I immediately left the tent without making a reply.

When I reached the Jerusalem Plank road which was but a few paces from Clark's tent, I turned down toward Jones' house. Some of the pickets honored me with a few bullets. Soon I heard some one running behind me, and soon Lieut. Edward Clark sang out to me: "Wait, Jud; I want to talk to you."

When he came up, he said: "The Captain sent me after you to see if you meant what you said while in the tent just now?"

"Certainly I meant it. You are sure to be attacked either this evening or early in the morning, and when it does come it will be from the west. You ought to have a strong breastwork thrown up facing that way instead of the one our guns are in now facing Petersburg."

The Lieutenant went back, and I skirmished for food, having eaten nothing in 24 hours. After the food question was settled I continued on my way to Army Headquarters. Long before reaching there I heard quite a row in the direction from which I had come, but too far away to tell exactly what it was, so I said nothing about where I had been or what I had seen, but concluded to let them hear through the regular channels. Twenty years after I got the following letter in answer to a query:

*Newark, N.J., April 24, 1884*

*Capt. JUDSON KNIGHT.[147]*

*MY DEAR CAPTAIN: You ask me if I recall y our being at the Jerusalem Plank road in June, 1864. I certainly do. You came to where I was stationed. Just to the left of the road as it crosses the ravine close to Fort Hell, and where Fort Davis was afterward placed, and told us that we would have lively work soon, as the enemy were going to attack, and although some of the infantry offices near did not put much faith in what you said, not knowing who you were, I, who did know you, was satisfied I should have warm work and prepared for it to the best of my ability. I told the officers when you left that you were a scout at Army Headquarters, and that your information could be fully relied on, and am satisfied that the attack, which was made in a very short time thereafter, would have proved much more disastrous than it did, but for your kindly warning.*

*Cordially yours,*

*A. J. Clark, late Captain, commanding*
*Battery B. N.J. Art.*

*The rear of Fort Sedgwick, or Fort Hell as it was more often called, past which Judson Knight frequently rode as he departed for his scouting forays into Confederate lines during the siege of Petersburg. Alfred R. Waud, Library of Congress, LC-DIG-ppmsca-22391.*

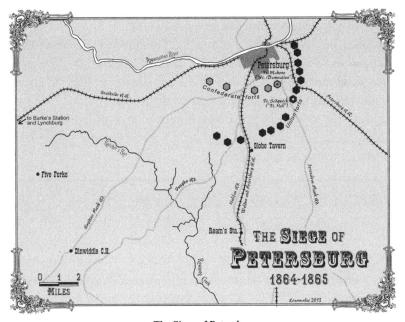

*The Siege of Petersburg.*

The Captain's modesty is only equaled by his bravery. When Lieut. Clark went back and told him what I had said, he not only set his own men at work, but obtained a detail of infantry and set up a strong work facing westward, and only had time to get his guns in it before the enemy came down the line from the left flank and had things their own way until they came to Clark. He had Napoleon guns, and used them with such effect that the Johnnies stopped in their wild career. McKnight, who was west of Clark, lost his battery, and a portion of another one was also captured. I have been told since that had it not been for Clark's battery that day the Army of the Potomac would most likely have met one of its worst reverses.

I have to own with deep humiliation, that I was rather pleased to hear that the regiment commanded by that colonel who said I was more scared than hurt was torn all to pieces. The feeling was entirely wrong, but I could not help it. The Colonel was from New York City, and named either Burns or Byrne; I never could get definite information from Lieut. Clark as to what it really was. He has kept a "gin-mill" in New York, somewhere on the East Side, and I spent several nights in searching for him, but never found him.

Since the war—in fact, within the last three years—in talking with my ex-Confederate friend, Mr. James Caperton, the one who introduced me to Byrd Lewis, I have been convinced that the attack on our left flank was under the leadership of the Confederate Gen. Mahone. He told me of their capturing a battery of iron guns and hauling them over our works with the horses of Demont's Maryland battery, in which he belonged.[148]

*HEADQUARTERS ARMY OF THE POTOMAC,*

*June 22, 1864—6 p.m.*

*Lieutenant-General GRANT:*

*Birney advanced this morning his left to envelop the enemy. Wright advanced on his left by a road that separated him somewhat from Birney. Wright soon found the enemy's skirmishers and reported them in considerable force. Fearing Birney's left would be exposed, Barlow was ordered to move back so as to make connection with Wright. While doing this he was vigorously attacked and thrown into some confusion. At the same time Gibbon on the plank road (Birney's right) was very warmly attacked and forced back from his first line, losing I regret to say, four guns. Order was soon restored, but in view of these facts I directed the withdrawal of Wright, so as to make a secure connection with Birney. At this time all is quiet. It is reported, but I fear not reliably, that Gibbon has retaken his rifle-pits and guns. I have ordered Birney and*

*Wright at 7 p.m. to make a vigorous attack and try to drive the enemy back. Prisoners report the whole of A. P. Hill's corps, with others, in our front. They say they marched out of their breastworks or fortifications, advancing nearly a mile. We have taken prisoners from each of the divisions of Hill's corps. The morale of the men is not so good as I would like it, but I deem it of the utmost consequence to take the offensive. Scouts on our left report Wilson at Reams' Station, on the Weldon railroad, at 10 a.m. today. They saw he burned the station and did other damage, but on retiring was attacked by cavalry and infantry. I hope to send you after dark some favorable news. A prisoner, who states he was on provost guard at Petersburg, reports the arrival there day before yesterday of troops from Johnston's army.*

GEO. G. MEADE,
*Major-General.*

*OR*, Vol. XL, Part 2, p. 304.

\* \* \*

*EDITOR'S NOTE: Patrick McEneany, whose supporting account is below, was one of Knight's closest associates among the scouts in the BMI.*

The National Tribune
August 17, 1891
Patrick McEneany, Pension Office, Washington, D.C.

McENEANY. After the Wilson raid the scouts were organized into parties. Judson Knight was made chief, and ordered to establish headquarters at City Point.[149] Four of us went with him. The Confederates were getting very annoying on the opposite side of the James River, and it was decided to keep a close watch in this direction. We had experienced a surprise in 1862 at Harrison's Landing, when the rebels did considerable damage. The 5th Cav. boys will remember that night.[150]

One morning, about the latter part of July, 1864, the mail boat started down the James River from City Point to Washington, and when nearing Harrison's Landing was fired upon by Rebel pieces of artillery posted behind a clump of willows. They fired too soon. She was out of range, escaped uninjured, and returned to City Point.

That evening the gunboat *Dawn* escorted her down the river and Knight, Hatton, Foster and I were sent on board a double-ender with a detachment of the 20th N.Y. to land at any point which Knight might select.[151] We were to signal the infantry in case we were attacked. Knight, Hatton and I started toward the Chickahominy, leaving Foster to look out for the signal. We had gone about a mile and a half when we came across the rebel battery. We hastened back and told the Captain of the gunboat what we had seen. Knight described the location, etc. The Captain gave a command to his men, and in a short time the two big guns on board were discharged.

The following evening we started on another trip. On the way one of the sailors gave me a dark-lantern to signal with. It was an improvement on our usual way of signaling, which was matches. I used to conceal this lantern in the hollow of an old willow tree, in a bend of the James River, between City Point and Harrison's landing. I left it in its hiding place. It was marked U.S. G.B. *Sassacus*.

When we landed Knight went alone to ascertain what damage had been done by the two shells from the gunboat, leaving us on the bank of the river to await his return. Toward morning he got back and reported that one shell exploded in the woods about 100 yards beyond the battery, cutting off a great many limbs from the trees, and the second one tore up the ground to the right and rear. That battery must have scampered up the Darbytown Pike toward Richmond in short order. After that there was a squadron of cavalry stationed at Harrison's Landing. I think it was the 1st Maine. The scouts were kept busy on the left flank and up the James River to Haxall's Landing, near Turkey Bend, where the gunboat *Commodore Morris* was anchored.[152]

Late one evening Knight and I started on a trip, and, going up to Haxall's Landing, we went on board the Commodore Morris, and informed the officer in charge who we were, telling him we would not return that night unless compelled to; that in case we did we would make ourselves known by a signal, which we would explain to the guard on the shore. We went ashore, and Knight explained everything to the guard.

Then we started in the direction of the "old gips." We kept on all night, and remained in the woods all the next day. Having obtained the desired information, we started back toward the river. It was a little too early in the evening for us to travel, and we went into an empty barn nearby. We were there but a short time when a Confederate scout—whom we knew, by the name of Roche—came up the road and stood looking in the direction from which we came. Either one of us could have killed him. After dark we started back. When we got close to the Landing Knight said to me, "Go ahead and give the signal," which I did. To our great surprise we heard the locks of their guns click, and we immediately dropped.

They fired over us. The guard then moved toward the gunboat, and we hastened toward them, shouting to them not to shoot. Lucky for us the two big guns on board did not open. The guard told us they were instructed not to hail any one, but to shoot. Just then a voice from the gunboat called: "Ashore, there!" The nervous Corporal answered: "Prisoners." Then the command came: "Bring your prisoners aboard!" We were taken on board, and could hear the Captain from his cabin bellowing: "Put them in irons!" He was evidently intoxicated. We did not see him at all. However, his orders were carried out. A big pompous-looking officer managed the affair, and ordered the Master-at-Arms to put them on Knight first. When the Master was putting the irons on me, I recognized him as an old comrade of mine, whom I had served with in Utah. His name was Bob Crawford, formerly of the 10th Infantry. I said: "Bob, put those on carefully, or I'll break them." He looked up, and recognizing me, exclaimed in great astonishment: "Mack, is that you?" He told the officer that I was a scout; that he knew me, and the result was we were released. We were well-treated by them after that. We had them to signal our tug, which was down the river some distance, and we boarded her and got back to Headquarters.

The whole trouble was the guard were 90-day men doing duty on the James River, and they were green at the business. If we had related our experience at Headquarters we would have gotten those officers into a serious scrape; but we had compassion on them, as they assured us that it would never occur again.

CARNEY. IN THE city of Richmond lived an intelligent lady, who furnished us with very valuable information. She was aided by a railroad man, who reported to her various movements (by rail) of rebel soldiers, artillery, ammunition, etc.[153] The news was sent to our lines by a man who worked his way past the rebel picket at night, and who was met by a couple of us scouts somewhere agreed on between the Chickahominy and James Rivers. We had a system of cipher, which was used for greater security, and even some of our scouts who carried the news were unable to read the messages. At one time during the winter of '64-65, I came into headquarters from a trip in Richmond, and reported to General Grant that with 1,000 good men I could walk into Richmond, as part of the line northeast of the city was very weak. The general did not act on this information, because he was not seeking Richmond so much as Lee's army. Lee's army was what he was after, and he got it, you bet!

Late in the fall of 1864, while eating dinner in our mess room at City Point, an orderly came in and said that General Grant wished to see me. On my return to the mess room I told the boys: "Grant wants to know what is done with our men who desert to the rebels? The enemy has been offering safe conduct to all our men who desert, and General Grant wants to know how they manage it." The boys asked me whether I was going to find out. I told them that the general offered me $300 extra pay if I would desert. I said I would sleep on it and give my answer in the morning. Next day I decided to go. I left our quarters in the afternoon; they did not see me again for seven weeks. They began to think I was a "goner," but one morning I stepped off the mail boat from Washington and walked into the quarters and asked for some breakfast. You can imagine whether the boys were surprised or not.

Before departing I had to secure a pass (as was necessary) to go through our picket lines. Before I reached the rebel picket lines I tore up the pass so as not to be suspected. I did not have far to go to be halted by a Johnny, who asked me what I wanted. I told him

The possible origin of Carney's mission is found in the message from Capt. John McEntee to Col. George H. Sharpe, Chief, Bureau of Military Information. Certainly, Carney matched McEntee's requirements.

*HEADQUARTERS, ARMY OF THE POTOMAC,*

*September 7, 1864*

*DEAR COLONEL: Have you a man down there who has good common sense and a good hard "mug" on him, one who is overflowing with the shine of adventure and desires to give it vent by a tough journey through Rebeldom? There is now a fine chance for sending deserters to the enemy, and even if he does nothing more and can ascertain how the business is done. I have a copy of the order from S. Cooper [adjutant general of the Confederate Army] which a man can put in his pocket and be sent north through their underground R.R. General Patrick approves of it. What do you think of the matter? Neither [scout] Phelps nor Hatton seem inclined to undertake the trip. Please, think the matter over. Deserters, prisoners of war and the Richmond papers say that the rebels [word illegible] there faster in this matter if they never do in any other....*

*Yours truly,*

*J. McENTEE*

Source: NARA, Microcopy 2096, Roll 35

I wanted to desert, as I had enough of fighting. I was told to come in and I was taken before a captain and examined as to our army, etc. I was well posted but was too sharp to betray any information of value. I was soon taken to Libby prison and there confined until thirty-seven of our deserters had come in. Then all were marched westward from Richmond under guard. On reaching the mountains the guards left the deserters, and some of the latter went north for the sake of reaching a part of the country where war was unknown. Some of the other deserters were taken south and run through the blockade on some outward bound rebel or English vessel.

In the mountains I was robbed of my clothes three times by rebels, Union deserters and bushwhackers, who had formed a sort of robbers' gang in the mountains. The first time I was robbed I was told I wore too good clothes and must exchange. After the third robbery my clothes became too poor to excite the envy of any one, and I was allowed to proceed in peace. Before leaving City Point [Grant's headquarters and main supply base for the siege of Richmond and Petersburg] I had taken the precaution to secure a $100 bill, which I concealed on my left arm under a sticking plaster. When robbed of my clothes I was asked what was the matter with my arm, and I replied that I had been wounded in battle and it seemed it would never heal up. I saved my money, and in due time I passed through Cumberland Gap and reached the headquarters of General Gregg. The soldier considered me a genuine deserter, but when I was taken to the general I revealed my mission and was sent to Cincinnati and thence to Washington.[154]

# X

# Getting into Richmond

*EDITOR'S NOTE: Shortly after the Armies Operating Against Richmond settled down into the Siege of Petersburg and Richmond, Grant was enormously embarrassed by the raid of Lt. Gen. Jubal Early's Second Corps of the Army of Northern Virginia that nearly captured Washington. He had chosen to believe that Early remained with Lee in Petersburg. Essentially, the wish became the father of the thought for him, disregarding Sharpe's increasing evidence that Early was not in Petersburg and was mostly likely in the Shenandoah Valley. That realization caused Grant to seriously rethink how military intelligence could best serve him. He reassigned the Provost Marshal of the Army of the Potomac as well as Col. Sharpe to his own headquarters. Sharpe's mission was to develop an agent network inside Richmond, and he was anxious to make contact with Elizabeth Van Lew and other Unionists. He quickly turned to the best man he knew for the job—Judson Knight.*

*The National Tribune*
May 4, 1893 (continued from Chapter 9.)
Judson Knight, Washington, D.C.

$\mathbf{K}$NIGHT. WITHIN TEN days of the mine explosion in front of Petersburg [July 30, 1864], which by the way, was the grandest sight I ever saw, Col. Sharpe, Deputy Provost-Marshal-General, told me to go down to City Pont and select some building for Headquarters of the scouts, then to select some 10 or 12 of the best men and go down there and open up communication with Richmond. It was easy to say, but proved quite an undertaking before getting things established so that we had a communication every day, which we did eventually.

On July 21 Brigadier General Patrick, the Army of the Potomac's Provost Marshal General, instructed Col. Sharpe to go to City Point to "get into Richmond," in other words, to establish intelligence contacts with agents in the Confederate capital. The very next day Patrick reported to Maj. Gen. Meade, commander of the Army of the Potomac, that Sharpe had notified him that he had "organized a system of information to Richmond...."
David S. Sparks, ed., *Inside Lincoln's Army*, p. 401.

In getting it we had some amusing experiences. I selected a small frame building that had been used as a marine hospital for quarters, and in two days or thereabouts, we were ready to begin operations of establishing daily communications between the Capital of the Confederacy and Gen. Grant's Headquarters at City Point. Sharpe had since removed from Headquarters of the Army of the Potomac to City Point, where "Headquarters Armies Operating Against Richmond" had been established.

In early July Grant had recognized that he needed Sharpe to work directly for him to replicate the intelligence operation of the Army of the Potomac for his army group, Armies Operating Against Richmond. In order to make the transfer more palatable for the touchy Meade, he transferred Brigadier General Patrick's entire

Provost Marshall General organization, which included Sharpe and the Bureau of Military Information. On July 7th the transfer was made. Meade flew into a rage, and in typical general officer fashion Grant and he made up by cutting the difference. Sharpe ended up working for both of them. As Sharpe wrote to his uncle, "I am now by the way alternating in my duties at H.Q. Army of the Potomac & here at H.Q. Armies of the U.S. in the field, of which [the] latter Genl Patrick is the Pro Mar Genl. He comes down occasionally for a day or two, & then I return to represent him. My interviews with Genl Grant are frequent—generally every day."

Letter, Sharpe to Jansen Hasbrouck, August 15, 1864, Sharpe Collection, Senate House Museum, Kingston, New York.

*Headquarters of the BMI scouts at City Point established in July 1864. It was from here that Judson Knight and Col. Sharpe planned the scouts' missions behind enemy lines during the siege of Petersburg and Richmond. Library of Congress, LC-DIG-cwpb-02158.*

We were but just fairly settled in our new quarters when Col. Sharpe sent to me by his Orderly a man named Powers, who had been forwarded to City Point from a gunboat called *Commodore Morris*. The *Commodore Morris* had been built for a ferryboat, and after being purchased by the Government altered into a gunboat. She was a double-ender and armed with heavy guns. She lay at Hexall's Landing, just below Malvern Hill, eight miles above City Point.

Upon questioning Powers I learned he had been a clerk for John N. Van Lew in Richmond. As soon as Van Lew's name was mentioned it refreshed my memory, and I remembered what he had told me at least two months before at Cold Harbor. Powers said the reason of his leaving Richmond was that he found he had to join the Confederate army, and that while ostensibly engaged in getting ready to join, he left Richmond the night before he was to report for duty.

* * *

The National Tribune
May 11, 1893
Judson Knight, Washington, D.C.

KNIGHT. IN MY last I spoke of being sent by Col. Sharpe to City Point to open up communications between Grant's Headquarters and the rebel Capital—Richmond, and of having a man named Powers sent to me who had served on the gunboat *Commodore Morris*, and who had worked for John Van Lew in Richmond, but who had escaped from that city.[155] When I asked Powers how he got out of Richmond past the Confederate pickets, he said he did not know how he passed them, as he had not seen any, but that a man by the name of Myers had helped him out of Richmond, and that he also brought a man and his wife out along with him, who were coming into the Union lines.[156] To this I said:

"Powers, Myers must have had a pass for you, also one for the man and his wife. He surely could not have passed the pickets without documents of some kind."

"All I can say is from the time we left Richmond until he left me on a path in the woods, telling me to follow it, and it would take me to the river, where I could wait on shore until daylight, when I would see a Yankee gunboat which would send a boat on shore upon being hailed and take me off, I followed his directions, and here I am."

After becoming satisfied that he was telling the truth, and learning that Myers was a Northern man, originally from New Jersey; that he had been imprisoned for his Unionism for two years at Salisbury, N.C. until recently; that he was now employed in the Quartermaster's Department under a Maj. Wood, who was stationed in Richmond, and that Myers had a roving commission to travel anywhere where he thought he could find material of war, such as clothing, blankets, arms, mules or horses that had been abandoned by the Yankees in possession of any citizens in the State of Virginia, in which case Myers was empowered to seize such material and turn it over to his superior, Maj. Wood, it seemed to me that Myers was a very desirable man to interview. Upon questioning Powers further he said he thought Myers intended to bring the man and his wife, who had been left two or three miles further up the country than where Powers had been released, down to the same place in the woods where he himself had been turned loose the night before. He also said Myers had told him that he owned a plantation somewhere in the vicinity of the place where he had been left.

After learning all this, I was very sure that Mr. Myers was more than a desirable acquaintance to make, and immediately proposed to Powers that he should go along with another man and myself to endeavor to meet Myers when he brought the man and his wife down that night. Very much to my surprise Powers positively refused to set his foot on the north side of the James that night or any other night for any purpose whatever. He was safely out of rebeldom, and did not propose to put himself in any position where by any possibility they could get him in their power again. Money was no temptation to him; $50 did not tempt him to go to Hexall's and show two of us the road he came through the woods.

Finding that no inducement I could offer had any effect on him, I began to question him about rocks, trees, streams of water, or anything he might have noticed as he came along. He had seen no rocks, no peculiar-shaped trees, and only one small stream of water, which, as he stepped across, he had noticed a large oak tree at the right hand close to the road; and he had also noticed that wagons had at some time passed over it, but not for several months he thought. The road was also larger than any other he saw after striking the river and before reaching Hexall's gate. He felt really certain that it was about four miles from the river where Myers left him. With this scant information, Anson B. Carney, now of Bradford County, Pa., and myself started about dark and were landed on the wharf at Hexall's about 2:30 p.m. Hexall's was eight miles above City Point. We soon found the river road, and as we journeyed inland began passing paths that Powers had mentioned. After a time we came to one larger than any we had before seen, and after a slight search discovered that wagons had formerly been in use of it.

When about a mile from the river we came to a small branch crossing the road, and on the left of the road as we were going stood a large oak tree. We knew we were right now, and went ahead. After leaving the branch we discovered we were on ascending ground. We presently made a turn to the left. We both thought we were four miles from the river and that we were just about where Myers would leave the man and his wife. We hid in the bushes and waited.

Carney and I not two weeks before had hid while waiting for a negro off southwest of Petersburg, and two of the most villainous-looking white men came out in the moonlight close to where we were hiding. Col. Sharpe always insisted that we must travel around through the country in such a way that the rebels should not suspect us of being around at night. We could neither kill nor take prisoners when on night expeditions.

We remained hidden in the bushes until it became very monotonous. Looking east through the tree-tops I became convinced we were close to a clearing, and proposed to Carney that we should go to it. After going about 50 yards we came to a field. There appeared to be a road on the other side of it. We crossed the field and found there was a small house on the other side of the road, with a number of outbuildings. A lane led from the road. Close to the gate was a picket on horseback. We went up the road beside the fence until we located another picket, then returned toward the first one until we were about half-way between them; then sneaked across the road into a field on the east side. Keeping at quite a distance from the road, we proceeded parallel with it until we came to another running at a right-angle with the first. A short distance from us was a log house on the second road.

I told Carney that I was going to knock at the door and see if we could not learn something. We went to the house and rapped at the door. A woman's voice inquired: "Who be there?"

"A friend."

"What do you want?"

"To speak to you."

"Who are you?"

"Capt. Phillips, of the 5th N.C. Cav. Open your door; I wish to ask you a few questions."

After some time she said: "I can't open my door this time of night. Go around to the back of the house, and I will open a window."

We went around as she ordered, and presently a small window was pushed sideways and she appeared. "Who did you say you was?"

"I am Capt. Phillips of the 5th N.C. Cav., and this is Serg't Robinson. Do you know a man named Myers?"

"Do you mean old Alec Myers?"

"Really I can't say what his first name is, but the man I mean used to live in this neighborhood, and has a plantation yet somewhere in this vicinity."

"Oh, that is old Alec. Now, Captain, I want to tell you something. Old Alec did not know that that good-for-nothing, stinking cousin of mine was going to the Yankees. I would like to make a shroud to lay him out in."

We were certainly learning something, although who her cousin was we as yet had no inkling. We also learned from her that she expected Myers to bring her a barrel of flour from Richmond that night, and that her name was Slater. Her husband, she said, was an Englishman named Joe Slater, and he belonged to "Parker's Artillery Company."

While she was volubly giving us a history of her husband Joe, another woman came to the window, whom Mrs. Slater introduced as "My sister Betty. Betty Roach, gentlemen." Of course, we were pleased to see Betty, and while Carney conversed with her mostly, I paid more attention to the very voluble Mrs. Slater. At a suggestion of mine that as it was so late I was doubtful if she saw her barrel of flour that night, she said it would make no difference, for she would get it soon in the morning, as sometimes, when Myers was late, he stopped at Moodey's.

"How far is Moodey's from here?" I asked.

"About a mile," she replied, and leaned out of the window, pointing in a northeasterly direction.

"Well, Mrs. Slater, if you will kindly give me the directions for finding the place, we will go there and see if we can find him."

"Oh, that would never do in the world! For if you did not find him right there at first, the Moodeys would tell him, and you never would catch him in the world. Moodey is a Yankee, same as Myers, only he is from Pennsylvania and Myers from Jersey. No, that would not do at all." Suddenly she said: "Look here, Captain; how is it they sent you down here to find him, and he in Richmond himself nearly all day, and you from North Carolina, too, and don't know anything about the country? Why, you would not be able to find Moodey's house if you were to try; and they could have sent so many men who know the country. Say, Captain, how did you get to my house?"

"I came right down the road."

"How did you pass the pickets?"

"What pickets do you mean?" "Why, the reserves, about 100 yards above my gate."

We were both glad to find that out. Putting on all the dignity I could muster, with as much hauteur as I could possibly assume, I sternly said: "Mrs. Slater, has not the war been going on nearly four years, and have you not learned by this time that a soldier when he receives an order from his superior officer, has but one thing to do, obey? Now, I can't say that Myers is wanted in Richmond, what he has done, or why he is wanted. I know nothing. I simply know that Gen. Winder, the Provost-Marshal-General of the Confederacy, ordered me about sundown to come down here and bring Myers to Richmond with me. Why I was sent on the errand I do not know. Why he did not send some one who knew the country better than we do it is impossible for me to say. Your insinuations as to how we passed the pickets led me to suspect you don't believe what I have told you. I supposed we were talking with a woman with intelligence enough to know that an officer of Gen. Winder's rank and ability would not send a man off on an errand of that kind without papers that would pass him anywhere, and that is what I have got. Perhaps I had better show them to you, and possibly, after seeing them you will believe I have not been telling you a pack of lies. Sergeant, have you a match?"

"No, Captain."

"Have you any way of striking a light, Mrs. Slater?"

She had wilted, and assured us that she had no doubt at all but we were just what we represented ourselves to be. We both wanted to get away, and an idea struck me by which we could make a dignified retreat, and I said, "I want both of you ladies to hold up your right hands and take an oath not to reveal to a soul, neither father, mother, brother, sister, husband, or lover, or any other person, that I have been here to-night inquiring for Myers, or to Myers himself, if you should see him before I do." They both took the oath, and Carney and I left for Hexall's Landing.

About 20 minutes after we left, Myers drove up to the gate, and Mrs. Slater and Betty had a race from the house to the gate to see which should tell him first to "Look out for Capt. Phillips, of the 5th N.C. Cav.," who was looking for him.

We got to the landing and went aboard of our steamer, which had been tied to the wharf all of the time we were gone, and ran down to City Point, which we reached before daylight. After a sleep I reported to Col. Sharpe and got papers from him to take any negro I might find at Bermuda Hundreds working for a Quartermaster, provided I found one willing to go with me.

By calling upon the Harbor master we could always get a steamboat or tug to take us anywhere we wished to go. After a call on him I went over to Bermuda Hundreds, and went to the home of a family who had lived there all through the war. As I expected, I found an old colored man who had remained at home all the time. The first question I asked him was if he knew any colored man who had refugeed from Charles City County, and pointing toward Malvern Hill, saying, "from this part of the County." After studying a few moments, he said he knew several from the County, and one from just across the river about four or five miles back. He said he was a free man and always had been, and was at work for a Quartermaster down at the wharf unloading oats from the schooner lying there. Bringing him along we went down to the wharf and stood where we could see all the hands pass until nearly 200 had gone by, each one carrying a bag of grain. Then he pointed to one of them, saying: "That is the man you want to see."

"What is the man's name," I asked.

"Lightfoot Charles," he replied.

* * *

*The National Tribune*
May 18, 1893
Judson Knight, Washington, D.C.

KNIGHT. LAST WEEK I told about getting permission to take a negro laborer from the Quartermaster at Bermuda Hundreds, who was born in the vicinity of Malvern Hill, by the name of Lightfoot Charles. The man pointed out was a slim, wiry, and black fellow, about 25 years of age, as one who did not know any more of the average African than myself would judge. He looked as though he had more "sprawl" (to use a Nova Scotia expression) in him than any man in the gang. Following him up until he dropped his sack of oats, I called him to one side and asked if he knew a man named Moodey, over the river in Charles County, about six miles from Hexall's Landing.

"Yes," said he; "I cut hoop-poles for him last Spring."

"Do you think you could find his place in the night?"

"I reckon so."

"Will you go over there to-night with another man and I, and show us to his house?"

"You don't catch me over thar, Boss, to-night or any other night; too many rebels over thar."

"Do you know Joe Slater?"

"Yes; he's in the rebel army."

"Two of us were at his house last night, and Mrs. Slater told us that we would be unable to find Moodey's house in the night, look it as we might."

"Why, Boss, you was nigh about thar when you was at Slater's. But I reckon she told you nigh about the truth. It's rather a blind place to find, that's a fact."

"Well, Lightfoot, two of us are going over there to-night, and we want you to go along. We can go to Slater's all right, but are afraid, after what Mrs. Slater and you say about it, we could not find the place if we go alone. Will you go?"

"I reckon not, Boss."

"See here, Lightfoot, there is no more danger in going over there as in walking down the dock."

"I'd rather walk down the dock."

In answer to an inquiry he told me what his pay was. I offered him $5 more, better rations, and only one, or at most two horses to take care of, and again told him there was not the slightest danger in going over there, and told him I had been doing that kind of thing ever since the war broke out. "The moment you show us Moodey's house we will never ask you to put your foot on the north side of the river again, and will give you $25 extra beside. We will give you just as good arms as we will have ourselves and the man Carney, who will go with us, is not afraid of anything on the face of the earth."

I also learned from him that he was born free. As with Powers, he was safe in our lines, and it began to look very doubtful if any inducement that he could be offered would tempt him to risk himself on the north side of the river. Finally, I called the old man who had pointed him out to me and told him the offers I had made. He said: "Why, Lightfoot, if I knew where Moodey lived I would go myself. Show yourself a man and go with him."

His next excuse was that the Quartermaster would not pay him if he left.

"Come right with me and see him. I will get your money for you." I said.

Then we went to the Quartermaster together, and upon my explanation of the matter he paid him in full and allowed him a full day's pay for the day, shook hands with and complimented him very highly on his bravery, and I got him off to City Point. There the boys all told him there was not the slightest danger of being either shot or captured.

About 8 p.m. Carney and myself with Lightfoot started away from City Point on a steamer, ran up to the wharf at Hexall's, and went ashore after the people who lived near the landing were in bed and probably sound-asleep. We let our guide follow us until we came to Joe Slater's, whose house we reached by pursuing the same tactics that we did the previous night. There, to reassure Lightfoot, we stopped and had a chat in whispers. We pointed out that the direction Miss Slater had said was the way to Moodey's, which he said was right. We then told him to take the lead, as we knew nothing about the country any further. He started ahead, and we followed. About a half-mile from Slater's we struck into a dense forest of small pines, none of them over 20 feet in height. We soon found a small path just wide enough for us to get through in Indian file. Every little way it was intersected by other small paths about the same size.

After some time, during which I was certain we had walked more than a mile, which Mrs. Slater had declared to be the distance to Moodey's, I asked Lightfoot if he was sure of his direction. Carney grumbled a good deal to me, and swore he did not believe the nigger knew the way at all. Lightfoot said he was all right, and we went on again until I became positive that our guide was completely bewildered, and was really scared very much, and said to him, "Lightfoot, we will give it up tonight and have another try at it tomorrow night." Carney declared he would fool around no more with that nigger.

If there was anything on which I prided myself more than another, it was what Col. Sharpe termed my topographical instinct, which a friend of mine by the name of Harry Seibert, in New York City, declared meant that I was like a mule—could find my way to the place where I was fed last. At all events, we got back to Hexall's all right.

Soon after making my report of a total failure to Col. Sharpe of the trip of the night before, three men were brought on shore at City Point and turned over to Col. Sharpe. Myers had brought them from Richmond. We had not seen or heard a thing from them. Two more disgusted men than Carney and myself probably could not have been found in the "Armies Operating Against Richmond." When night came I took Lightfoot and went alone with him. Carney absolutely declining to go.

Our English ancestors took delight in what they called a "maze"; thought it was very cunning to build a place that when you once entered it, it would be tedious work to find your way out. Lightfoot declared the narrow paths which led to nearly every point of the compass were made by hogs. (No reflection on our English ancestors intended.) We traveled until I was certain we had gone at least two miles, when I became certain in my own mind that we were simply traveling over and over the same paths. At last, every time we turned from one path into another, I would stoop down, pick up a small dead limb that can always be found under a thick growth of pines, and break a piece about eight inches long and set it up against the tree nearest the intersection of two paths. I could do this without Lightfoot knowing anything about it, as I was following him. After pursuing this course for about an hour, I began finding the sticks that I had already set up. When this happened I said to Lightfoot: "It is getting late, and we must get back to Hexall's without being seen by anyone, so we will give it up now, and try it again to-morrow night."

After following him a short distance I asked him where he was going. His answer was, "To Hexall's Landing." "You are going as straight as can toward Richmond. You follow me now"; and I turned in the opposite direction and soon crossed the road that passed Slater's house, got into the field, and passed the house where Carney and I had the interview with Mrs. Slater and her sister. Lightfoot then acknowledged he had been perfectly lost. Before we reached Hexall's I found that the first house Carney and I saw was owned by an Englishman named Hill; and from what I heard from Lightfoot, I came to the conclusion he could not be much of a rebel sympathizer.

Soon after reporting to Col. Sharpe next morning, a batch of eight or 10 men were forwarded from the gunboat *Commodore Morris*, who had been brought through the rebel lines by Myers. I had been in the country over there nearly all night, and had not heard or seen anything of them. I did not know what to think. The next night I told Lightfoot we would not go again until the following night. Soon after dark I took a boat and ran down the river about two miles opposite the upper Harrison place. We had to anchor in the south channel, about a mile-and-a-half from shore. Two of the steamboat's crew volunteered to put me ashore in a small boat with muffled oars. In crossing the flats between the two channels the boat dragged in the mud for a long distance, which made it very hard pulling. After reaching the shore we had a consultation as to what was best to be done. Finally we

*U.S. Navy gunboats such as this carried Judson Knight and his scouts up and down the James River to land them on the Confederate shore to slip and out of Richmond with intelligence gathered by the Van Lew Ring.  Library of Congress, LC-B811- 2547.*

*Elizabeth Van Lew, the Union spy mistress of Richmond.  Author's collection.*

came to an agreement. The boys were to pull across the north channel and wait about an hour; if they saw three lights from the lighting of matches, they were to come ashore and take me off. If no lights were shown, they were to return to the steamer and have the watch keep a good lookout for the three lights. It was a crude way of signaling, but one not liable to attract attention, if the one who was doing it held his coat open, so that the light could only be seen directly in front.

\* \* \*

*The National Tribune*
May 25, 1893
Judson Knight, Washington, D.C.

KNIGHT. MY LAST letter told how I had been set ashore by two of a steamboat's crew at the upper Harrison place, and making arrangements to signal them to return upon seeing me burn three matches.

The place I intended to visit was called the upper Harrison house, and could not be seen from the river on account of the trees. Below this, about a mile, was another Harrison house, in full view from the river bank. It was a mile above Harrison Landing to which McClellan changed his base in 1862. When I saw the upper Harrison house I recognized it as the place where Bob McNair, a comrade of Co. H, 2d N.J., and I had found the 8th Ill. Cav. in 1862, when we were so nearly taken in by rebel cavalry the morning after Malvern Hill.

Now I went straight to the house and knocked. I found three negro men there—Emanuel, Ben, and Joe. I got some information from them, and engaged one of them to lead me to Moodey's house the next night. The man Joe met Carney and me the next night.

Joe took us into a hidden negro path, but did not find Moodey's for us. So we failed again.

But I had found out two things from these negroes. One was that Hill was more of a Union sympathizer than a rebel,[157] and the other was that a man named William Henry Tallman, who lived near Hexall's Landing, had about 30 mounted men acting as couriers and scouts. Tallman personally spent the greater part of the day time on Epp's Island at the turn in the river where it bends at City Point at nearly a right angle. He watched the arrival of troops, supplies, etc., sending off his men as couriers when necessary.

Two nights later I made my way to Hill's house about an hour before midnight. Just before crossing the road a man came down the road, stopped and talked a while with the picket at Hill's gate, and then both went off up the road. I went around to the back of Hill's house and rapped at the door. He was much surprised to see me, and particularly in the very new and bright uniform I had on, which shone in the moonlight. I asked him the road to Richmond. He wanted to know how I came there, and why the picket did not stop me, and I told him what I had just seen.[158]

"Well," he said, "the road you left when you came into the lane will take you to Richmond."

Then he declared I would never get there with that new suit of clothes, as it would be taken from me. I told him I had $800 with me, and he said, that I would soon be relieved of that.

I pretended to be much disturbed, and then said I could go back before daylight, and no one would know I had been away.

"Where did you come from, anyway?" he said.

"From Bermuda Hundred," I replied. I added that I had crossed the river in a boat I had found not locked.

"See here!" he exclaimed; "you go back—go back by all means." He was evidently in earnest.

"Mr. Hill," said I, "I am not one of the kind that desert."

"How did you know my name?" he demanded.

I told him I had heard much of him from negroes, and my conclusion was that he was not much of a rebel. He admitted he was not, and did not dare say so around there.

Then I got down to business. I told Hill I wanted him to go into Richmond for me the next day. He declared he could not; that he had no excuse for going.

"Can't you kill a shoat and take it to market? I will pay you $25 for it."

At that he consented. He promised to do what I requested, which was that he should be ready the next night to tell me what he had seen and heard in Richmond on the following day. I wanted him to find out from what States the different regiments he saw were, and their numbers. I also asked him to go to a market gardener, an Englishman like himself, who lived below Rockett's, on the left side of the York River Railroad, and who, I believed, was a Union man, and to find out if it was so.

The next morning I told Sharpe what I had done.

As was frequently the case, the gunboat *Morris* had forwarded a batch of refugees, who told the same story that I had already tired of, "Myers brought us through." Myers was the man wanted now, and Col. Sharpe had told me to tell him when I met him to stop bringing people out of Richmond, as they were bound to tell how they were got away from rebeldom, and at length the rebel authorities would hear of it, and Myers's goose would be cooked.

I saw Hill the next night, but he had accomplished little. However, he had brought me a copy of each of the Richmond papers. This was good, for I had been trying now for over a week to get communications with Richmond. Hill agreed to go to Richmond again in a few days.

The day following four of us started early in the morning on horseback, crossed the Appomattox and James Rivers, and reached Gen. Hancock's Headquarters in good time. I carried a message to Gen. Hancock from Col. Sharpe, requesting him to turn over to me a military map that he had written Sharpe had been found on the dead body of Gen. Chambliss.[159]

The General told me that he had sent the map away to City Point to be photographed. I explained how we had hunted so long for Moodey's house, and thought the map might help us, and he gave me a note to Gen. Gregg, commanding the cavalry on the extreme right of the line, who, he thought, might have some refugees or prisoners from whom I might get exact information about the location of Moodey's house.

So we went to Gen. Gregg. He did not have anyone with him who could do anything for us. But he recommended me to the Ladd Brothers, Quakers, who, he said, kept a store on the river road at the foot of Malvern Hill; he had met them when he was there in 1862, and they had seemed very loyal men.

He was much surprised when I acquainted him with the fact that the Ladds were now in the Old Capitol Prison in Washington, put there for shooting the pilots on our gunboats when they had come up the river the Spring before. They were the last men in the world, the General said, that he would have suspected.

"Have you any troops on Malvern Hill?" I then asked.

"Yes; Maj. McCabe is there with the 13th Pa. Cav."

So I decided to go to Maj. McCabe. When we rode up McCabe recognized us, and wanted to know our errand. I told him, and also that we believed Moodey's place was within four miles of Malvern Hill, and also that we were going to hunt for it once more.

"How far do you think you will get into these woods over there before you will have your heads shot off?"

"Why, Major, are they as thick as that?"

"You four men would not get a hundred yards into the woods before you would all go up. Let me tell you what to do. Write to Gen. Gregg asking him to let me go with you, and I will take the regiment and we will go through them like a dose of salts. I will send an orderly with the note."

We all thought this was a good idea, and rested easy.

McCabe had been on a couple of expeditions with us the previous May just before Spotsylvania, and rather enjoyed our kind of trips. Six p.m. came presently, and so did a note from Gen. Gregg, that said: "Maj. McCabe will proceed to Deep Bottom immediately."

* * *

*The National Tribune*
June 1, 1893
Judson Knight, Washington, D.C.

KNIGHT. I HAD now become very much ashamed of my repeated failures both up and down the river. Nearly every morning the Gunboat Morris forwarded refugees from Richmond to City Point, with the same old story that Myers had brought them through. It was necessary to find Myers soon.

One night Carney and I went out with Lightfoot. I set sticks as before. After we had wandered for some time we came to an intersection of two paths. I said: "Lightfoot, when we come here we always turn to the east, I notice. Suppose you take the other path."

So after traveling on that for awhile we came to another intersection and Lightfoot stopped, while I felt to see if I had placed a stick there. There was no stick. We had struck a new lead.

We followed it, and in less than a hundred yards distance came to a rail fence. Over we climbed. There was a large barn standing in certain position with regard to log houses near it, which convinced Lightfoot that it was Moodey's.

Carney and Lightfoot withdrew to one side, and I tapped on the window of the house. The curtain was raised and a woman's face appeared. She raised the window slightly and asked: "Are you caught?"

"No," I replied. "Where is Myers?"

"He is out in the kitchen. Go around to the other side, and I will come out as soon as I can."

When she came outside and saw three of us with pistols in our hands she was frightened, but made no noise. Bidding her lead the way, we followed closely. She opened the door of the log house and entered. After stirring the ashes in the fireplace they sprang into flame and revealed a large room with two beds in it, and the figure of a man in each.

Upon being questioned she indicated which one was Myers. I shook the sleeper, who awoke with a start, and I ordered him up and out-of-doors.

I took him into the cornfield, where we could not be seen or overheard. I told him who we were, so as to allay his fears. I talked to him about his bringing so many refugees through, and advised him to stop it at once, as we did not want the people, and I explained to him the danger he was in. To all of this he did not say a word. I talked to him a long while, and at last managed to draw him into conversation. He told me of his coming to Slater's and the women having the race to see which should be first to tell him look out for Capt. Phillips. Upon my telling him how Mrs. Slater would not open the door, he said there were two rebel scouts sleeping there that night, who begged her to make us go to the back of the house; they were John Gillem and Harry Brandy, both of South Carolina.

During all the time we had been looking for Myers I had carried a letter in my pocket for Miss E. N. Van Lew. I now gave it to Myers to deliver, and I made him promise to meet me in the woods the next night if Miss Van Lew answered the letter.

The following night Carney and I met Myers. He had a letter from Miss Van Lew, which contained some news and a promise to furnish more whenever she could.

Myers from that time stopped bringing refugees through. After that he often met us at night, and usually had valuable information. However, the Headquarters people wanted to hear from Richmond every day. Without saying anything to Hill or Myers, I got Moodey to go. He knew one Loman, a rebel detective, with whom he communicated.

As the war advanced and the army closed around Richmond, I was able to communicate with General Butler and General Grant, but not so well with General Butler, for there was too much danger in the system and persons. With General Grant, through his Chief of Secret Service, General George H. Sharpe, I was more fortunate.
Elizabeth Van Lew

Elizabeth R. Varon, *Southern Lady, Yankee Spy: The True Story of Elizabeth Van Lew, A Union Agent in the Heart of the Confederacy*, 2003, p. 158.

*The Van Lew mansion in Richmond to which Judson Knight was a frequent visitor.*
*Library of Congress. Library of Congress, LC-D4-33908.*

We returned to City Point, and one day two men, named Major and Wardwell, came and told us they had been hidden in a chamber of Major's mother-in-law's, a Mrs. Gill, about seven miles from Wilcox's Landing, for several days. They said Mrs. Gill was at heart a Unionist, and that she would be glad to go into Richmond one day in every week for us; but they would not take the risk in going to show us where she lived.

However, down in Bermuda Hundred, we secured an old colored man named Johnson [not the Richard Johnson referred to earlier] to lead us. We reached Wilcox's Landing one night at an hour when most people would naturally be in bed. We anchored out in the stream, and were pulled ashore with muffled oars. It was a long tramp from the landing that night, and the old negro could not find the place. But he said he was sure he could find it in the daylight, so we directed him to make the search the next day, and meet us in the evening.

We had nearly reached the landing the next night when we suddenly saw a flash of fire from the top of the bluff and heard several heavy reports. The rebels had a battery on the hill, and we soon saw that they were firing upon what looked like a transport coming up the river, but which proved to be a gunboat. She opened fire, and in a very short time the rebels had disappeared from the bluff, and by the time we had dropped down opposite the gunboat the affair was over.

The men on board hailed our steamer, and we scouts went on board to explain our business. The gunboat was the *Sassacus*, a double-ender, under Lieut. Commander Lee, who later rose to the rank of Rear-Admiral, and died some five years ago.[160] We staid on board the *Sassacus* until time to land, but when we did land no Johnson came.

The next evening we ran down again, and I found the Steamer *Dawn* instead of the *Sassacus*. We could not hear anything about Johnson, and were sure the rebs had caught him.

In the morning the Captain of the *Dawn* let me have 50 men and an officer, and we went up on top of the plateau to the house of Col. Wilcox. We informed the old gentleman that if any more firing took place from his plantation upon Union transports or gunboats, we should burn his house down. The old Colonel began to argue that he could not prevent it, but we silenced him.

At intervals while talking I had noticed a wooly head bobbing up at the southwest corner of the house. I strolled in that direction, and came upon a negro boy. When I got out of sight of the others I went up to him, and he volunteered the information that a Col. Garey and a lot more were coming to the house to breakfast soon, and warned me that we had all better get away, as they would be too many for us.

I immediately ran to the top of a small mound west of the house, out of sight of the porch where the Colonel and his family were sitting. Toward Richmond I saw a cloud of dust a mile and a half away. I returned and strolled around the corner of the house as if I had just been looking around. As I passed the officer of the detachment, who was talking to the Colonel, I said in a low voice, "Give your men the order to about-face. We will go to the river."

It did not take us long to get away, and the rebs did not come in sight until we had gone down the bluff, so we did not encounter them after all.

* * *

*The National Review*
June 8, 1893
Judson Knight, Washington, D.C.

KNIGHT. WE RETURNED to City Point without Johnson. Foster and I concluded that he must have been caught by the rebels the night they fired on the *Sassacus*.

Meanwhile some of the boys were meeting Myers every few nights. Dodd, McCord, Phil Carney, S. McGee, and others were sent to Washington to communicate with Silver, who had moved away from his place above Fredericksburg and was now on a farm below the town.

Hill told me one night that he knew of a man named Carter who would do the work he was doing a good deal better. He had been a soldier of the old army and in the recruiting service in Richmond years before. He was then near White Oak Swamp. He was all right, and Hill had told him about me and the man wanted to see me.

A few nights later I had an interview with the man and decided to trust him. I gave him a letter for Miss Van Lew and set him to work otherwise.

The second time Moodey went to Richmond he came back so badly frightened that we were obliged to take him to City Point. To that place his wife came from Harrison's Landing. They went North in a few days, and we heard no more of them. I have always asked myself whether it was a put-up job, or whether Moodey was really afraid to stay. I never learned what scared him.

Myers proved an excellent man to have, and never seemed to fear danger. Although four rebel scouts were prowling through that part of the country night after night, and knew he was down there two or three nights a week, yet he never seemed to take any precautions against being watched by them. We often changed our meeting place, but that was all. We never told Myers what Carter was doing for us.

Myers introduced us to Henry Roach, a cousin of John Roach, the scout, who wanted to go through our lines. Roach gave me a description of the obstructions in the river and directions how to pass them without striking the torpedoes. (I went through them the next Spring and found out that he was correct.) He told me of a new torpedo the rebels were making at that time in Richmond. He gave me the name of a man who was at work on them, and I got Myers to bring him out. We got the exact description. A drawing was made of the torpedo, and the matter was published in the *Scientific American*. I give herewith a drawing of the torpedo, with the letter that was sent to the journal which published it:

*EDITOR'S NOTE: In this* National Tribune *article, Knight only included that part of his article that described the mechanism. Provided here is the entire article that appeared in* Scientific American *under the title, "New Rebel Torpedo."*[161]

KNIGHT. TORPEDOES HAVE come to be recognized as very formidable mechanisms in offensive warfare, and the damages they have inflicted on our navy, during the war, have been very great. These machines are being continually experimented with, and are much more reliable than they were formally. We illustrate herewith one of the latest inventions of the rebels in this line, and append the letter of an obliging correspondent in the army who has furnished us with the sketch. The sketch is indistinctly drawn as regards the details of the lock; it would not work as now shown. The principle of the thing is, however, correctly delineated, and any common musket lock will answer the purpose as well as another. As the propeller revolves by the action of the current, it draws away from the lever, which liberates the trigger and explodes the cap on the nipple. It is a very crude affair and poorly arranged as to its details. It is expected to swing up against the side of a vessel (two torpedoes being connected together by a line) and heading downstream the screw is intended to turn with the current as before explained. We subjoin the report of our correspondent:

> *Having formerly been a reader of your paper, and knowing that you are always interested in new inventions, and of undoubted loyalty, I take pleasure in sending you the accompanying sketch of a torpedo lately invented in Richmond, hoping you will publish it, as I believe it is calculated to do a vast amount of damage. This description will enable you to understand it: A is the shell containing the powder, with the tube, B: fastened into it is a rod of seven-eighths iron (round with a thread cut on it). D is a flat bar of iron (there is one on each side) one inch by one-fourth, fastened to the rod, C, far enough apart to allow the torpedo, A, to just pass in between them, to which it is soldered or brazed. E is the propeller, which has a thread cut inside the hub. F is a lever, and G is a*

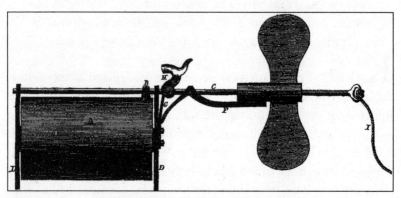

*Judson Knight's torpedo. Scientific American.*

*spring fastened near one end by rivets; the other end works in a slot in the hammer, H. I is a cord by which two torpedoes are intended to be fastened together. To operate them it is intended to have them buoyed so that they will float four or five feet below the surface; they will be stretched apart the length of the cord, and placed in the water at ebb tide above the vessel that it is intended to destroy. They are then to be floated down until the cord comes foul of the ship's cable or the ship herself, when the two torpedoes will swing around under the ship's side. The propeller then begins to operate; as soon as the hub has passed the end of the lever, F, the hammer falls upon the cap on the tube, and the explosion occurs.*

*City Point, Va., Sept. 21, 1864*

KNIGHT [resuming his *National Tribune* article]. It was not long before I had a large number of copies of the paper distributed to the fleet, and I had a copy dropped in the box of Confederate Secretary of War Seddon. This had the effect of stopping the work, and we found a lot of these torpedoes unfinished when we went into Richmond in the Spring.

*EDITOR'S NOTE: In the following section Scout Carney describes how he required passes with the highest authority to make sure he could pass through Union lines. The first two passes for Anson B. Carney are written in the hand of Maj. Gen. George G. Meade, commander of the Army of the Potomac, and were signed by both him and Brig. Gen. Marsena R. Patrick, Provost Marshal General.[162]*

Headquarters Army of the Potomac

Office of the Provost Marshal General

July 17, 1864

The bearer, Anson Carney, (and one colored man) has permission to pass outside the lines and return on special service. Pass also A. W. Loyd, 6th U.S. Cavalry. This pass good for one trip only. By command of MAJ.-GENL. MEADE.

This pass will expire July 18, 1864

M.R. PATRICK
Provost Marshal General,
Army of the Potomac

Headquarters Army of the Potomac
Office of the Provost Marshal General

Aug 8, 1864

The bearers, A. Carney and McCord have permission to pass outside
the lines on the left and return to these Headquarters.
This pass will Expire Aug. 9, 1864

By command of

MAJ.-GEN. MEADE

M.R. PATRICK

Provost Marshal General

Army of the Potomac

Office of the Provost Marshal General,
Armies Operating Against Richmond.

Dec. 5, 1864

LIEUT. CARR,

In charge of the *Washington Irving*
You will please convey (per steamer *Wash'n Irving*) Carney and
Phelps to such point on the James River as they may direct.

By order of

GEN. PATRICK
MCENTEE, CAPT.

CARNEY. With regard to the pass dated Dec. 5, 1864, "per steamer," I would go up the James River and be rowed ashore in a small boat after dark and work my way through the enemy's lines by creeping through a dark and deep ravine, called "Mill Hole." After passing the rebel pickets I would call at the house of a lady named Gill. She was loyal to the Union, and sometimes I could get her to go to Richmond and carry a letter (in cipher) to a Mrs. Van Lew, who resided in the city and at whose house rebel General Winder had his headquarters. She would bring back the answer "in cipher." If Mr. Gill

RICHMOND LADIES GOING TO RECEIVE GOVERNMENT RATIONS.—Sketched by A. R. Waud.—[See the First Page.]
"Don't you think that Yankee must feel like shrinking into his boots before such high-toned Southern ladies as we?"

*The Van Lew spy ring regularly reported on the increasing privations of the population and garrison of Petersburg and Richmond during the siege. Here women of Richmond line up for rations during the siege. Alfred R. Waud, Library of Congress, LC-USZ62-116427.*

would not go, I went into the city myself, going to her son-in-law named Brown, who kept a small stall in the market.[163] Brown would conceal me at his house, deliver the letter to Mrs. Van Lew and bring me the answer. This I would convey to General Grant at City Point.

The other two passes I had were used when I desired to go through the enemy's lines on the left to visit a negro family in Petersburg. It was more difficult to get through on the left, as the rebel picket was closer together; quite often I was fired upon and had to run the gauntlet to get back and then try it over at some other point. If late, I would lay over in the woods. Then sometimes I would get back to headquarters and wait till things cooled down, then try again. I generally succeeded on the second trip.

The man with me "on the left" would watch the horses until my return; the man on the "Richmond trip" would remain on the steamer to watch my signals upon my return from the rebel city, as we could not always trust the deck hand in keeping awake—the steamer being anchored on the opposite side of the river awaiting my return. I would signal with a dark lantern, which I had concealed on shore.

Comments of the editor of *The Boys in Blue* to Carney's account.

"The following high testimonial shows the esteem, in which Comrade Carney was held by the Department in which he served:"

Office of the Provost Marshal General,

Armies Operating Against Richmond.

31st January, 1865

Anson B. Carney, private Co. G., 5th U.S. Cavalry, enlisted the 25th of October, 1862, and has been in service of Special Service Bureau of this Department for the last 22 months. During this time he has been of valuable important service to the Government and we cheerfully recommend him as a faithful, energetic, brave and trustworthy soldier, and particularly valuable in the line of duty he was engaged.

PAUL A. OLIVER, Capt.[164]

*EDITOR'S NOTE: Capt. Oliver's above commendation of the scout Carney, "faithful, energetic, brave, and trustworthy," is a fitting epitaph for Judson Knight and the other scouts of the BMI. But for Knight and many others these attributes were also in order: They were clever, cunning, resourceful, and determined. Knight especially had that cool head and capacity for mimicking the enemy with an almost breathtaking boldness.*

*His narrative in* The National Tribune *unfortunately ended in 1893 with the rest of this story to the end of the war untold. Most likely the deterioration of his health was a cause. We are left only the tantalizing evidence of Grant's payments to him for "special services," from December 1864 to June 1865, of large sums that together equaled his own pay as a lieutenant general, the most senior officer in the United States Army, and acclaimed victor in the terrible War of the Rebellion.*

# Appendix

**MEMBERS OF THE BUREAU OF MILITARY INFORMATION (BMI), ARMY OF THE POTOMAC, 1863–1865, AND THE ARMIES OPERATING AGAINST RICHMOND, 1864–1865**

The following is the list of 234 names of members of the Bureau of Military Information (BMI), the intelligence operation of the Army of the Potomac and the Armies Operating Against Richmond.[165] Except for the officers in the analytical staff, the list was largely derived from the payrolls of that organization and correspondence of the BMI since there are so many surviving personnel rosters of the BMI. These men initially were paid for what was considered a unique service from a special War Department Secret Service Fund. Subsequently, they were paid through regular quartermaster channels.[166]

Under the heading below of Scouts and Guides are the names compiled from the overall payroll heading of Guides. The heading causes some confusion since guides were not considered to be scouts who were on the permanent roles of the army as soldiers or contract civilians with wide-ranging reconnaissance and intelligence collection duties. Guides were local men who had a knowledge of the immediate area of operations. Often they were African American slaves, most of whom were considered to have little knowledge outside of a five-mile radius of the plantations or farms on which they lived.

Clearly, this category of Guides included both scouts and guides, though there are only a few indications of who was a scout and who

234

was a guide. However, in those cases where the individual is named as a colored guide, his pay is at the lower rates of one to two dollars a day. Some of the guides and most of the civilian staff were identified in the payroll as either white or colored. All soldier scouts were presumed to be white. The status of most of the scouts and guides remains unknown.

It should be noted that the date an individual first appears on the payrolls is sometimes preceded by mention as a scout in earlier correspondence of the BMI. There appears to be some lag in some cases between beginning work as a scout and appearance on the payroll.

The total of 234 men is broken down into the following categories:

Analytical Staff            5

Scouts & Guides          182

Civilian Support Staff      46

Military Mail Agent         1

This total represents all the personnel working for the BMI over the entire life of that organization. There were never at any one time more than seventy men in the BMI, with forty to fifty being the usual number, depending on the mission requirements. Major General Meade, Commander of the Army of the Potomac, was not supportive of any large increase in the size of the organization.

| Name | Unit/Status | Joined BMI |
|---|---|---|
| **Analytical Staff**[167] | | |
| Babcock, John C. | Civilian Analyst | 02-13-63 |
| McEntee, John C. | Capt., 20th NY State Militia[168] | 03-22-63 |
| Manning, Frederick L. | Lieut., 148th NY Infantry | 03-08-63 |
| Oliver, Paul A. | Lieut., 12th NY Infantry | 01-65 |
| Sharpe, George H. | Col., 120th NY Infantry | 02-13-63 |

| Name | Unit/Status | On BMI Payroll [170] | Contract[169] Date |
|---|---|---|---|
| **Scouts and Guides** | | | |
| Anderson, Allen | Civilian White [171] | 03-63 | 03-10-63 |
| Ball, J. P. | Unknown | 09-63 | |
| Bates, Rueben | Unknown | 10-63 | |
| Battle, Lewis[172] | Unknown | 06-63 | |
| Bensen, John | Unknown | 09-64 | |
| Beverley | Unknown | 07-63[173] | |
| Blake, William | Unknown | 04-63[174] | |
| Botts, Thomas | Unknown | 05-64 | |
| Bremen, M. H. | Unknown | 01-64 | |
| Bromly?, John | Unknown | 07-63 | |
| Brooks, Isaac | Unknown | 10-63 | |
| Brown, R. J. | Unknown | 06-63 | |
| Brown, Carter | Unknown | 10-63 | |
| Bryant, Jerry | Unknown | 09-63 | |
| Cammack, James M. | Unknown | 09-63 | |
| Carney, Anson B.[175] | G/5th U.S. Cavalry | 04-19-63 | 05-03-63 |
| Carney, Edward A. | G/5th U.S. Cavalry | 04-19-63 | 05-03-63 |
| Carney, Philip | F/5th NY Cavalry | 07-05-63 | |
| Carter, Dick | Unknown | 10-63 | |
| Charles, Jack | Unknown | 09-63 | |
| Chase, William H. | B/20 NYSM | 04-63 | 04-01-63 |
| Cline, Milton W. | C/3rd IN Cavalry | 04-63[176] | 04-01-63 |
| Cline, Walter[177] | Civilian White | 10-63 | |
| Coburn, H. M. | Unknown | 04-63 | |
| Cole, Daniel R. | D/3rd IN Cavalry | 04-63[178] | 04-16-63 |
| Cole, Samuel R. | Unknown | 06-64 | |
| Danes, Robert | Unknown | 01-65 | |
| Davis, Robert | Unknown | 01-65 | |
| Dawson?, John | Unknown | 01-64 | |
| Dillard, Charles L. | Unknown | 05-64 | |
| Dodd, Henry Wood | H/1st OH Light Artillery | 04-63[179] | 04-14-63 |
| Doughty, James R. | Unknown | 10-63 | |

| Name | Unit/Status | On BMI Payroll [6] | Contract[5] Date |
|---|---|---|---|
| Doughty, John G. | Unknown | 10-64 | |
| Dushal, Clark | Unknown | 12-63 | |
| Dykes, Joel R. | Unknown | 10-64 | |
| Edwards, Aaron | Civilian Colored | 03-65 | |
| Edwards, Eugene | Unknown | 04-64 | |
| Evans, Henry[180] | Civilian Colored | 11-64 | |
| Fay, William[181] | Civilian White | 06-64 | |
| Flomer, Henry | Unknown | 09-64 | |
| Flomer, Samuel | Unknown | 09-64 | |
| Ford, Ben | Unknown | 08-64 | |
| Forrestal, Charles | Unknown | 04-64 | |
| Foster, J. D. | Unknown | 06-64 | |
| Fox, James | Unknown | 04-64 | |
| Frazier, Cezar | Unknown | 05-64 | |
| Gaines, Benjamin F. | Unknown | 05-64 | |
| Gardener, Alfred | Unknown | 04-64 | |
| Gardener, Dan | Unknown | Unknown | |
| Goldman, William | Unknown | 05-64 | |
| Graham, Michael | Civilian White | 11-63 | |
| Green, Bushrod | Unknown | 07-63 | |
| Greenwood, Joseph W. | Unknown | 06-63 | |
| Gunn, John | A/1st NJ Cavalry | 01-65 | |
| Gutheridge, R. | Unknown | 04-63 | 04-10-63 |
| Halleck, Ebenezer[182] | Unknown | 02-65 | |
| Harding, John | Civilian White | 01-63 | 01-12-63 |
| Harding, Phillip | Civilian White | 03-63 | 03-10-63 |
| Hiram, Harris | Unknown | 08-64 | |
| Harrison, Benjamin | Civilian Colored | 12-64 | |
| Harter, Thomas O. [183] | Civilian White | 11-64 | |
| Hart, Major | Unknown | 05-64 | |
| Hatch, J. M. | 1st ME Cavalry | 04-64 | |
| Hatton, James | D/3rd IN Cavalry | 04-64 | |
| Hawkins, J. W. | Unknown | 09-64 | |
| Hill, Thomas | Unknown | 09-64 | |

| Name | Unit/Status | On BMI Payroll [6] | Contract [5] Date |
|---|---|---|---|
| Hirth, Frederick | Unknown | 06-64 | |
| Hodges, Thomas | Unknown | 05-63 | 05-01-63 |
| Hogan, Martin | E.[184] | I/1st IN Cavalry | 06-64 |
| Holmes, Essex | Unknown | 05-64 | |
| Homer, Henry | Unknown | 09-64 | |
| Homer, Samuel | Unknown | 09-64 | |
| Hopkins, Edward P. | H/1st OH Light Artillery | 04-63 | 04-14-63 |
| Howard, Moses | Unknown | 08-64 | |
| Hyson, Fielding | Unknown | 02-64 | |
| Humphreys, Joseph M. | Civilian White | 03-63[185] | 03-11-63 |
| Hunnicutt, Mordecai P. | I/73rd OH Infantry | 04-63 | 04-14-63 |
| Irby, James | Unknown | 04-64 | |
| Jack, Charles | Unknown | 09-64 | |
| James, Watkins | Unknown | 07-63 | |
| Johnson, Dick | Civilian Colored | | 05-06-64 |
| Johnson, Richard[186] | Unknown | | |
| Johnson, Oliver | Civilian Colored | 12-64 | |
| Johnson, William | Unknown | 09-64 | |
| Jones, John | D/3rd IN Cavalry? | 01-65 | |
| Jones, Ned | Unknown | 07-64 | |
| Jones, Stephen | Civilian Colored | 03-65 | |
| King, Samuel | Unknown | 12-63 | |
| Knight, Judson | Civilian White[187] | 10-63 | |
| Lee, William J. | Civilian White | 11-63 | |
| Leitch, Benjamin | Unknown | 12-63 | |
| Lesh*, James | Unknown | 10-63 | |
| Lewis, Philip | Unknown | 10-63 | |
| Lickland, George | Unknown | 07-63 | |
| Littral, William | Unknown | 03-63 | 03-10-63 |
| Lloyd, Adolphus W. | Unknown | 04-64 | |
| Lymmerick, James | Unknown | 12-63 | |
| Lyon, Jack | Unknown | 05-64[188] | |
| Mahoney, Frank | Unknown | 05-64 | |

| Name | Unit/Status | On BMI Payroll [6] | Contract[5] Date |
|---|---|---|---|
| Major, Charles[189] | Civilian White | 07-64 | |
| Marcus, P. M. | Unknown | 05-63 | 05-01-63 |
| McCord, Benjamin Frank | H/1st OH Light Artillery | 04-63 | 04-14-63 |
| McCraken, Thomas | Unknown | 05-64 | |
| McFarlane, I. H. | Unknown | 01-64 | |
| McGee, Ebenezer | Civilian White | 04-63 | 04-01-63 |
| McGee, Robert M. | Civilian White | 12-63 | |
| McGee, Sandford | Civilian White | 12-63 | |
| McEneany, Patrick | Unknown | 04-64 | |
| Maybee, Thomas | Unknown | 06-63 | |
| Menito?, E. | Unknown | 11-63 | |
| Merritt, Edward | Unknown | 08-63 | |
| Miller, James | Unknown | | 04-64 |
| Miller, William H. | Unknown | 07-63 | |
| Mitchell, James A. | Unknown | 04-64 | |
| Moore, Isaac E. | Unknown | 06-63 | |
| Morris, James F. | Unknown | 04-64 | |
| Myers, Alexander[190] | Civilian White | 10-64 | |
| Myers, John | Unknown | 09-64 | |
| O'Boyline, Joseph | Unknown | 01-64 | |
| O'Conner, Richard | Unknown | 12-63 | |
| Orrick, Robert | Civilian White | 05-64 | |
| Otto, D. G.[191] | NY Cavalry | Unknown | |
| P.?, John | Unknown | 11-64 | |
| Parum, Sidney | Unknown | 02-65 | |
| Patrick, B. B. | Unknown | 12-64 | |
| Payne, ?. R. | Unknown | 12-63 | |
| Pelham, John | Unknown | 07-63 | |
| Pettis, Major | Unknown | 11-63 | |
| Phelps, Charles A. | 5th NY Cavalry | 04-64 | |
| Plew, Daniel | C/3rd IN Cavalry | 05-63[192] | |
| Poole, Albert | Unknown | 02-64 | |
| Powell, John M. | F/3rd IN Cavalry | 05-64 | |

| Name | Unit/Status | On BMI Payroll [6] | Contract[5] Date |
|---|---|---|---|
| Price, Isaac | Unknown | 01-64 | |
| Price, James | Unknown | 02-64 | |
| Prince, George | Unknown | 07-64 | |
| Randall, Richard | Unknown | 09-63 | |
| Reed?, D. C. | Unknown | 09-63 | |
| Reese, William | Unknown | 02-65 | |
| Roach, Henry | Unknown | 09-64 | |
| Robison, John | Unknown | 12-63 | |
| Roses, Edmond | Unknown | 02-64 | |
| Rose, William | Unknown | 09-64 | |
| Rowen, M. | Unknown | 05-64 | |
| Russ, Lewis | Unknown | 09-64 | |
| Sanford, Henry | Unknown | 04-64 | |
| Scott, Alexander | Unknown | 12-64 | |
| Scott, S. F. | Unknown | 07-63 | |
| Scott, Thomas | Unknown | 07-64 | |
| Sheppard, Henry | Unknown | 09-63 | |
| Sherman, Thomas | Unknown | 01-65 | |
| Silver, Isaac | Civilian White | 09-63 | |
| Silver, John | Civilian White | 08-64 | |
| Simons, William | Unknown | 04-65 | |
| Simpson, John | Unknown | 08-63 | |
| Skinker, John Howard | Civilian White | 03-63 | 03-08-63 |
| Skinker, M. H. | Civilian White | 01-64 | |
| Skinner, W. H. | Unknown | 02-64 | |
| Smith, E. P. | Unknown | 04-63 | 04-15-63 |
| Smith, Charles W. | Unknown | 11-64 | |
| Smith, George S. | Civilian White | 04-64 | 04-01-63 |
| Smith, James H. B. | Unknown | 11-64 | |
| Staian, J. L. | Unknown | 04-64 | |
| Stile, E. W. | Unknown | 09-63 | |
| Stevens, John F. | Unknown | 05-64 | |
| Swicher, Jacob | I/1st IN Cav | 06-63 | |
| Thomas, Barrett | Unknown | 08-64 | |

| Name | Unit/Status | On BMI Payroll [6] | Contract[5] Date |
|------|-------------|--------------------|------------------|
| Toppin, William | Unknown | 10-64 | |
| Tuisley, Charles | Unknown | 11-64 | |
| Tyson, John "Jack" | Unknown | 03-63 | 03-01-63 |
| Vadden, John | Unknown | 08-64 | |
| Van Pelt, A M. | Unknown | 01-64 | |
| Wagoner, I. S. | Unknown | 07-63 | |
| Walker, Dabney[193] | Civilian Colored | 06-63 | |
| Weams, William | Civilian White | 02-63 | 02-02-83 |
| Weaver, William | Unknown | 11-02-63[194] | |
| Weekly, Benjamin | Unknown | 10-63 | |
| Weekly, Calhoun | Unknown | 10-63 | |
| White, Daniel | Unknown | 11-64 | |
| Williams, Joseph | Unknown | 09-64 | |
| Wilson, William[195] | White | 09-63 | |
| Wood, James R. | Unknown | 02-64 | |
| Yager, Ernest | Unknown | 05-63 | 05-01-63 |

## Civilian Support Staff

**Clerks**

| | | | |
|------|-------------|--------------------|------------------|
| Ransom, A. F. | Civilian Clerk | 06-63 | |
| Taylor, M. B. | Civilian Clerk | Q. M. D. | 03-64 |

**Wagon Masters**

| | | | |
|------|-------------|--------------------|------------------|
| Algaien, Elias | Civilian | | 06-63 |
| Fox, David E. | Civilian | | 09-64 |

**Teamsters**

| | | | |
|------|-------------|--------------------|------------------|
| Averson, Henry | Civilian Colored | 04-65 | |
| Brom, Armistead | Civilian Colored | 02-65 | |
| Brown, Samuel | Civilian White | 11-64 | |
| Bug, Henry | Civilian Teamster | 12-63 | |
| Coin, Abram[196] | Civilian White | 12-63 | |
| Davis, Washington | Civilian Colored | 09-64 | |

| | | |
|---|---|---|
| Elmendorf, Edgar | Civilian White | 03-64 |
| Edwards, Aaron | Civilian Colored | 03-65 |
| Evans, Robert | Civilian White | 04-64 |
| Fingle, William | Civilian Colored | 11-64 |
| Franise, Hiram | Civilian White | 12-64 |
| Fry, Thorton | Civilian Colored | 06-64 |
| Green, Samuel | Civilian White | 11-64 |
| Harris, George | Civilian Colored | 05-64 |
| Hill, John | Civilian Colored | 08-64 |
| Hills, George | Civilian Colored | 11-64 |
| Jackson, Jerry | Civilian Colored | 04-65 |
| Johnson, William | Civilian Colored | 02-65 |
| Jones, Addison | Civilian Colored | 12-64 |
| Jones, Eugene | Civilian Colored | 06-64 |
| Jones, Stephen | Civilian Colored | 03-65 |
| Logan, Joseph | Civilian Colored | 04-65 |
| Low, George | Civilian White | 12-64 |
| Marshall, S. | Civilian Colored | 04-65 |
| Mason, Samuel | Civilian Colored | 09-64 |
| Maury?, E. S. | Civilian teamster | 06-63 |
| Merriweather, Israel | Civilian Colored | 06-63 |
| Miner, Robert | Civilian Colored | 07-63 |
| Oliver, Robert | Civilian Colored | 07-63 |
| Pendleton, Nathan | Civilian Colored | 09-63 |
| Quales, Henry J. | Civilian Colored | 07-64 |
| Scott, Lewis | Civilian Colored | 06-64 |
| Scott, Warren | Civilian Colored | 12-64 |
| Thomas, Jefferson | Civilian Colored | 11-64 |
| Watts, Oliver | Civilian White | 06-64 |
| Widey, Nelson | Civilian Colored | 06-64 |
| Young, Albert | Civilian Colored | 04-65 |

**Other**

| | | |
|---|---|---|
| Elmendorf, Edgar | Blacksmith White | 01-65 |
| Hawkins, George | Cook | 09-64 |
| Miner, Robert | Cook | 09-64 |

| Palmer, E. W. | Blacksmith | 11-64 |
| Quales, Henry J. | Blacksmith Colored | 08-64 |

## Also Paid On BMI Payroll

**Mail Agent**

| Parker, David B | Mail Agent, 72d NY[1] Inf | 07-64 |

# Notes

## Foreword:

1  U. S. War Department, *The War of the Rebellion: Compilation of the Official Records of the Union and Confederate Armies*. Ser. 1, vol. 46, pt. 1:481. (Washington, DC: Government Printing Office, 1880-1901). [henceforth *OR*]

2  Baron Antoine Henri Jomini, *The Art of War*, trans. by Capt. G. H. Mendell and Lt. W. P. Craighill (Westport, CT: Greenwood Press, 1971), 269.

3  Edwin C. Fishel, "The Mythology of Civil War Intelligence," *Civil War History* 10 (December 1964): 345, 352.

4  *OR* 27, pt. 3: 175.

5  Frederick C. Newhall, *With General Sheridan in Lee's Last Campaign* (Philadelphia: J. B. Lippincott, 1866), 53.

6  U. S. Congress, House of Representatives, *Report on the Impeachment of the President*, 40th Cong., 1st sess., 1867, H. Rept. 7: 111.

7  *OR* 46, pt. 1: 481.

## Introduction:

8  "About *The National Tribune*. (Washington, D.C.) 1877-1917," http://chroniclingamerica.loc.gov/lccn/sn82016187/, accessed March 12, 2013. The *National Tribune* (based in Washington, D.C.)

was founded as a monthly newspaper for Civil War veterans and their families in October 1877. Its aim was "to secure to soldiers and sailors their rights, and to expose their wrongs to public inspection so that correction may be made...." The *Tribune* included articles on the experiences of both commanding officers as well as ordinary soldiers, ranging from detailed battle descriptions to personal narratives.

The paper showed a particular interest in the Civil War as its founder, George E. Lemon, was himself a Union veteran. An attorney and accountant, Lemon intended the *National Tribune* to advocate on behalf of veterans rights and specifically for laws to ensure the receipt of pensions by veterans and their families. Later, in 1881, Lemon added to the paper's motto a quotation from Abraham Lincoln's second inaugural address: "to care for him who shall have borne the battle and for his widow and his orphan...."

During its first few years of publication, the *National Tribune* covered Congressional news related to pension laws and the Pension Office, as well as providing narratives, tables, and statistics about past wars. Relying on his background as a lawyer, Lemon frequently printed simple yet valuable advice to veterans on claiming their pensions. The paper also covered lighter topics and included anecdotes, poems, and jokes. Large illustrations, many drawn by Thomas Nast, a well-known political cartoonist for *Harper's Weekly*, appeared on its front page. Later the *Tribune* became known for its regular feature, "Fighting Them Over: What Our Veterans Have to Say About Their Old Campaigns," which solicited memoirs from veterans of all ranks and backgrounds. This column established the *National Tribune* as a forum for discussion, debate, and reminiscence for veterans around the country, eventually becoming the official paper of the Grand Army of the Republic.

Like many other papers, the *National Tribune* underwent changes over the course of its history. On August 20, 1881, it shifted to a weekly publication schedule and adopted a new masthead and motto. The *Tribune* gave rise to several special interest papers focusing on the veterans of specific wars, including the *American*

*Standard* and the *National Guardsman.* Eventually, the *Tribune* absorbed these titles, changing its name in 1917 to the *National Tribune, incorporating the National Guardsman and the American Standard.* Between 1926 and 1927, the paper was briefly renamed the *National Tribune, Stars and Stripes, the National Guardsman, the American Standard,* preceding the penultimate name change on January 7, 1926, when it became known as the *National Tribune, the Stars and Stripes,* representing a merger with the *Stars and Stripes,* the official publication of the American Expeditionary Force from World War I. A final name change to *Stars and Stripes, the National Tribune,* followed in 1963, and afterwards it was printed as an independent newspaper reporting on the activities of the Department of Veterans Affairs and veterans' organizations, as well as veterans legislation in Congress.

9   William Gilmore Beymer, Introduction by William B. Feis, *Scouts and Spies of the Civil War* (Lincoln: University of Nebraska Press, 2003), 164-84.

10  Spies were usually Northern persons imbedded within the Confederacy posing as Southerners or Northern sympathizers to obtain information. Agents were loyal Union persons living within the Confederacy who would obtain information from their local area. Scouts were either military or civilian contract personnel who would penetrate into the Confederacy to trace enemy movements and dispositions. Guides were local persons who knew the immediate area well and could literally guide military formations around the countryside. Quite often they were slaves.

11  Horace Porter, *Campaigning with Grant* (New York: The Century Company, 1897), 232. He also said in the same sentence that Sharpe was known for "his skill in examining prisoners and refugees."

12  John Esten Cooke, *Wearing of the Gray: Being Personal Narratives and Adventures of the War* (Baton Rouge, LA: Louisiana State University Press, 1997), 468.

13  *Or,* Series 1, Vol. XXXVI, Part 2, p. 34, letter from Sharpe to Hancock, May 2, 1864.

14  National Archives, Pension File of Judson Knight, Deposition A, Case of Judson Knight, No. 409.319, December 18, 1899.

15  National Archives, Pension File of Judson Knight, War Department Record and Pension Office summary of service and Certificate of Disability for Discharge, Dec. 18, 1862.

16  National Archives, Military Personnel File of Judson Knight, Company Muster Role May-June 1861. In *The National Tribune*, October 8, 1899, Knight states in this article that he was transferred on August 17th.

17  National Archives, Military Service Record of Judson Knight, Company Muster Role, July-August 1861.

18  National Archives, Military Service Record of Judson Knight, Company Muster Role, Nov.-Dec. 1861; Certificate of Disability for Discharge, Dec. 18, 1862.

19  NARA, letter from Taggert to Grey, RG 110, Entry e31, Box 2, File 80.

20  Certificate of Disability for Discharge, Dec. 18, 1862; Letter from Dr. J.H. Knight [Sgt. Knight's brother] to Maj. Gen. George Meade, January 1, 1867; H Company, 2nd NJ Infantry, muster rolls, July 1861 to February 1863; Military Service Record for Judson H. Knight, (NARA). Report No. 467, March 6, 1888 (U.S. Senate) and Report No. 1839, April 22, 1888 (U.S. House of Representatives), both to accompany bill S. 1192, 50th Congress, 1st Session, Military Pension File of Judson Knight.

21  NARA, RG, Entry 0910.

22  Milton Cline was also a member of the 3rd Indiana Cavalry.

23  J. W. Landegon, *The National Tribune* (July 24, 1890).

24  David S. Sparks, ed., *Inside Lincoln's Army: The Diary of General Marsena Rudolph Patrick, Provost Marshal General of the Army of the Potomac* (New York: A. S. Barnes & Co., 1964), 11.

25  The term "The Debatable Land" comes from the border region of England and Scotland, the playground of raiders for centuries.

26  Judson Knight, "How Scouts Worked: Serg't Knight Tells How They Went About Getting Information," *National Tribune* (April 27, 1897).

27  NARA, RG 92, Entry 0447 for 1864 (BMI Payrolls).

28  David D. Ryan, ed., *A Yankee Spy in Richmond: The Civil War Diary of "Crazy Bet" Van Lew* (Mechanicsburg, PA: Stackpole Books, 1996), 101-103.

29  NARA, RG 92, Entry 238, Files 0447 for 1864 and 0447 for 1865 (BMI Payrolls); http://www.civilwarhome.com/Pay.htm, accessed February13, 2013.

30  NARA, RG 92, Entry 238, File 0447 for 1865 (BMI payrolls).

31  National Archives, Pension File of Judson Knight, Deposition A, December 18, 1899; Philip A. Melanson, *The Secret Service: The Hidden History of an Enigmatic Agency* (New York: Carroll & Graf Publishers, 2003), 20. "Over the next three years, the Secret Service shadowed Klan leaders, discovered their meeting places, and pounced throughout the rural South, arresting and prosecuting one thousand persons involved in Klan activities; many were handed sentences of up to ten years."

32  National Archives, Military Service Record of Judson Knight, Letter of J. H. Knight [Sgt. Knight's brother] to Meade, January 1, 1867; Letter from Sharpe to Headquarters, Department of the East, January 25, 1867; National Archives, Pension File of Judson Knight, Deposition A, Case of Judson Knight, No. 409.319, Dec. 18, 1899.

33  50th Congress, 1st Session, Senate, Report No. 467, and House of Representatives, Report No. 1839.

34  50th Congress, 1st Session, Senate, Report No. 467, and House of Representatives, Report No. 1839.

35  50th Congress, 1st Session, Senate, Report No. 467, and House of Representatives, Report No. 1839.

[36] 50th Congress, 1st Session, S. 1192 [Report No. 1839] entitled "An Act Granting a pension to Judson Knight."

[37] NARA, Military Pension File of Judson Knight, Appeal of John Hunter [Knight's Attorney], Certificate No. 409, 319, February 17, 1902.

[38] National Archives, Pension File of Judson Knight, document, Department of the Interior, Board of Review Division, "Decision to Appellant, June 38, 1902."

**Chapter 1:**

[39] Trevor N. Dupuy, et al., *The Harper Encyclopedia of Military Biography* (New York: Harper Collins, 1992), 396.

[40] Ezra J. Warner, *Generals in Blue: Lives of the Union Commanders* (Baton Rouge, LA: Louisiana State University Press, 1964), 259. Eicher, John H. and David J. Eicher, *Civil War High Commands* (Stanford, CA: Stanford University Press, 2001), 328. Gen. Kearn(e)y's Gallant Charge at Chantilly, Library of Congress. http://www.loc.gov/shop/index.php?action=cCatalog.showItem& cid=77&scid=570&iid=3630; accessed November 21, 2012.

[41] Brett Schulte, "'I've Been Ordered Up to Fight!': Phil Kearny to the Rescue at Williamsburg," TOCWOC—A Civil War Blog, http://www.brettschulte.net/CWBlog/best-of-tocwoc-a-civil-war-blog/, accessed November 21, 2012.

[42] National Archives, Military Service Record of Judson Knight, Company Muster Role, May-Jun 1861. Knight's muster role entries state he was transferred for special duty on August 20, 1861.

[43] Secesh was a derogatory term for secessionists and rebels in general.

[44] Frederick Samuel Dellenbaugh, *George Armstrong Custer* (New York: The Macmillan Company, 1917), 22. A few days after Custer's company of the 2[d] Cavalry Regiment arrived in Arlington, Virginia, immediately after the battle of First Bull Run, it was assigned to the newly arrived Jersey Brigade of Brig. Gen. Phil

Kearny. As Kearny did not have a staff, he detailed Custer to serve as his aide-de-camp.

[45] Lt. Col. Joseph Cooke Jackson, 26th New Jersey Volunteer Infantry Regiment, was brevetted brigadier general of U.S. Volunteers on March 13, 1865. His brevet was confirmed March 2, 1867.

[46] *New York Times*, February 13, 1892; http://www.civilwarintheeast. com/USA/NY/NY040.php, accessed November 18, 2012. Lt. Col. Madison Mott Cannon (1840-1892) commanded the 40th New York Volunteer Infantry Regiment also known as the Mozart Regiment or the Constitution Guard. He rose from captain to lieutenant colonel between September 6 and 15, 1864, during the siege of Petersburg.

[47] Maj. James Chatham Duane (1824-1897) was the Chief Engineer of the Army of the Potomac (1863-1865) and an expert bridge-builder. He served forty years on active duty (1848-1888). Letter from Warren to Humphries, June 8, 1864, *OR*, Vol. XXXVI, Part 3, p. 698. Maj. Gen. Gouveneur Warren refers to Major Duane's map of Virginia and that it was two inches to the mile.

[48] *The National Tribune*, Dec. 17, 1891. Two months after this article written by Knight, another former scout, Jonathan Roberts, wrote to argue that he, and not Knight, was the creator of this map. "[H] e claims to have been the principal in making that map of the country around Annandale, Va., now in the War Department, furnished by Gen. Kearny, when, in fact, 'that map' was made by me for Gen. McClellan. But before I had the chance to give it to him I showed it to Kearny at Bishop John's house, near the Seminary, at Alexandria, which he (Kearny) wanted me to give to him.

"I told Gen. Kearny that it was intended for Gen. McClellan, and then he asked me to let him copy it, to which I consented, and he set his clerk at it, tracing it on tissue paper; and while this was being done Kearny and I were talking out on the porch of the house. In the midst of our conversation Gen. Kearny jumped up, excused himself, and when he returned out of the house he held a $20 gold piece to me and said he wanted that map. I told him he might have it and I would make another for Gen. McClellan; and so I got the $20 gold piece and he got the map, which he soon afterwards deposited in the War Department, and it was credited on the margin to Gen. Kearny."

[49] Brig. General William S. Harney (1800-1889) distinguished himself in the Florida War against the Creeks and the Seminoles, against the Mexicans at the battle of Cerro Gordo, and thereafter against the plains Indians in the West. He was relieved of his command of the Department of the West in the Civil War in 1863 for perceived pro-Southern sympathies and retired.

**Chapter 2:**

[50] Edwin Fishel, *The Secret War for the Union: The Untold Story of Military Intelligence in the Civil War* (Boston: Houghton Mifflin, 1996), 272. Knight is referring to Ebenezer McGee, one of several McGee families living on the turnpike six to eight miles west of Fredericksburg and one of his neighbors, Isaac Silver, whom Knight misremembered as Sylvia.

[51] The U.S. Ford is on the Rappahannock River just south of the union of that river with its tributary, the Rapidan River. Knight confuses the two rivers, but his placement of the McGee and Silver Farms is correct.

[52] The Bull Pen was the stockade maintained by the Provost Marshall at the headquarters, Army of the Potomac, for the incarceration of prisoners of war and suspect persons.

[53] http://www.wtv-zone.com/civilwar/gshadburne.html, accessed November 4, 2012. "During the summer of 1864 Shadburne became one of Hampton's notorious 'Iron Scouts,' who hid along the Blackwater River just two miles from Grant's lines near City Point, Va. Wearing Yankee uniforms, they skillfully eluded capture while they killed and captured Union pickets and couriers and interfered with wagon trains and telegraph lines. Shadburne also informed Hampton of some 2,500 head of poorly protected cattle that were just five miles south. Shadburne helped lead the

Beefsteak Raid, which netted much needed meat, Union supplies, and 304 Yankee prisoners. Shadburne was captured on March 6, 1865, near Fredericksburg. He was sent to Fort Monroe, Va., then to Union prison barge at City Point. Charged with being a spy, he faced hanging, but escaped on March 10th and returned to the Iron Scouts. After the war he went to San Francisco, where he became a lawyer and family man."

[54] Edward G. Longacre, *Gentleman and Soldier: The Extraordinary Life of General Wade Hampton III* (Nashville, TN: Rutledge Hill Press, 2003), 211-14. These pages give a good account of the raid of 14 September 1864 in which Wade Hampton's cavalry penetrated Union lines and made off with a herd of almost 3,000 beef cattle to Grant's intense embarrassment.

## Chapter 3:

[55] Fishel, *The Secret War,* 421, 649 n. 78.

[56] Colonel Harry Gilmor, *Four Years in the Saddle* (New York: Harper & Brothers, Publishers, 1866). Gilmor's narrative has a gap for March-April 1864 which would have covered the events described by Knight.

[57] William Gilmor Beymer, *On Hazardous Service* (Harper & Brothers, 1912), 181-84.

[58] Carney is probably referring to Isaac Silver, an agent of the BMI.

## Chapter 4:

[59] Since Lee was going to pass himself off as a sutler, it makes no sense for him to be wearing a Confederate uniform. A sutler was a civilian merchant attached to a regiment who sold a variety of necessities and luxuries unavailable through normal commissary and supply channels.

[60] The Army of Northern Virginia did not organize its artillery by regiments but by battalion, one of which was assigned to each corps.

These battalions were not tactical but administrative formations to which a large number of batteries were assigned. Artillery was employed by batteries, individually and in groups.

61  Lieut. Gen. James Longstreet commanded the First Corps of the Army of Northern Virginia, considered by many to be one of the finest offensive formations in American military history. Longstreet's corps was still in Tennessee at the time of the Mine Run Campaign, as Judson Knight in the subsequent article will make clear in no uncertain terms. Longstreet was referred to as "Pete" Longstreet, never as "Pap Longstreet."

62  William B. Feis, *Grant's Secret Service: The Intelligence War from Belmont to Appomattox* (Lincoln: University of Nebraska Press, 2002), 203. Knight is correct that Longstreet was still in Tennessee at this time; however, he is off by a month himself on the return of Longstreet's First Corps to the Army of Northern Virginia. The Bureau of Military Information, on April 25, 1864, had identified Longstreet's arrival in Charlottesville, Virginia, and on the 29th identified his arrival at Gordonsville where Lee himself arrived to review the returned First Corps.

63  Knight is correct on the location of the Silver Farm which was about 4¼ miles east of Chancellorsville on the Orange Plank Road. Fishel, *The Secret War,* 317.

64  Samuel Ruth was the Superintendent of the Richmond, Fredericksburg, and Potomac Railroad and headed a ring of loyal unionists in Richmond. His position gave him sources of vital intelligence which he passed on to Sharpe. He also did as much as possible to make his railroad, one of the most important lines of communication for the Confederate war effort in Virginia, as inefficient as possible without raising suspicion.

65  John C. Babcock was at this time a civilian employee of the Bureau of Military Information (BMI) and served as Col. Sharpe's chief order-of-battle analyst and also served effectively as his deputy. He was addressed with the honorific of "Captain."

66  The First Corps was commanded by Maj. Gen. John Newton. Maj. Gen. William H. French commanded Third Corps at this time.

67  Knight is correct in this assessment. French marched too slowly, and the opportunity to beat Lee's two corps in detail was lost. Vincent J. Esposito, ed., *The West Point Atlas of American Wars, Vol. I, 1689-1900* (New York: Frederick A. Praeger Publishers, 1959); see narrative for Map 119.

68  Brig. Gen. Henry Prince commanded 2nd Division, III Corp at this time.

69  French in his after action report attempts to excuse Prince's marching off in the wrong direction in the absence of a guide. "That without a guide the head of the column lost its road and had to retrograde on the night of the 26th" [November]; *OR*, Vol. 29, Part I, p. 736.

70  http://dictionary.reference.com/browse/boiled+shirt, accessed November 13, 2012. A "boiled shirt" is a formal or semiformal dress shirt with a starched front.

71  Brig. Gen. Marsena Patrick was the Provost Marshal-General of the Army of the Potomac. He would have been responsible for issuing passes and safeguards to the local civilian population.

72  http://ranger95.com/civil_war/virginia/cavalry/rosters/43rd_cav_bn_rost_h.html, accessed Nov. 14, 2012. The Prince William Cavalry mentioned by Knight probably refers to the Prince William Rangers, Co. H, 15th Virginia Cavalry Regiment, commanded by Captain James C. Kincheloe. The Prince William Rangers was disbanded on Dec. 4, 1864, and the unit was absorbed by Mosby's Partisan Rangers (43rd Virginia Battalion) on April 9, 1865, as Co. H, in which Kincholoe is listed as a private.

73  Samuel Sprigg "Red" Carroll (1832–1893) was a career army officer who rose to the rank of brigadier general during the Civil War. He was known for his command of the famed "Gibraltar Brigade" that played a key role during the defense of Cemetery Hill

at Gettysburg, as well as in repulsing a portion of Pickett's Charge. Wounded three times in the Overland Campaign, he was invalidated out of the Army in 1869 with the rank of brevet major general.

**Chapter 5:**

74  William B. Feis, *Grant's Secret Service: the Intelligence War from Belmont to Appomattox* (Lincoln: University of Nebraska Press, 2002), 238, no. 38; 304. Feis identifies those members of the BMI accompanying Kilpatrick as Capt. John McEntee, Milton Cline, and Joseph M. Humphreys. Anson Carney, Martin Hogan, J. R. Dykes, Jacob Swicher, and William H. Chase rode with Dahlgren. Carney in this chapter identified his cousin Philip Carney as accompanying him. Also in this chapter Joseph Humphreys identifies William H. Chase as being with Dahlgren's group. Capt. McEntee in his account in this chapter also mentions 1st Lieut. Frederick L. Manning, another BMI member, who appears to have been along with the Kilpatrick group. That would make the ten members of the BMI that Carney states went on the expedition. The importance that Col. Sharpe attached to supporting this expedition is shown by the assignment of his only two other officers in the BMI and eight of his best scouts.

75  Duane Schultz, *The Dahlgren Affair: Terror and Conspiracy in the Civil War* (New York: W. W. Norton & Company, 1999), 108-10. Dahlgren's command departed Stevensburg on the afternoon of 28 February. Kilpatrick's main body did not depart Stevensburg until 11 p.m. It is some fifteen miles from Stevensburg to Ely's Ford. By the time Kilpatrick's main body passed through Spotsylvania Court House at 8 a.m. the next morning, Dahlgren's command had already passed through earlier.

76  NARA, Military Service Record of Martin E. Hogan who was a twenty-two-year-old Irish immigrant and member of Co. A., 1st Indiana Cavalry where he served as a scout. He had already been captured once on August 5, 1862, and paroled and exchanged. Sharpe had requested his transfer to the BMI in on June 6, 1863. He was to be captured again on this expedition and escape in January 1865.

77  The negro guide was provided by Col. Sharpe's BMI as shown by
the note that his deputy, John Babcock, sent to Dahlgren shortly
before the expedition departed. "At the last moment I have found
the man...well acquainted with the James River from Richmond
up....Question him five minutes and you will know him the very
man you want....He crossed the Rapidan last night, and has late
information."

Official Records, Series I, Vol. XXXIII, p. 221. The man's name
was Martin Robinson, a freedman, who had belonged to David
Meems in Gouchland County, the very area the expedition was
traveling through.

78  According to a cavalryman writing thirty years later, when Dahlgren ordered the destruction of a store of whiskey they had come
across, as described by Knight, the men, including Martin, helped
themselves, and Robinson helped himself so much that thereafter
"he lost his head, and the right road." This is the very incident of
the peach brandy described by Knight. Dahlgren was not aware of
Robinson's condition. When they arrived at the river it was swollen by a rainstorm and any ford would have become impassable.
Robinson then directed them upriver where they ran into a Confederate fort at which time Dahlgren became convinced Robinson had
deceived him.

As much as he lacked moral justification for the execution of
Robinson, Dahlgren did have legal justification for his action.
General Orders No. 100, dated April 24, 1863, stated that "Guides,
when it is clearly proved that they have misled intentionally, may
be put to death." According to the chaplain of the 5th New York
Cavalry, Dahlgren pointedly told Robinson that if he betrayed
them, he would hang him and that Robinson said he understood.

How well that justification could have held up under scrutiny
is another question. Clearly, Dahlgren was under great stress and
must have reacted with rage when he found that he had been misled, whether intentionally or not. He saw his chance to fulfill his
mission in ruins at that point and in his mind the man's guilt was
"clearly proved."

79  NARA, Military Service Record of Philip Carney who enlisted in Co. F, 5th N.Y. Cavalry on 7 Feb. 1862. He joined the BMI in July 1863. He was captured in this expedition but escaped from Richmond in June 1864. Another relative, Edward Carney, Co. G, 5th N.Y. Cavalry also served in the BMI.

80  Here Landegon (also spelled Langegan) obviously misread the text of Carney's account. He never states that it was Brig. Gen. Kirkpatrick who praised him. Carney is clearly referring to Col. Dahlgren.

81  Again Landegon is mistaken because as the testimony of another participant showed that store of whiskey or peach brandy was not entirely destroyed as Dahlgren ordered but spirited away by many of the men.

82  Letter from McEntee to Sharpe, March 4, 1864, NARA, RG 393, Entry 3988.

83  1st Lieut. Frederick L. Manning was the junior most officer in the BMI. He wrote many of the reports of interrogation of deserters for the BMI. By 1865 he was promoted to lieutenant colonel and put in charge of intelligence operations in the Army of the James.

84  After the Civil War, Humphreys was appointed head of the Customs House in Richmond where he came into conflict with Elizabeth Van Lew, who had been appointed Postmistress of the city by President Grant. Humphreys coveted her position for a subordinate.

85  Captain John McEntee, 20th N.Y. State Militia (80th NY Vols.) was one of three officers in the BMI and was generally in charge of scouting operations. He accompanied Kilpatrick on this expedition.

86  Fishel, *The Secret War,* 272, 316-7. Ebenezer McGee was one of the best scouts in the BMI and came from a unionist family in Northern Virginia living only a few miles south of the Rappahannock River along the Orange Plank Road between Chancellorsville and Fredericksburg; he did vital work for Col. Sharpe. One of Sharpe's most important early scouts was John Howard McGee. Another family member was Sanford McGee.

87 Capt. Harry P. Clinton was the finance officer for the Provost Marshal General's Department of which Sharpe's Bureau of Military Information (BMI) was a part. Clinton paid the scouts, guides, and other members of the BMI from secret service funds. Sharpe and the other officers were paid from the normal Quartermaster payrolls.

## Chapter 6:

88 David S. Sparks, ed., *Inside Lincoln's Army: The Diary of General Marsena Rudolph Patrick, Provost Marshal General of the Army of the Potomac* (New York: A.S. Barnes & Co., 1964), 11. Brig. Gen. Marsena R. Patrick (1811-1888) Knight's recollection is an accurate reflection of the lack of affection felt by the men of the Army of the Potomac for Patrick.

89 2nd New Jersey Infantry, http://www.oocities.org/nj2ndregt/, accessed June 13, 2013. "The First NJ Brigade has earned its distinction as being the only Brigade in the Union Army to retain its single state composition for the duration of the Civil War."

90 The Red St. Andrew's Cross was the cap badge of the 1st Division of the 6th Corps. The cap badges were created under Maj. Gen. Joseph Hooker when he commanded the Army of the Potomac. The cross was the 6th Corps badge. In each corps the badge was colored by division with the 1st division in red, the 2nd in White, and the 3rd in blue.

91 Lieutenant Colonel James N. Duffy had been an aide to Major General George G. Meade, and after the war became a commissioner of the New Jersey Gettysburg Battlefield Commission, which was responsible for the creation and placement of New Jersey monuments at the Gettysburg National Military Park.

92 Col. John Hammond (1827-1889). Hammond recruited Co. H, 5th NY Cavalry from his own community and through ability rose "from captain to colonel. Hammond eventually commanded the entire 5th New York Cavalry Regiment. On June 22, 1867, he was appointed brevet brigadier general for faithful and meritorious service. After

the war, he became president of the Whitehall & Plattsburgh Rail-road Company. In 1878, he became a member of Congress. At the outset of the Battle of the Wilderness, Hammond and a detachment of about 500 soldiers, armed with Spencer carbines, held off the advance of Lt. Gen. A. P. Hill's III Corps for almost six hours near Parker's Store." *America's Civil War*, Jan 1998.

[93] "22nd Cavalry Regiment," New York State Military Museum and Veterans Research Center, http://dmna.ny.gov/historic/reghist/civil/cavalry/22ndCav/22ndCavMain.htm, accessed Oct. 31, 2012. The companies of the 22nd New York Cavalry were only mustered into service between December 1863 and February 1864. The regiment left the state in March and was only assigned to the Cavalry Corps of the Army of the Potomac in early May, just in time to see their first combat in the battle of the Wilderness.

[94] Isaac Silver was a southern unionist who worked for the Bureau of Military Information.

[95] "The United States Sanitary Commission," http://en.wikipedia.org/wiki/United_States_Sanitary_Commission, accessed Oct. 31, 2012. "The United States Sanitary Commission was a private relief agency created by Federal legislation on June 18, 1861, to support sick and wounded soldiers of the U.S. Army during the Civil War. It operated across the North, raised its own funds, and enlisted thousands of volunteers. It was directed by Frederick Law Olmsted."

[96] Col. Otto Harhaus commanded the 2[d] New York Cavalry at this time. Apparently, the charges were dismissed because he was still in command of his regiment at Petersburg in July.

[97] The 13th Pennsylvania Cavalry was also the 117th Pennsylvania Regiment. That may have been the origin of Knight's confusion about the 17th Pennsylvania. The 13th Pennsylvania was part of Col. John Irvin Gregg's 2nd Cavalry Brigade, Brig. Gen. David M. Gregg's Cavalry Division, Cavalry Corps, Army of the Potomac. The two Greggs were cousins. McCabe's regiment was at all those places which Knight associates with it in 1864.

[98] Fishel, *The Secret War,* 292, and Military Service files, National Archives. Sergeant Daniel R. Cole and Private Daniel Plew, 3rd Indiana Cavalry, were on detached duty as scouts with the Bureau of Military Information recruited by Col. Sharpe.

[99] Brig. Gen. Alfred Thomas Archimedes Torbert (1833-1880) was a career army officer who had commanded the New Jersey Brigade at the battles of Fredericksburg, Chancellorsville, and Gettysburg. By the time Knight encountered him he had been promoted to brigadier general and given command of the 1st Division, Cavalry Corps, Army of the Potomac.

[100] Daniel Coleman DeJarnett, Sr. (1822-1881) represented the 3rd District of Virginia in the U.S. House of Representatives (1859-1861) and Virginia in the Confederate House of Representatives (1861-1863).

[101] Corbin's Bridge was about three miles south of the right of the Union line at the battle of Spotsylvania. See Brig. Gen. Vincent J. Esposito, *The West Point Atlas of American Wars, Volume I, 1689-1900* (New York: Frederick A. Praeger, 1959), Maps 125ba-b.

[102] Union soldiers frequently referred to the Confederates as "the chivalry" in derision for their aristocratic airs.

[103] Civil War Talk, http://civilwartalk.com/threads/coffee-cooler.70013/.John D. Wright, *The Language of the Civil War* (New York: Greenwood Publishing Group, 2001), 65. Coffee cooler referred to soldiers who hid behind the battle lines during combat, brewing, drinking coffee until the danger was passed; often used derisively for someone who habitually shirked his duties in the camp.

[104] *OR*, Vol. 36, Part 2, p. 699. Sharpe refers to Tinsley's's Mill in his report of Knight's reconnaissance as Tinder's Mill.

[105] James Hatton was a member of D Company, 3rd Indiana Cavalry.

[106] Knight confuses the issue by referring to Spotsylvania here as the next battle since his earlier references to reconnaissance towards Corbin's Bridge, and Sharpe's report of May 13th, show

that the battle of the Wilderness had already taken place. His earlier description of finding Hancock's men on the Union right after coming in from his reconnaissance in the direction of Corbin's Bridge, as well as their subsequent move to the southeast again, fits with events during operations at Spotsylvania. Despite this, he picks up the Spotsylvania narrative again at this point.

[107] Knight is referring to the attack on the Confederate salient known as the Muleshoe at Spotsylvania on May 10, 1864, by twelve Union regiments. The Union force burst through the Confederate lines and captured most of Johnson's Division, including the Stonewall Brigade, among the 6,000 prisoners. However, powerful Confederate counterattacks then drove the Union regiments out of the Confederate position.

[108] Emory Upton (1839–1881) was a Union general and military strategist, who led a successful attack on entrenched Muleshoe positions at the Battle of Spotsylvania Court House and was considered one of the most accomplished officers in either army. His work, *The Military Policy of the United States*, which analyzed American military policies and practices and presented the first systematic examination of the nation's military history, had a tremendous effect on the U.S. Army when it was published posthumously in 1904.

[109] "121st Infantry Regiment," New York State Military Museum and Research Center, http://dmna.ny.gov/historic/reghist/civil/infantry/121stInf/121stInfMain.htm, accessed October 30, 2012. The 121$^{st}$ New York was raised in Ostego and Herkimer Counties and joined the Army of the Potomac and served in the 2d Brigade, 1st Division, 6th Corps, from September 9, 1862 until discharged after Appomattox. "The losses of the regiment at Spotsylvania amounted to 19 Killed, 106 wounded. In the magnificent charge of Upton's storming party at Spotsylvania, the strong works of the enemy were carried after a hand-to-hand struggle. Said Gen. Upton in a private letter: 'Bayonet

wounds and sabre cuts are very rare. But at Spotsylvania there were plenty of bayonet wounds, and no picture could give too exalted an idea of the gallantry of the 121st N. Y., 5th Me., and 96th Pa., as they led the assaulting column of twelve picked regiments over the formidable intrenchments.'"

[110] Babcock was considered more a deputy of Col. Sharpe than a private secretary.

[111] Knight is referring to a photographic negative of a map, in use at the time, which to be seen correctly had to be viewed against a light from its reverse side.

[112] Sharpe's report on Knight's observations at 6 p.m. on May 13, and the subsequent movement of a major part of the Army of the Potomac by the left beginning late that very night, gives some credence to Knight's belief that he had something to do with that.

[113] Brig. Gen. John H. Winder (1800–1865) served as provost marshal of Richmond (1862–1864) and commissary general of Confederate prisons (1864–1865). Elizabeth Van Lew offered him free room and board as a cover for her efforts to smuggle escaped Union prisoners out of Richmond and back into their own lines.

[114] John N. Van Lew (b. 1823) was the younger brother of Elizabeth Van Lew. Mr. Van Lew never exhibited the same degree of courage in the support of the Union as did his gallant sister.

[115] C. F. Heverely, *Our Boys in Blue: Heroic Deeds, Sketches and Reminiscences of Bradford Country Soldiers in the Civil War*, Vol. 1, 1899.

[116] By the time of the battle of Chancellorsville in early May 1863, the Army of the Potomac had had very reliable and accurate order-of-battle of its mighty opponent, the Confederate Army of Northern Virginia. In that case it was within two percent of its actual present-for-duty strength. This was all due to the analysis of the BMI of which the scouts were a vital component.

**Chapter 7:**

[117] Sergeant John W. Landegon was detached from the C Company, 2nd New York Cavalry, known as the Harris Light Cavalry, to serve as a scout for Maj. Gen. Judson Kilpatrick's 3rd Cavalry Division of the Cavalry Corps of the Army of the Potomac. He would later become chief of scouts for Maj. Gen. Sheridan when he became commander of the Cavalry Corps. In 1864 when his enlistment was up, he joined Gen. Kilpatrick as his chief scout on a contract basis.

[118] "3rd New Jersey Cavalry," http://3rdnjcavalry.com/ArticleVuksicBarbasic.html, accessed June 10, 2013; information derived from V. Vuksic and Z. Grbasic, *Cavalry: The History of a Fighting Elite 650 BC–AD 1914*, (London: Cassell, 1993). Clyde A. Risley and Frederick P. Todd, "3rd New Jersey Cavalry Regiment, 1864–1865 (1st Regiment, U.S. Hussars)." In contrast to the U.S. Army's standard blue cavalryman's uniform, the 3rd New Jersey Volunteer Cavalry Regiment wore a hussar-style uniform, loaded with buttons and yellow braid, that earned them the epithet of the "Butterflies." They were also known as the 1st United States Hussars and the Trenton Hussars. A large number of Germans were recruited into the regiment although they only predominated in Co. I.

[119] William Gilmore Beymer's book was originally titled, *On Hazardous Service: Scouts and Spies of the North and* South and was originally published by Harpers in 1912. The book was republished as *Scouts and Spies of the Civil War*, with an introduction by William B. Feis, by University of Nebraska Books in 2003.

[120] Ibid.,175-76.

[121] Ibid.,176.

[122] Ibid.,176-77.

[123] Ibid.,177.

[124] Ibid.

[125] Ibid.,180.

[126] Ibid. Landegon told the Dews of his fears about who "took his gray clothes and buried them in the garden."

[127] Ibid., 181. Jack Williams had served with Landegon in the 2nd New York Cavalry.

## Chapter 8:

[128] Guides were not considered to be scouts who were on the permanent roles of the army as soldiers. Guides were local men who had a knowledge of the immediate area of operations. Often they were African-American slaves, most of whom were considered to have little knowledge outside of a five-mile radius of the plantations or farms on which they lived.

[129] Maj. Gen. William Farrar Smith 1824–1903, nicknamed Baldy, was one of Grant's favorite generals from the Western theater; he brought him east with him in early 1864. He had commanded a division with great valor at Antietam and Fredericksburg, but his conspiracy to replace the commander of the Army of the Potomac, for incompetence, resulted in his ultimate transfer to the Army of the Cumberland as chief engineer. He was responsible for opening the "cracker line" of supply to the starving and besieged Army of the Cumberland at the siege of Chattanooga. His hesitation, however, in attacking the defenses of Richmond during the Overland Campaign, when the city was largely undefended, led to his relief.

[130] Colonel H. T. Collis, commanding 114th Pennsylvania Volunteers, known as Collis' Zouaves. The regiment was assigned to the brigade of the Provost Marshal General's guard on April 18, 1864.

[131] The Algonquin-speaking Pamunkey nation was one of the most powerful groups of the Powhatan chiefdom when the English first arrived in Virginia. They inhabited the coastal tidewater of Virginia on the north side of the James River near Chesapeake Bay. The Pamunkey reservation is located on some of its ancestral land on the Pamunkey River, adjacent to present-day King William County, Virginia. The Pamunkey number about 200 people today.

[132] Colonel William Pinckey Shingler was in command of the 7th South Carolina Cavalry, Colquitt's Cavalry Division, Army of Northern Virginia, at this time. See *OR*, Series 1, Vol XXXVI, Part I (Washington, DC: US Government Printing Office, 1891), p. 205. Colquitt's Division, with the 7th SC Cavalry, took part in the battle of Drewry's Bluff on May 16, 1864.

[133] "Tunstall's in the dark," is probably a double entendre referring to nearby Tunstall Station or to Robert Louis Stevenson, *The Black Arrow: a Tale of Two Roses (*Scribner's*, 1888).

[134] Knight was indeed correct; Confederate cavalrymen brought their own horses to war.

[135] Ananias appears in the *New Testament* (Acts 5) as a Jewish Christian of Jerusalem who was struck dead for lying.

[136] *Oxford English Dictionary* cites dornick as an American dialectical term originating in the mid-19th century, meaning "pebble, stone or small boulder," perhaps deriving from Irish "dornog" (small stone).

[137] The bull-pen was the stockade for prisoners of war, spies, etc., maintained by the Provost Marshal-General of the Army of the Potomac.

[138] The 20th N.Y. was actually the 20th New York State Militia Regiment. The regiment proudly insisted on being called by its prewar militia number even though its war number was 80th N.Y. Volunteers. At this time it was part of the Provost Brigade at army headquarters.

[139] Knight is referring to Colonel George H. Sharpe (1828-1900), who served not only as Deputy Provost Marshal-General but as Chief, Bureau of Military Information (BMI), the first all-source intelligence organization in American history, from February 1863 to the end of the war. He also served in a dual capacity in the same role directly for Grant's army group (Armies Operating Against Richmond). Grant promoted him to major-general and considered him one of his family of generals whom he would appoint to high office after the war.

**Chapter 9:**

[140] S. F. Adams to Babcock, January 12, 1903, John C. Babcock Collection, Library of Congress. After the war, John C. Babcock retained the services of guide Richard Johnson as his coachman and that of his wife, Sarah, as cook. After the turn of the century, a niece of Johnson's widow implored Babcock's help in obtaining Sarah a pension, but to no avail, as Babcock's health was also failing.

[141] Major Thomas W. Doswell "was a volunteer aide-de-camp to Gen. Starke. He inherited the property "Bullfield" from his father. From 1850 he was the owner, breeder, and trainer of race horses there. The stable was famous for the quality of racing and hospitality it had. Every spring brought exciting matches and many notables came out for the lavish affairs. T. W. Doswell served as a staff officer in the Civil War and was sheriff of Richmond for eleven years. He signed Jefferson Davis' bail bond. The hamlet where Bullfield was has been re-named Doswell in his honor." http://www.findagrave.com/cgi-bin/fg.cgi?page=gr&GRid=6177817, accessed November 22, 2012.

[142] National Archives, Military Service of Phillip Carney, 5th New York Cavalry; he was on detached duty as a scout with the Bureau of Military Information (BMI) from September 1863.

[143] Dodd and McCord were experienced scouts and had joined the BMI in March 1863, shortly after it was established.

[144] Heverely, *Our Boys in Blue.*

[145] General Robert E. Lee was also referred to by Union troops with a mixture of awe and respect as Bobby Lee.

[146] William Gilmore Simms (April 17, 1806–June 11, 1870) was a poet, novelist, and historian from the American South. His writings achieved great prominence during the 19th century, with Edgar Allan Poe pronouncing him the best novelist America had ever produced. Simms wrote a number of popular novels between 1830 and 1860, usually focusing on the pre-colonial and colonial periods of Southern history; his biographies of early Southern leaders were

enormously popular. Simms was one of the best, and most respected, historians of his day. He was a vehement supporter of slavery and strongly opposed Harriet Beecher Stowe's *Uncle Tom's Cabin*.

[147] The salutation is purely honorific; there is no record in Knight's Military Service Record or Pension Record at NARA to show that he was ever a commissioned officer.

[148] Francis A. Walker, *General Hancock* (New York: D. Appleton and Company, 1894), p. 24344. Knight was referring to the Confederate attack by Mahone's, Johnson's, and Wilcox's divisions of A. P. Hill's 3rd Corps against Birney's Division of Hancock's II Corps on June 22, 1864. Mahone's Division was the main attacking force. McKnight's battery of the 12th New York Battery lost four guns. The Confederates additionally captured 1,700 prisoners from II Corps.

[149] "City Point served as the headquarters of the Union armies under the command of Lieutenant General Grant during a crucial time in the Civil War. It was from this site that Grant planned and organized the Siege of Petersburg, which ultimately helped bring about the end of the Civil War in Virginia. It was at City Point that President Lincoln, Grant, and key military leaders met to discuss how to reunify the country once the war was over. As a result, this site holds special significance in American history. Providing food, clothing, and medical supplies to 100,000 Union soldiers and 65,000 horses and livestock was no small task for Ulysses S. Grant and his army during the Civil War....

"In Civil War times, one of the most efficient means of transportation was by way of the river. And that is why, in his effort to bring an end to the Civil War, General Grant strategically set up his headquarters next to the James River in City Point, Virginia. (The town of City Point is now known as Hopewell.) City Point was at the center of the Union Army's operations. The area was a hub of activity with tons of supplies arriving daily, via the James River. In fact, City Point became one of the busiest ports in the world for a brief, 10-month period during the war. Logistical operations were enormous. An elaborate railroad, ship supply, and communications operation was set up at City Point to distribute supplies to men in the field. A bakery was erected and produced over 100,000 rations of bread each day. In addition, seven hospitals were located at City Point. One of those hospitals, the Depot Field Hospital, would actually treat 6,000 patients on an average day and as many as 10,000 on a busy day." United States Park Service, http://www.nps.gov/history/logcabin/html/cp.html, accessed November 22, 2012.

[150] Knight was not made chief of scouts until August 1864 upon the departure of Sgt. Milton Cline who had been chief of scouts since the inception of the BMI in February 1863.

[151] The 20th New York State Militia Regiment (NYSM) was part of the Provost Brigade of the Headquarters, Army of the Potomac, and was subordinate to the Provost Marshal General, Brig. Gen. Marsena R. Patrick. He preferred his home state's regiments for this assignment. Although the regiment had been given the war designation of 80th New York, it had such pride in its militia origin that it always referred to itself as the 20th NYSM (New York State Militia) and is shown as such in the orders-of-battle of the Army of the Potomac in the *OR*. The 20th NYSM was also the original regiment of Col. George H. Sharpe even though he later raised and commanded the 120th New York. He chose that number to associate it forever with the 20th NYSM, and he remained devoted to both regiments for the rest of his life. He paid for a monument of his 120th NY in their home town of Kingston, NY. He was the only Union general to erect a statue to his men, rather than the other way around.

[152] Haxall's Landing was McClellan's initial base of supply on the north bank of the James River during the Peninsular Campaign of 1862. It is adjacent to Malvern Hill and approximately five miles north of the confluence of the James and Appomattox Rivers. The negotiations for the exchange of prisoners known as the Dix-Hill Cartel took place here on July 22, 1862. It was the end point for Sheridan's cavalry raid on Richmond May 9-24, 1864.

[153] Carney is referring to Samuel Ruth, Superintendent of the Richmond, Fredericksburg and Potomac Railroad. The route of the railroad ran from Richmond to a terminus five miles south of Fredericksburg, and through much of the war was a vital element in the supply of Lee's Army of Northern Virginia. Ruth, an ardent Unionist, did everything in his power to manage the railroads inefficiently. After Grant's forces through their siege around Richmond and Petersburg, he was the source of accurate reports on Confederate troop movements.

[154] Heverely, *Our Boys in Blue.*

## Chapter 10:

[155] *OR*, Series 1, Vol. XLII, Part 2, pp. 629-30; NARA, RG 108, Entry 112. The gunboat *Commodore Morris* was a major player in patrolling the James River and transporting Knight and other scouts across the river to Confederate territory. It also picked up numerous refugees from the city.

[156] NARA, RG 92, Entry 328, Files 0447 (1864) and 0447 (1865). Alexander Myers was hired by Sharpe as a scout, and he proved to be extremely valuable in getting in and out of Richmond.

[157] British immigrants living in the South were frequently Union sympathizers, and several ended up working for Sharpe in one capacity or another.

[158] Apparently Knight was wearing a Confederate uniform at this time.

[159] John Randolph Chambliss, Jr. (January 23, 1833–August 16, 1864) was a career U.S. Army officer who joined the Confederate forces when the Civil War broke out. He was eventually promoted to brigadier general and commanded a cavalry brigade with distinction. He was killed in a cavalry battle on the Charles City Road, on the north side of the James. His death fixes the time of Knight's narration at this point.

[160] Acting Rear Admiral Philip S. Lee (February 13, 1812–June 7, 1897) commanded the North Atlantic Blockading Squadron which

had command of naval forces in the James River supporting Grant's siege of Richmond. Lieut. Cmdr. J. L. Davis commanded the USS *Sassacus* at this time.

[161] Judson Knight, "New Rebel Torpedo," *Scientific American*, 1011, no. 15 (Oct. 8, 1864), 288.

[162] Heverely, *Our Boys in Blue.*

[163] Elizabeth R. Varron, *Southern Lady, Yankee Spy: The True Story of Elizabeth Van Lew, A Union Agent in the Heart of the Confederacy* (New York: Oxford University Press, 2003), 162. This appears to be an "African American farmer named Sylvanus J. Brown.... Brown possessed a pass to into Richmond to sell goods at the market."

[164] Capt. Paul A. Oliver had only a few weeks before being asked by Sharpe to join his tiny staff. His endorsement carried some weight because he had a sterling combat record, did excellent work for Sharpe, and was brevetted to colonel after the war for that reason.

**Appendix:**

[165] This list is not comprehensive but was pieced together from various sources to include BMI reports, Military Service Records, and pension records held by NARA.

[166] Fishel, *The Secret War,* 295.

[167] These officers' ranks are those held when they joined the BMI. Sharpe was brevetted brigadier general in January 1865 and to major general after the war; McEntee, Manning, and Oliver were all promoted to lieutenant colonel before the end of the war. They were brevetted to full colonel after the war.

[168] Also known as the 80th New York Infantry.

[169] NARA, RG92, Entry 0910 (1863). Scout contract dates were only listed for payrolls Jan-May 1863.

[170] NARA, RG92, Entries 0910 (1863), 0447 (1964), 0447 (1865).

[171] Allen's father, Thomas, was a resident of Fauquier County and was considered to be "off color," a quarter black, and was denied the right to vote. The entire family was strongly Unionist.

[172] Fishel, *The Secret War,* 295. Fishel states that Louis Battail (Lewis Battle) and Dabney Walker "went on the payroll as cooks," although they are listed as guides on the June 1863 payroll.

[173] NARA, Microcopy 2096, Roll 34, letter from Sharpe to Williams, July 9, 1863. Although Beverely is not listed in the payrolls, Sharpe definitely writes of him as "one of our scouts" in this report.

[174] Blake was not listed on the BMI payrolls but was identified as a scout in the company of Judson Knight in NARA, RG 110, Entry e31, Box 2, File 80, by a letter dated April 13, 1863.

[175] Anson Carney earlier served in B Co., 20th NY State Militia.

[176] Cline's Military Service Record at NARA states he was on detached duty at Army of the Potomac headquarters since February 25. 1863.

[177] Walter Cline was the teenage son of Chief of Scouts Milton Cline.

[178] Cole's Military Service Record at NARA contains a letter from Col. Sharpe attesting to Cole's presence in the BMI as of March 5, 1863.

[179] First mention of Dodd with the BMI was in March 1863.

[180] NARA, RG92, Entries 0410 (1864) and 0410 (1865). A Henry Evans is listed in the November 1864 payroll, and a Henry Evans described as colored is listed in the March 1865 payroll.

[181] Willliam Fay, shipbuilder, was one of the runners for the Richmond Unionist spy ring run by Elizabeth Van Lew.

[182] Ebenezer Halleck, grocer on Main St., was one of the runners for the Richmond Unionist spy ring run by Elizabeth Van Lew.

[183] Harter had been a member of the Co. I, 1st IN Cavalry until his discharge on October 9, 1863, after which he was employed by the BMI as a civilian scout.

[184] NARA, Military Service Record of Martin E. Hogan. Hogan was a twenty-two-year-old Irish immigrant and member of Co. A.,

1<sup>st</sup> Indiana Cavalry where he served as a scout. He had already been captured once on August 5, 1862, and paroled and exchanged. Sharpe had requested his transfer to the BMI on June 6, 1863. He was to be captured again on the Dahlgren Raid.

[185] First mention of Humphreys in the BMI was Feb. 13, 1863.

[186] John C. Babcock Collection, Library of Congress. This may well be the colored guide, Richard Johnson. In 1902 a lawyer for Johnson's widow inquired of Babcock if he could confirm Johnson's service, and cited May 64 as the date he joined the BMI.

[187] NARA, Military Service Record for Judson Knight. Knight had been in H Co., 2<sup>nd</sup> New Jersey Infantry before being medically discharged on Dec. 31, 1862. He then joined the BMI as a civilian.

[188] Jack Lyon is referred to as a scout in a BMI report of April 5, 1863.

[189] Charles Major was one of the runners for the Richmond Unionist spy ring run by Elizabeth Van Lew.

[190] Alexander Myers was one of the runners for the Richmond Unionist spy ring run by Elizabeth Van Lew.

[191] Fishel, *The Secret War,* 292. Fishel identifies D. G. Otto as an early scout for Sharpe who had proven himself scouting for Pleasanton; however, there is no D. G. Otto in the Military Service Records at NARA.

[192] Daniel Plew's Military Service Record at NARA states he was on detached duty as a scout with the Secret Service at the headquarters of the Army of the Potomac as of June 14, 1863.

[193] Fishel, *The Secret War,* 295. Fishel states that Dabney Walker and Louis Battail (Lewis Battle) "went on the payroll as cooks," although they are listed as guides on the June 1863 payroll.

[194] Weaver is identified by Sharpe in a message dated August 11, 1863 (NARA, BMI files), as employed by the BMI although his name does not appear on the payrolls.

[195] William Wilson appears in Library of Congress photos, LC-USZ62-108336, by James Gardner, and identified by name as a

scout with the Headquarters, Army of the Potomac. Wilson's name does not appear in the BMI payroll records.

[196] Abram Coin had been a wagoner in the 20th NYSM, which was part of the Provost Brigade, and was wounded in the explosion of the ammunition ship at City Point in August 9, 1864. He was mustered out at City Point on September 18th. He appeared on the BMI payroll only once, in December 1864, as a teamster. He's an example of how fluid was the personnel make up of the BMI.

# Selected Bibliography

Beymer, William Gilmore. *On Hazardous Service: Scouts and Spies of the North and South.* London: Harper & Brothers, Publishers, 1912. This book was subsequently republished with an introduction by William B. Feis, as *Scouts and Spies of the Civil War.* Lincoln: University of Nebraska Press, 2003.

Editors of Time-Life Books. *Spies, Scouts and Raiders: Irregular Operations.* Civil War Series. Alexandria, VA: Time-Life Books, 1985.

Esposito, Vincent J., ed. *The West Point Atlas of American Wars, Vol. I, 1689-1900.* New York: Frederick A. Praeger Publishers, 1959.

Feis, William B. *Grant's Secret Service: The Intelligence from Belmont to Appomattox.* Lincoln: University of Nebraska Press, 2002.

Fishel, Edwin C. *The Secret War for the Union: The Untold Story of Military Intelligence in the Civil War.* Boston: Houghton Mifflin, 1996.

Kane, Harriet T. *Spies for the Blue and Gray.* New York: Hanover House, 1954.

Markle, Donald E. *Spies and Spymasters of the Civil War.* New York: Barnes & Noble, 1995.

Ryan, David D., ed. *A Yankee Spy in Richmond: The Civil War Diary of "Crazy Bet" Van Lew.* Mechanicsburg, PA: Stackpole Books, 1996.

Schutz, Duane. *The Dahlgren Affair: Terror and Conspiracy in the Civil War.* New York: W. W. Norton & Company, 1996.

Sheehan-Dean, Aaron, ed. *Struggle for a Vast Future: The American Civil War.* Oxford: Osprey, 2006.

Sparks, David S., ed. *Inside Lincoln's Army: The Diary of Marsena Rudolph Patrick, Provost Marshal General of the Army of the Potomac.* New York: Thomas Yoseloff, 1964.

Varon, Elizabeth. *Southern Lady, Yankee Spy: The True Story of Elizabeth Van Lew, A Union Agent in the Heart of the Confederacy.* New York: Oxford University Press, 2003.

*The War of the Rebellion: A Compilation of the Official Records of the Union and Confederate Armies.* Series 1, Vols XXV, XXVII, XXIX, XXX, XXXIII, XXXVI, XL, XLII. U.S. Government Printing Office.